M000251271

Carolyn M. West, PhD
Editor

Violence in the Lives of Black Women: Battered, Black, and Blue

Violence in the Lives of Black Women: Battered, Black, and Blue has been co-published simultaneously as *Women & Therapy*, Volume 25, Numbers 3/4 2002.

Pre-publication REVIEWS, COMMENTARIES, EVALUATIONS . . .

"Carolyn West has brought together a stellar group of experts who present the most nuanced and COMPREHENSIVE OVERVIEW OF VIOLENCE AGAINST BLACK WOMEN AVAILABLE TODAY. The book represents the best in feminist research methodology. The works included use both quantitative and qualitative methods to elaborate our understanding of black women's experiences of childhood sexual abuse, partner violence, sexual assault, workplace harassment, and street violence. The book is noteworthy because it MOVES BEYOND THE TERRIBLE TOLL OF VIOLENCE TO CATALOGUE BLACK WOMEN'S STRENGTHS AND RESILIENCE. Liberally illustrated with quotes from literature and song, the book is A MUST READ FOR ANYONE CONCERNED WITH INCREASING THEIR CULTURAL COMPETENCY."

Mary P. Koss, PhD
Professor, Public Health, Family and Community Medicine, Psychiatry, and Psychology, University of Arizona

More pre-publication
REVIEWS, COMMENTARIES, EVALUATIONS . . .

"A RARE OPPORTUNITY to review a range of approaches that address physical, psychological, and spiritual consequences of intimate violence in one volume. . . . BRINGS TOGETHER SOME UNDERSTUDIED THEMES in intimate violence research, such as battered black lesbians, racialized sexual harassment of black women, battered black women who have experienced brain trauma, and femicide–black women who have been murdered by their intimate partners. The book has a very strong emphasis on intervention strategies that WILL BE USEFUL TO THERAPEUTIC PRACTITIONERS AS WELL AS SURVIVORS of intimate violence. . . . A FRESH APPROACH."

Traci C. West, PhD, Author
Wounds of the Spirit: Black Women, Violence, and Resistance Ethics

"FILLS A CRITICALLY IMPORTANT VOID . . . A SCHOLARLY AND COMPREHENSIVE look at a serious problem that often goes undiscussed. West and her contributors shed light on an important issue for Black women that has often been shrouded in secrecy, shame, and silence. This book will be useful to mental health clinicians as well as administrators of programs whose scope includes violence against women. It is written in accessible language and is suitable for training mental health clinicians and researchers as well as experienced professionals."

Beverly Greene, PhD, ABPP
Professor of Psychology, Diplomate in Clinical Psychology, St. John's University

The Haworth Press, Inc.
New York

Violence in the Lives of Black Women: Battered, Black, and Blue

Violence in the Lives of Black Women: Battered, Black, and Blue has been co-published simultaneously as *Women & Therapy*, Volume 25, Numbers 3/4 2002.

The *Women & Therapy* Monographic "Separates"

Below is a list of "separates," which in serials librarianship means a special issue simultaneously published as a special journal issue or double-issue *and* as a "separate" hardbound monograph. (This is a format which we also call a "DocuSerial.")

"Separates" are published because specialized libraries or professionals may wish to purchase a specific thematic issue by itself in a format which can be separately cataloged and shelved, as opposed to purchasing the journal on an on-going basis. Faculty members may also more easily consider a "separate" for classroom adoption.

"Separates" are carefully classified separately with the major book jobbers so that the journal tie-in can be noted on new book order slips to avoid duplicate purchasing.

You may wish to visit Haworth's website at . . .

http://www.HaworthPress.com

. . . to search our online catalog for complete tables of contents of these separates and related publications.

You may also call 1-800-HAWORTH (outside US/Canada: 607-722-5857), or Fax 1-800-895-0582 (outside US/Canada: 607-771-0012), or e-mail at:

getinfo@haworthpressinc.com

Violence in the Lives of Black Women: Battered, Black, and Blue, edited by Carolyn M. West, PhD (Vol. 25, No. 3/4, 2002). *Helps break the silence surrounding Black women's experiences of violence.*

Exercise and Sport in Feminist Therapy: Constructing Modalities and Assessing Outcomes, edited by Ruth L. Hall, PhD, and Carole A. Oglesby, PhD (Vol. 25, No. 2, 2002). *Explores the healing use of exercise and sport as a helpful adjunct to feminist therapy.*

The Invisible Alliance: Psyche and Spirit in Feminist Therapy, edited by Ellyn Kaschak, PhD (Vol. 24, No. 3/4, 2001). *"The richness of this volume is reflected in the diversity of the collected viewpoints, perspectives, and practices. Each chapter challenges us to move out of the confines of our traditional training and reflect on the importance of spirituality. This book also brings us back to the original meaning of psychology–the study and knowledge of the soul." (Stephanie S. Covington, PhD, LCSW, Co-Director, Institute for Relational Development, La Jolla, California; Author,* A Woman's Way Through the Twelve Steps.)

A New View of Women's Sexual Problems, edited by Ellyn Kaschak, PhD, and Leonore Tiefer, PhD (Vol. 24, No. 1/2, 2001). *"This useful, complex, and valid critique of simplistic notions of women's sexuality will be especially valuable for women's studies and public health courses. An important compilation representing many diverse individuals and groups of women." (Judy Norsigian and Jane Pincus, Co-Founders, Boston Women's Health Collective; Co-Authors,* Our Bodies, Ourselves for the New Century)

Intimate Betrayal: Domestic Violence in Lesbian Relationships, edited by Ellyn Kaschak, PhD (Vol. 23, No. 3, 2001). *"A groundbreaking examination of a taboo and complex subject. Both scholarly and down to earth, this superbly edited volume is an indispensable resource for clinicians, researchers, and lesbians caught up in the cycle of domestic violence." (Dr. Marny Hall, Psychotherapist; Author of* The Lesbian Love Companion, *Co-Author of* Queer Blues)

The Next Generation: Third Wave Feminist Psychotherapy, edited by Ellyn Kaschak, PhD (Vol. 23, No. 2, 2001). *Discusses the issues young feminists face, focusing on the implications for psychotherapists of the false sense that feminism is no longer necessary.*

Minding the Body: Psychotherapy in Cases of Chronic and Life-Threatening Illness, edited by Ellyn Kaschak, PhD (Vol. 23, No. 1, 2001). *Being diagnosed with cancer, lupus, or fibromyalgia is a traumatic event. All too often, women are told their disease is 'all in their heads' and therefore both 'unreal and insignificant' by a medical profession that dismisses emotions and scorns mental illness. Combining personal narratives and theoretical views of illness,* Minding the Body *offers an alternative approach to the mind-body connection. This book shows the reader how to deal with the painful and difficult emotions that exacerbate illness, while learning the emotional and spiritual lessons illness can teach.*

For Love or Money: The Fee in Feminist Therapy, edited by Marcia Hill, EdD, and Ellyn Kaschak, PhD (Vol. 22, No. 3, 1999). *"Recommended reading for both new and seasoned professionals. . . . An exciting and timely book about 'the last taboo.' . . ." (Carolyn C. Larsen, PhD, Senior Counsellor Emeritus, University of Calgary; Partner, Alberta Psychological Resources Ltd., Calgary, and Co-Editor,* Ethical Decision Making in Therapy: Feminist Perspectives*)*

Beyond the Rule Book: Moral Issues and Dilemmas in the Practice of Psychotherapy, edited by Ellyn Kaschak, PhD, and Marcia Hill, EdD (Vol. 22, No. 2, 1999). *"The authors in this important and timely book tackle the difficult task of working through . . . conflicts, sharing their moral struggles and real life solutions in working with diverse populations and in a variety of clinical settings. . . . Will provide psychotherapists with a thought-provoking source for the stimulating and essential discussion of our own and our profession's moral bases." (Carolyn C. Larsen, PhD, Senior Counsellor Emeritus, University of Calgary, Partner in private practice, Alberta Psychological Resources Ltd., Calgary, and Co-Editor,* Ethical Decision Making in Therapy: Feminist Perspectives)

Assault on the Soul: Women in the Former Yugoslavia, edited by Sara Sharratt, PhD, and Ellyn Kaschak, PhD (Vol. 22, No. 1, 1999). *Explores the applications and intersections of feminist therapy, activism and jurisprudence with women and children in the former Yugoslavia.*

Learning from Our Mistakes: Difficulties and Failures in Feminist Therapy, edited by Marcia Hill, EdD, and Esther D. Rothblum, PhD (Vol. 21, No. 3, 1998). *"A courageous and fundamental step in evolving a well-grounded body of theory and of investigating the assumptions that, unexamined, lead us to error." (Teresa Bernardez, MD, Training and Supervising Analyst, The Michigan Psychoanalytic Council)*

Feminist Therapy as a Political Act, edited by Marcia Hill, EdD (Vol. 21, No. 2, 1998). *"A real contribution to the field. . . . A valuable tool for feminist therapists and those who want to learn about feminist therapy." (Florence L. Denmark, PhD, Robert S. Pace Distinguished Professor of Psychology and Chair, Psychology Department, Pace University, New York, New York)*

Breaking the Rules: Women in Prison and Feminist Therapy, edited by Judy Harden, PhD, and Marcia Hill, EdD (Vol. 20, No. 4 & Vol. 21, No. 1, 1998). *"Fills a long-recognized gap in the psychology of women curricula, demonstrating that feminist theory can be made relevant to the practice of feminism, even in prison." (Suzanne J. Kessler, PhD, Professor of Psychology and Women's Studies, State University of New York at Purchase)*

Children's Rights, Therapists' Responsibilities: Feminist Commentaries, edited by Gail Anderson, MA, and Marcia Hill, EdD (Vol. 20, No. 2, 1997). *"Addresses specific practice dimensions that will help therapists organize and resolve conflicts about working with children, adolescents, and their families in therapy." (Feminist Bookstore News)*

More than a Mirror: How Clients Influence Therapists' Lives, edited by Marcia Hill, EdD (Vol. 20, No. 1, 1997). *"Courageous, insightful, and deeply moving. These pages reveal the scrupulous self-examination and self-reflection of conscientious therapists at their best. An important contribution to feminist therapy literature and a book worth reading by therapists and clients alike." (Rachel Josefowitz Siegal, MSW, retired feminist therapy practitioner; Co-Editor,* Women Changing Therapy; Jewish Women in Therapy; *and* Celebrating the Lives of Jewish Women: Patterns in a Feminist Sampler*)*

Sexualities, edited by Marny Hall, PhD, LCSW (Vol. 19, No. 4, 1997). *"Explores the diverse and multifaceted nature of female sexuality, covering topics including sadomasochism in the therapy room, sexual exploitation in cults, and genderbending in cyberspace." (Feminist Bookstore News)*

Couples Therapy: Feminist Perspectives, edited by Marcia Hill, EdD, and Esther D. Rothblum, PhD (Vol. 19, No. 3, 1996). *Addresses some of the inadequacies, omissions, and assumptions in traditional couples' therapy to help you face the issues of race, ethnicity, and sexual orientation in helping couples today.*

A Feminist Clinician's Guide to the Memory Debate, edited by Susan Contratto, PhD, and M. Janice Gutfreund, PhD (Vol. 19, No. 1, 1996). *"Unites diverse scholars, clinicians, and activists in an insightful and useful examination of the issues related to recovered memories." (Feminist Bookstore News)*

Classism and Feminist Therapy: Counting Costs, edited by Marcia Hill, EdD, and Esther D. Rothblum, PhD (Vol. 18, No. 3/4, 1996). *"Educates, challenges, and questions the influence of classism on the clinical practice of psychotherapy with women." (Kathleen P. Gates, MA, Certified Professional Counselor, Center for Psychological Health, Superior, Wisconsin)*

Lesbian Therapists and Their Therapy: From Both Sides of the Couch, edited by Nancy D. Davis, MD, Ellen Cole, PhD, and Esther D. Rothblum, PhD (Vol. 18, No. 2, 1996). *"Highlights the power and boundary issues of psychotherapy from perspectives that many readers may have neither considered nor experienced in their own professional lives." (Psychiatric Services)*

Feminist Foremothers in Women's Studies, Psychology, and Mental Health, edited by Phyllis Chesler, PhD, Esther D. Rothblum, PhD, and Ellen Cole, PhD (Vol. 17, No. 1/2/3/4, 1995). *"A must for feminist scholars and teachers . . . These women's personal experiences are poignant and powerful." (Women's Studies International Forum)*

Women's Spirituality, Women's Lives, edited by Judith Ochshorn, PhD, and Ellen Cole, PhD (Vol. 16, No. 2/3, 1995). *"A delightful and complex book on spirituality and sacredness in women's lives." (Joan Clingan, MA, Spiritual Psychology, Graduate Advisor, Prescott College Master of Arts Program)*

Psychopharmacology from a Feminist Perspective, edited by Jean A. Hamilton, MD, Margaret Jensvold, MD, Esther D. Rothblum, PhD, and Ellen Cole, PhD (Vol. 16, No. 1, 1995). *"Challenges readers to increase their sensitivity and awareness of the role of sex and gender in response to and acceptance of pharmacologic therapy." (American Journal of Pharmaceutical Education)*

Wilderness Therapy for Women: The Power of Adventure, edited by Ellen Cole, PhD, Esther D. Rothblum, PhD, and Eve Erdman, MEd, MLS (Vol. 15, No. 3/4, 1994). *"There's an undeniable excitement in these pages about the thrilling satisfaction of meeting challenges in the physical world, the world outside our cities that is unfamiliar, uneasy territory for many women. If you're interested at all in the subject, this book is well worth your time." (Psychology of Women Quarterly)*

Bringing Ethics Alive: Feminist Ethics in Psychotherapy Practice, edited by Nanette K. Gartrell, MD (Vol. 15, No. 1, 1994). *"Examines the theoretical and practical issues of ethics in feminist therapies. From the responsibilities of training programs to include social issues ranging from racism to sexism to practice ethics, this outlines real questions and concerns." (Midwest Book Review)*

Women with Disabilities: Found Voices, edited by Mary Willmuth, PhD, and Lillian Holcomb, PhD (Vol. 14, No. 3/4, 1994). *"These powerful chapters often jolt the anti-disability consciousness and force readers to contend with the ways in which disability has been constructed, disguised, and rendered disgusting by much of society." (Academic Library Book Review)*

Faces of Women and Aging, edited by Nancy D. Davis, MD, Ellen Cole, PhD, and Esther D. Rothblum, PhD (Vol. 14, No. 1/2, 1993). *"This uplifting, helpful book is of great value not only for aging women, but also for women of all ages who are interested in taking active control of their own lives." (New Mature Woman)*

Refugee Women and Their Mental Health: Shattered Societies, Shattered Lives, edited by Ellen Cole, PhD, Oliva M. Espin, PhD, and Esther D. Rothblum, PhD (Vol. 13, No. 1/2/3, 1992). *"The ideas presented are rich and the perspectives varied, and the book is an important contribution to understanding refugee women in a global context." (Contemporary Psychology)*

Women, Girls and Psychotherapy: Reframing Resistance, edited by Carol Gilligan, PhD, Annie Rogers, PhD, and Deborah Tolman, EdD (Vol. 11, No. 3/4, 1991). *"Of use to educators, psychotherapists, and parents–in short, to any person who is directly involved with girls at adolescence." (Harvard Educational Review)*

Professional Training for Feminist Therapists: Personal Memoirs, edited by Esther D. Rothblum, PhD, and Ellen Cole, PhD (Vol. 11, No. 1, 1991). *"Exciting, interesting, and filled with the angst and the energies that directed these women to develop an entirely different approach to counseling." (Science Books & Films)*

Jewish Women in Therapy: Seen But Not Heard, edited by Rachel Josefowitz Siegel, MSW, and Ellen Cole, PhD (Vol. 10, No. 4, 1991). *"A varied collection of prose and poetry, first-person stories, and accessible theoretical pieces that can help Jews and non-Jews, women and men, therapists and patients, and general readers to grapple with questions of Jewish women's identities and diversity." (Canadian Psychology)*

Women's Mental Health in Africa, edited by Esther D. Rothblum, PhD, and Ellen Cole, PhD (Vol. 10, No. 3, 1990). *"A valuable contribution and will be of particular interest to scholars in women's studies, mental health, and cross-cultural psychology." (Contemporary Psychology)*

Motherhood: A Feminist Perspective, edited by Jane Price Knowles, MD, and Ellen Cole, PhD (Vol. 10, No. 1/2, 1990). *"Provides some enlightening perspectives. . . . It is worth the time of both male and female readers." (Comtemporary Psychology)*

Monographs "Separates" list continued at the back

Violence in the Lives of Black Women: Battered, Black, and Blue

Carolyn M. West, PhD
Editor

Violence in the Lives of Black Women: Battered, Black, and Blue has been co-published simultaneously as *Women & Therapy*, Volume 25, Numbers 3/4 2002.

The Haworth Press, Inc.
New York • London • Oxford

Violence in the Lives of Black Women: Battered, Black, and Blue has been co-published simultaneously as *Women & Therapy*™, Volume 25, Numbers 3/4 2002.

The development, preparation, and publication of this work has been undertaken with great care. However, the publisher, employees, editors, and agents of The Haworth Press and all imprints of The Haworth Press, Inc., including The Haworth Medical Press® and Pharmaceutical Products Press®, are not responsible for any errors contained herein or for consequences that may ensue from use of materials or information contained in this work. Opinions expressed by the author(s) are not necessarily those of The Haworth Press, Inc. With regard to case studies, identities and circumstances of individuals discussed herein have been changed to protect confidentiality. Any resemblance to actual persons, living or dead, is entirely coincidental.

Cover design by Marylouise Doyle

Library of Congress Cataloging-in-Publication Data

Violence in the lives of black women : battered, black, and blue / Carolyn M. West, editor.
    p. cm.
    "Co-published simultaneously as Women & therapy, Volume 25, Numbers 3/4 2002"–P.
    Includes bibliographical references and index.
    ISBN 0-7890-1994-9 ((hard) : alk. paper) – ISBN 0-7890-1995-7 ((pbk) : alk. paper)
    1. Women–Violence against–United States. 2. African American women–Violence against.
3. African American women–Abuse of. 4. Victims of violent crimes–United States–Psychology.
5. Abused women–United States–Psychology. 6. Abused women–Rehabilitation–United States.
I. West, Carolyn M. (Carolyn Marie)
HV6250.4.W65 V5677 2002
362.88′082–dc21

                                           2002013253

Indexing, Abstracting & Website/Internet Coverage

This section provides you with a list of major indexing & abstracting services. That is to say, each service began covering this periodical during the year noted in the right column. Most Websites which are listed below have indicated that they will either post, disseminate, compile, archive, cite or alert their own Website users with research-based content from this work. (This list is as current as the copyright date of this publication.)

Abstracting, Website/Indexing Coverage......... Year When Coverage Began

- *Academic Abstracts/CD-ROM* **1995**
- *Academic ASAP <www.galegroup.com>* **1992**
- *Academic Index (on-line)* **1992**
- *Academic Search Elite (EBSCO)* **1994**
- *Alternative Press Index (print online & CD-ROM from NISC)*
  <www.altpress.com> **1982**
- *Behavioral Medicine Abstracts* **1996**
- *Child Development Abstracts & Bibliography (in print & online)*
  <www.ukans.edu> **1994**
- *CINAHL (Cumulative Index to Nursing & Allied Health*
  Literature) **2000**
- *CNPIEC Reference Guide: Chinese National Directory*
  of Foreign Periodicals **1996**
- *Contemporary Women's Issues* **1998**
- *Current Contents: Social & Behavioral Sciences*
  <www.isinet.com> **1995**
- *e-psyche, LLC <www.e-psyche.net>* **2001**
- *Expanded Academic ASAP <www.galegroup.com>* **1992**
- *Expanded Academic Index* **1993**

(continued)

- *Sociological Abstracts (SA) <www.csa.com>* **1997**
- *Studies on Women Abstracts <www.tandf.co.uk>* **1982**
- *SwetsNet <www.swetsnet.com>* **2001**
- *Violence and Abuse Abstracts: A Review of Current Literature on Interpersonal Violence (VAA)* **1995**
- *Women Studies Abstracts* **1991**
- *Women's Studies Index (indexed comprehensively)* **1992**

*Special Bibliographic Notes related to special journal issues
(separates) and indexing/abstracting:*

- indexing/abstracting services in this list will also cover material in any "separate" that is co-published simultaneously with Haworth's special thematic journal issue or DocuSerial. Indexing/abstracting usually covers material at the article/chapter level.
- monographic co-editions are intended for either non-subscribers or libraries which intend to purchase a second copy for their circulating collections.
- monographic co-editions are reported to all jobbers/wholesalers/approval plans. The source journal is listed as the "series" to assist the prevention of duplicate purchasing in the same manner utilized for books-in-series.
- to facilitate user/access services all indexing/abstracting services are encouraged to utilize the co-indexing entry note indicated at the bottom of the first page of each article/chapter/contribution.
- this is intended to assist a library user of any reference tool (whether print, electronic, online, or CD-ROM) to locate the monographic version if the library has purchased this version but not a subscription to the source journal.
- individual articles/chapters in any Haworth publication are also available through the Haworth Document Delivery Service (HDDS).

Violence in the Lives
of Black Women:
Battered, Black, and Blue

CONTENTS

Introduction   1
    Carolyn M. West

OVERVIEW OF VIOLENCE

Battered, Black, and Blue: An Overview of Violence
   in the Lives of Black Women   5
    Carolyn M. West

Black Women and Community Violence: Trauma, Grief,
   and Coping   29
    Esther J. Jenkins

TYPES OF VIOLENCE

Childhood Sexual Abuse in the Lives of Black Women:
   Risk and Resilience in a Longitudinal Study   45
    Victoria L. Banyard
    Linda M. Williams
    Jane A. Siegel
    Carolyn M. West

Grounding Our Feet and Hearts: Black Women's Coping
   Strategies in Psychologically Abusive Dating Relationships   59
    April L. Few
    Patricia Bell-Scott

"The Straw That Broke the Camel's Back":
  African American Women's Strategies for Disengaging
  from Abusive Relationships   79
    Janette Y. Taylor

Living at the Intersection: The Effects of Racism and Sexism
  on Black Rape Survivors   95
    Roxanne Donovan
    Michelle Williams

Racialized Sexual Harassment in the Lives
  of African American Women   107
    NiCole T. Buchanan
    Alayne J. Ormerod

MARGINALIZED POPULATIONS

"There's a Stranger in This House": African American Lesbians
  and Domestic Violence   125
    Amorie Robinson

Head and Brain Injuries Experienced by African American
  Women Victims of Intimate Partner Violence   133
    Martha E. Banks
    Rosalie J. Ackerman

BREAKING SILENCE: ACTIVISM AND HEALING

Talking Back: Research as an Act of Resistance and Healing
  for African American Women Survivors
  of Intimate Male Partner Violence   145
    Janette Y. Taylor

Fragmented Silhouettes   161
    Salamishah Tillet

Using Celluloid to Break the Silence About Sexual Violence
  in the Black Community   179
    Aishah Shahidah Simmons

Striving for a More Excellent Way   187
    Rosalyn R. Nichols

"I Find Myself at Therapy's Doorstep": Summary
    and Suggested Readings on Violence in the Lives
    of Black Women   193
    Carolyn M. West

Index   203

ABOUT THE EDITOR

Carolyn M. West, PhD, is Assistant Professor of Psychology at the University of Washington, Tacoma. She received her doctorate in Clinical Psychology from the University of Missouri, St. Louis, completed a clinical and teaching postdoctoral fellowship at Illinois State University, and completed a National Institute of Mental Health Research postdoctoral fellowship at the Family Research Laboratory at the University of New Hampshire. Dr. West is a frequent speaker at national conferences and has published numerous articles and book chapters on violence in the lives of Black women. She has previously been a consultant for the Centers for Disease Control and the National Institute of Justice, and is currently a consultant for the National Violence Against Women Prevention Research Center. In 2000, the University of Minnesota's Institute on Domestic Violence in the African American Community presented Dr. West with the Outstanding Researcher Award.

Introduction

How do feminist therapists, researchers, advocates, activists, and survivors begin a dialogue about violence in the lives of Black women? The discussion often starts with the familiar tag line, "Domestic violence is a problem that affects all women, regardless of race and social class." This statement is true. To some extent, violence in the home, on the streets, and in the workplace is *color blind*. In our patriarchal society, any woman is vulnerable. Other scholars have considered violence to be a problem that plagues people of color, particularly African Americans. In some respects, this statement is also true. Race, class, and gender inequalities place Black women at an increased risk for many forms of victimization. Therapists and scholars face the challenge of articulating the many similarities among survivors, without negating the particular experiences of Black women. Simultaneously, we need to acknowledge racial differences without perpetrating the stereotype that African Americans are inherently more violent than other racial/ethnic groups.

This challenge requires us to develop a Black feminist analysis of violence in the lives of African American women. Such a perspective would not privilege gender oppression over race or class oppression. Instead, a Black feminist approach would consider how living at the intersection of race, class, and gender oppression, and other forms of oppression, such as homophobia, converge to shape Black women's experiences with violence. For example, when compared to poor women and lesbians, social class and heterosexual privilege can protect middle-class or heterosexual Black women from some types of aggression. At the same time, racism can make it difficult for Black women, regardless of their economic status or sexual orientation, to escape racially-based forms of violence.

[Haworth co-indexing entry note]: "Introduction." West, Carolyn M. Co-published simultaneously in *Women & Therapy* (The Haworth Press, Inc.) Vol. 25, No. 3/4, 2002, pp. 1-4; and: *Violence in the Lives of Black Women: Battered, Black, and Blue* (ed: Carolyn M. West) The Haworth Press, Inc., 2002, pp. 1-4. Single or multiple copies of this article are available for a fee from The Haworth Document Delivery Service [1-800-HAWORTH, 9:00 a.m. - 5:00 p.m. (EST). E-mail address: getinfo@haworthpressinc.com].

All these forms of oppression and violence are deeply rooted in history. For example, slavery created institutionalized forms of violence, including rape and forced breeding. Oppressive images were created to "normalize" this violence. It was easier to perceive Black women as sexually promiscuous Jezebels rather than as rape victims. Although this history is unpleasant, it continues to influence institutional responses to Black survivors. Some mental health, legal, and medical professionals continue to minimize the violence in Black women's lives. However, Black feminist scholars also emphasize Black women's long history of resistance to violence in their lives and communities. We see examples of this resistance in Black women's literature, music, and spirituality.

The authors of this volume are therapists, researchers, community activists, and survivors of violence. Most of the authors are African American women, and all are deeply committed to ending violence in the lives of women. They write from a Black feminist perspective. Such a framework requires us to broaden our definition of violence to include violence in intimate relationships, violence in the workplace, and violence in the community. Accordingly, the first section of this volume is a literature review. In the first article, I focus on childhood sexual abuse, dating violence, partner abuse in intimate relationships (both dating and married couples), sexual assault, and sexual harassment. In the second article, Esther Jenkins reviews the literature on community violence, with a focus on witnessing violence and the loss of an intimate to homicide. Both articles provide prevalence rates and risk factors, and discuss the most common psychological sequelae associated with each form of victimization.

The second section of this volume delves into each type of violence in more detail. The goal is to focus on violence across the life span, beginning with violence during childhood. Victoria Banyard, Linda Williams, Jane Siegel, and Carolyn West used a longitudinal study, whose sample consisted primarily of African American women, to investigate the long-term physical and mental health consequences associated with childhood sexual abuse. They discovered that many survivors of child sexual abuse are vulnerable to re-victimization in the forms of partner violence and rape in their adult relationships. These findings indicate that violence in the lives of Black women is not an isolated incident. Instead, violence is often a "complex web of trauma exposure," which influences many areas of Black women's lives.

The abuse experience is further complicated when survivors live at the intersection of multiple forms of oppression. As evidence, NiCole

Buchanan and Alayne Ormerod conducted focus groups with professional African American women. They discovered that racism and sexism converged to form what they describe as "racialized sexual harassment." Roxanne Donovan and Michelle Williams explore how living at the intersection of racism and sexism can make it difficult for Black women to disclose having been raped. Consistent with Black feminist theory, the authors explain how Black women's history of sexual violence and the history of oppressive images influence how contemporary Black women experience sexual harassment and rape.

The diversity among African American women will obviously shape their experiences with violence. Accordingly, the third section of this volume focuses on battered African American women who are further silenced by their marginalized status. Amorie Robinson addressed the unique challenges faced by battered lesbians, such as internalized and institutionalized homophobia. Martha Banks and Rosalie Ackerman focus on Black battered women who had experienced traumatic head and brain injuries. The authors used cases studies to allow Black women from these marginalized groups to speak for themselves.

Despite the challenges, many Black women are survivors and active change agents. Banyard and her colleagues investigate characteristics that are associated with resilience among Black survivors of childhood sexual abuse. Other authors also contribute to our knowledge in this area. Specifically, several authors used interviews to investigate the decision-making and termination process that Black women use to escape abusive intimate relationships. April Few and Patricia Bell-Scott focus on violent dating relationships, and Janette Taylor extends this discussion with her focus on marital relationships. Regardless of their relationship status, leaving is a process that requires many women to identify their partners' behavior as abusive, to disengage from their partners, and finally to move toward healing.

Black feminist scholars value testimonials offered by survivors and believe that a variety of methods can be used to raise awareness about violence in the lives of Black women and thus promote healing. Consequently, the final section of this volume is devoted to activism and healing. Janette Taylor conducted interviews to demonstrate how formerly battered Black women used the research process to heal themselves and to help others. Salamishah Tillet and Aishah Simmons draw on their personal experiences as rape survivors. Both authors have used the media and the arts to depict their vision of a world where Black women are free from sexual violation. Rev. Rosalyn Nichols represents the voice of a spiritual leader and community member. Reliance on faith and courage inspired her to develop a program to address violence in her community. In the final article, I summarize the authors' findings, review their suggestions for intervention, and provide a list of references and resources.

This volume is entitled *Battered, Black, and Blue* because we know that too many Black women are battered in their intimate relationships, communities, and workplaces. Furthermore, Black women are battered when social institutions are unresponsive to their plight. In addition, as the title suggests, many Black women are *blue*. The color blue represents the physical and emotional bruises caused by the violence in their lives. The color blue represents the depression and other negative mental and physical consequences associated with abuse and victimization. Finally, the color blue represents a form of music that Black women developed to resist the violence in their lives. Although one volume cannot provide all of the answers, it is clear that violence in the lives of Black women is a serious problem. It is our hope that this volume will help feminist therapists, researchers, advocates, activists, and survivors begin a dialogue about violence in the lives of Black women.

Carolyn M. West

OVERVIEW OF VIOLENCE

Battered, Black, and Blue:
An Overview of Violence in the Lives
of Black Women

Carolyn M. West

Carolyn M. West, PhD, is Assistant Professor of Psychology in the Interdisciplinary Arts and Sciences Program, University of Washington, Tacoma, where she teaches a course on Family Violence. She received her doctorate in Clinical Psychology from the University of Missouri, St. Louis (1994), and has completed a clinical and teaching postdoctoral fellowship at Illinois State University (1995) and a National Institute of Mental Health research postdoctoral research fellowship at the Family Research Laboratory, University of New Hampshire (1995-1997). In 2000, the University of Minnesota's Institute on Domestic Violence in the African American Community presented Dr. West with the Outstanding Researcher Award.

Address correspondence to: Carolyn M. West, PhD, Interdisciplinary Arts & Sciences, Box 358436, 1900 Commerce Street, Tacoma, WA 98402-3100 (E-mail: carwest@ u.washington.edu or www.drcarolynwest.com).

Deep appreciation is expressed to Drs. Ellyn Kaschak, Beverly Greene, Suzanna Rose, and Laurie Roades for their support and encouragement, to Bronwyn Pughe for her generous editing, and to Karin Dalesky for her research assistance.

[Haworth co-indexing entry note]: "Battered, Black, and Blue: An Overview of Violence in the Lives of Black Women." West, Carolyn M. Co-published simultaneously in *Women & Therapy* (The Haworth Press, Inc.) Vol. 25, No. 3/4, 2002, pp. 5-27; and: *Violence in the Lives of Black Women: Battered, Black, and Blue* (ed: Carolyn M. West) The Haworth Press, Inc., 2002, pp. 5-27. Single or multiple copies of this article are available for a fee from The Haworth Document Delivery Service [1-800-HAWORTH, 9:00 a.m. - 5:00 p.m. (EST). E-mail address: getinfo@haworthpressinc.com].

5

SUMMARY. The purpose of this article is to review the many forms of violence in the lives of African American women, including childhood sexual abuse, dating violence, intimate partner violence, sexual assault, and sexual harassment. The first section will address definitions of violence, prevalence rates and risk factors, and suggest new directions for research. The second section is a review of the most common psychological sequelae associated with Black women's victimization. The final section is devoted to activities that promote healing, including therapy, participation in research studies, and activism. *[Article copies available for a fee from The Haworth Document Delivery Service: 1-800-HAWORTH. E-mail address: <getinfo@haworthpressinc.com> Website: <http://www.HaworthPress.com> © 2002 by The Haworth Press, Inc. All rights reserved.]*

KEYWORDS. Blacks, battered women, rape, sexual abuse, sexual harassment, violence

Take all my money, blacken both of my eyes
Give it to another woman, come home and tell me lies

> *–Black Eye Blues* by Gertrude "Ma" Rainey

I woke up this mornin', my head was sore as a boil
My man beat me last night with five feet of copper coil

> *–Sweet Rough Man* by Gertrude "Ma" Rainey
> (as cited in Davis, A.Y., 1998, p. 204 & 247)

Battered Black women have a long history of singing the blues. During the 1920s and 1930s, blues women like Bessie Smith, Billie Holiday, and others used music to document their abuse, depression, and ultimate triumph over the violence in their lives. According to Angela Y. Davis (1998), this music was important because it "named domestic violence in the collective context of blues performance and therefore defines it as a problem worthy of public discourse" (p. 28).

In the tradition of Black feminist scholarship, this article will identify the various types of violence experienced by African American women across the lifespan. More specifically, I will define each type of violence, discuss prevalence rates and risk factors, and suggest new directions for research. The second section is a review of the most common psychological sequelae associated with violence in the lives of Black women, such as substance abuse, depression, and suicide attempts. Finally, I will discuss activities that promote healing, such as therapy, participation in research, and activism.

TYPES OF VIOLENCE

This section will focus on Black women's experience with childhood sexual abuse, dating violence, intimate partner violence, sexual assault, and sexual harassment. Although each type of violence will be discussed separately, it is common for multiple forms of violence to co-occur. For example, battered women are often victims of marital rape (Campbell & Soeken, 1999a).

Childhood Sexual Abuse

There is no universal definition of *childhood sexual abuse* (CSA). However, researchers (Fergusson & Mullen, 1999) have identified two overlapping but distinguishable types of interactions: (a) forced or coerced sexual behavior imposed on a child; and (b) sexual activity, whether or not obvious coercion is used, between a child and an older person, for example, when there is a five-year age discrepancy or more between the victim and perpetrator. Sexual abuse can be categorized as intrafamilial and involve a father, uncle, or brother, or extrafamilial and involve a baby sitter, neighbor, or authority figure, such as a coach, teacher, or clergy member. Although males are perpetrators in many cases of child sexual abuse, there have been documented cases of female offenders. Perpetrators commit a wide range of sexually abusive behaviors, which can be categorized as contact abuse (e.g., fondling or oral, anal, or digital penetration) or noncontact abuse (e.g., exhibitionism or taking pornographic pictures of the child).

Estimates of CSA have varied widely. In small San Francisco (Wingood & DiClemente, 1997a) and Baltimore (Banyard, 1999) samples of low-income Black women, approximately 14% reported a history of childhood sexual abuse. However, almost one-third of the surveyed Black women in a community sample of Los Angeles residents had been victims of CSA, a prevalence rate that has remained stable over a ten-year period (Wyatt, Loeb, Solis, Carmona, & Romero, 1999). This is consistent with the rates reported by Black women in a variety of samples, including Black adolescent girls in a community-based health program (23%) (Cecil & Matson, 2001), Black college women (21%, 44%)

(Kenny & McEachern, 2000; Urquiza & Goodlin-Jones, 1994, respectively), and Black welfare recipients (37%) (Marcenko, Kemp, & Larson, 2000).

Although African American women report a range of sexually abusive experiences in childhood, they are especially vulnerable to severe forms of violence, such as vaginal, anal, or oral penetration. Nearly two-thirds of Black girls whose medical records were reviewed (61%) (Huston, Prihoda, Parra, & Foulds, 1997), Black girls treated at child abuse clinics (53%, 65%) (Shaw, Lewis, Loeb, Rosado, & Rodriguez, 2001; Sanders-Phillips, Moisan, Wadlington, Morgan, & English, 1995, respectively), and Black girls in foster care (73%) (Leifer & Shapiro, 1995) reported some form of forced penetration. A similarly high percentage of Black women in a community sample reported childhood sexual abuse that involved attempted or completed oral sex, anal sex, or rape (Wyatt et al., 1999).

What accounts for these high rates of severe childhood sexual abuse? Penetration is more likely to occur if the child is older or if the perpetrator is the mother's boyfriend (Huston et al., 1997). Black girls are often overrepresented in these categories. On average, Black women are eight years old when they experience the first incidence of sexual abuse (West, C. M., Williams, & Siegel, 2000), and, due to marital patterns in the African American community, a substantial number of Black girls will be exposed to stepfathers or their mothers' boyfriends (Abney & Priest, 1995). Both of these demographic factors may leave Black girls more vulnerable to sexual abuse.

Many Black survivors of CSA will be re-victimized in adulthood, defined as the occurrence of at least one incident of sexual abuse during childhood followed by a subsequent incident of adult physical or sexual victimization (West, C. M. et al., 2000; Wyatt, Notgrass, & Gordon, 1995). In addition, they are often exposed to community violence, in the form of witnessing assaults or losing family members to homicide (Jenkins, 2002 [This volume]). Banyard, Williams, Siegel, and West (2002 [This volume]) use a longitudinal study, whose sample consisted primarily of Black women, to investigate mental health consequences, re-traumatization, and resilience.

Dating Violence

The National Center for Injury Prevention and Control (1997) defined *dating violence*:

As the perpetration or threat of an act of violence by at least one member of an unmarried couple on the other member within the context of dating or courtship. This violence encompasses any form of sexual assault, physical violence, and verbal and emotional abuse. (p. 1)

Researchers have been investigating dating violence, also referred to as *courtship violence* or *premarital abuse*, since the early 1980s (Lewis & Fremouw, 2001). This form of aggression has been documented among Black high school students (Coker et al., 2001; O'Keefe, 1997; Valois, Oeltmann, Waller, & Hussey, 1999; Watson, Cascardi, Avery-Leaf, & O'Leary, 2001) and Black college students (Clark, Beckett, Wells, & Dungee-Anderson, 1994; DeMaris, 1990).

Similar to their White counterparts, verbal and psychological abuse are the most commonly reported forms of courtship violence. The majority (90%) of Black college students had used verbal aggression, such as swearing, insulting, and name-calling, in the context of a dating relationship (Clark et al., 1994). Substantial rates of physical violence have been reported as well. Approximately one-third of Black undergraduates were victims or perpetrators of physical aggression, such as pushing, slapping, and hitting (Clark et al., 1994). Disturbingly high rates of dating aggression also have been discovered among adolescents. Almost one-half of African American high school students in a South Carolina sample had been victims or perpetrators of severe dating violence, defined as beating, kicking, or knocking a partner down (Coker et al., 2000).

A review of the literature indicates that women are equally or more likely to inflict dating violence as their male counterparts (Lewis & Fremouw, 2001). A similar pattern of gender aggression has been found among African Americans. Black college women inflicted more aggression than their male peers (Clark et al., 1994), and Black adolescent males and females inflicted and sustained equal rates of physical aggression (Valois et al., 1999; Watson et al., 2001). However, when researchers considered the types of aggression enacted, women experienced forms of violence that were more injurious. For example, West, C. M., and Rose (2000) discovered that the Black adolescent women in their sample made threats, threw objects, and hit their partners. They were also more likely to have their feelings hurt and to be victims of severe violence, such as choking and attempted rape. In contrast, the young men made their partners feel inferior, degraded them, and were more likely to use sexual aggression, including forced breast fondling and attempted rape. This pattern of abuse suggests that although young Black women may inflict dating aggression, they also endure severe forms of violence, which may increase their risk of injury.

Black women who experienced violence in another area of their lives were at increased risk for dating aggression. Specifically, Black college women who had witnessed parental fighting were more likely to be victimized by their boyfriends (DeMaris, 1990). In addition, low-income Black adolescent girls appear to be especially vulnerable to premarital abuse (Brown & Gourdine, 1998; Hunt & Joe-Laidler, 2001). For instance, in a sample of Black youths who were enrolled in a government-sponsored vocational training program, almost one-fourth had been threatened with a weapon, and nearly one-third had been beaten by a date (West, C. M. & Rose, 2000). Researchers believe that exposure to community violence, which can spill over into intimate relationships, may partially account for the high rates of dating violence among impoverished Black youths (Malik, Sorenson, & Aneshensel, 1997).

After more than two decades of research, there continues to be a dearth of information on dating aggression among African Americans. In particular, there needs to be more research on how Black women assign meaning to the psychological, physical, and sexual violence in their dating relationships. In this volume, Few and Bell-Scott (2002) investigate the coping strategies used by psychologically abused Black college women.

Intimate Partner Violence

Intimate partner violence, also referred to as *domestic violence* or *wife battering*, often involves a broad range of abusive behaviors including:

> Physical violence, sexual violence, threats of violence against the woman and children or other loved ones, emotional/psychological abuse, economic exploitation, confinement and/or control over activities outside the home (e.g., social life, working), stalking, property destruction, burglary, theft, and homicide. (Mahoney, Williams, & West, C. M., 2001, p. 145)

More researchers are beginning to focus on violence in lesbian relationships (Kaschak, 2001). However, with few exceptions (e.g., Butler, 1999), researchers have neglected violence in the lives of Black lesbians. Although the dynamics of abuse are often similar across sexual orientation, lesbian batterers can use homophobic control as a method of psychological abuse. For example, an abuser may *out* her partner by revealing her sexual orientation to unsupportive relatives or co-workers. In this volume, Amorie Robinson (2002) addresses issues concerning this population.

To date, most researchers have investigated violence in heterosexual Black relationships, which will be the focus of this literature review. Based on national surveys, Black women experience an alarmingly high rate of intimate partner violence. For example, in the National Family Violence Survey, 17% of Black wives had been victims of at least one violent act in the survey year (Hampton & Gelles, 1994). In the more recently administered Violence Against Women Survey, one-quarter of the Black women surveyed had been victims of physical partner violence, and 4% had been stalked (Tjaden & Thoennes, 2000).

When rates of severe violence were considered, Black women were frequent victims of wife battering (Kessler, Molnar, Feurer, & Appelbaum, 2001). For instance, 7% had been kicked, choked, beaten, or assaulted with a weapon (Hampton & Gelles, 1994). The battering often continues when the woman becomes pregnant. In a sample of women, primarily African American, who sought emergency treatment at an Atlanta gynecologic and obstetric clinic, 50% had a history of abuse or were currently in an abusive relationship. Fractures were the most commonly reported injuries. Other patients listed moderate to severe injuries, including head injuries, nerve damage, and miscarriage (Geary & Wingate, 1999). These types of injuries, particularly head and brain injuries, may impair a survivor's future physical and psychological functioning (Banks & Ackerman, 2002 [This volume]). In the most severe cases of abuse, Black women have been murdered. In fact, homicide by intimate partners is the leading cause of death for African American women between the ages of 15 and 24 (National Center for Health Statistics, 1997).

Women from all economic and social backgrounds are victims of wife abuse (Hampton & Gelles, 1994). However, the demographic profile of victims indicates that women who are African American, young, divorced or separated, impoverished, and residents in urban areas are the most frequent victims of partner violence (Rennison & Welchans, 2000). Among indigent Black women, those who received food stamps or other forms of government assistance were especially vulnerable to physical (67%) and psychological abuse (95%) (Honeycutt, Marshall, & Weston, 2001). Other high-risk groups included Black women with a history of violence in their families of origin (Hampton & Gelles, 1994;

Huang & Gunn, 2001), incarcerated Black women (Richie, 1994), substance abusing Black women (Davis, R. E., 1997; Curtis-Boles & Jenkins-Monroe, 2000), and HIV positive Black women (Wyatt, Axelrod, Chin, Carmona, & Loeb, 2000).

Many battered women eventually terminate their abusive relationships. Although researchers are beginning to consider cultural differences in the termination process (Kearney, 2001), with few exceptions (Burke, Gielen, McDonnell, O'Campo, & Maman, 2001), little research has focused on the process that battered Black women use to disengage from their violent partners. In particular, more research should focus on how African American women survive in abusive relationships, how they prepare to leave, and how they cope with the initial crisis after leaving. In this volume, Few and Bell-Scott (2002) investigate the process that Black college women use to terminate their abusive dating relationships. Married Black women face additional challenges when they flee violence in their homes, such as protecting their children and locating housing. Janette Taylor (2002a) investigates Black women's strategies for terminating violent marital and long-term relationships.

Sexual Assault

Similar to intimate partner violence, sexual assault can involve a broad range of aggressive behaviors, including:

> sex without consent, rape, sexual control of reproductive rights, and all forms of sexual manipulation carried out by the perpetrator with the intention or perceived intention to cause emotional, sexual, and physical degradation to another person. (Abraham, 1999, p. 552)

Although stranger rape does occur, women are more likely to be raped by acquaintances, boyfriends, and husbands (Bachar & Koss, 2001).

According to the National Crime Victimization Survey, nearly 3 Black women per 1,000 had been raped or sexually assaulted (Rennison & Welchans, 2000). In another national study, 7% of Black women identified themselves as rape survivors (Tjaden & Thoennes, 2000). When self-reports were used, researchers discovered even higher rates of sexual violence. For example, approximately 20% of Black adolescent females had been raped (Valois et al., 1999). Although Black teenage girls are sometimes sexually aggressive in their dating relationships, they are more likely to be victims of a wide range of sexual violence, including forced kissing, forced breast and genital fondling, and attempted rape (West, C. M. & Rose, 2000). Even higher rates of rape, more than 30%, were reported by Black women in community samples (Molitor, Ruiz, Klausner, & McFarland, 2000; Wyatt et al., 1999) and in samples of Black college women (Carmody & Washington, 2001; Urquiza & Goodlin-Jones, 1994).

Similar to victims of domestic violence, low-income Black women (Kalichman, Williams, Cherry, Belcher, & Nachimson, 1998) and Black women who received public assistance (Honeycutt et al., 2001) experienced elevated rates of sexual assault. Women who are battered are also at increased risk of partner rape. This pattern of violence creates an extremely dangerous situation for victims. When compared to Black women who experienced physical abuse only, victims who were both beaten and raped were more likely to be psychologically abused and to experience physical violence that was severe and potentially lethal (Campbell & Soeken, 1999a).

Although substantial numbers of African American women have been raped, many survivors never disclose their sexual assaults (Pierce-Baker, 1998; Washington, 2001). In order to understand their reluctance to seek help, scholars and therapists must begin to contextualize rape (Neville & Heppner, 1999). This entails investigating how discrimination and negative images of Black women, which depict them as sexually promiscuous and thus not legitimate victims, can create barriers to the help-seeking efforts of Black rape survivors (Neville & Hamer, 2001). In this volume, Donovan and Williams (2002) explore how two historical images of Black women, the Jezebel and Matriarch, may potentially influence the disclosure patterns of Black rape survivors.

Sexual Harassment

According to the Equal Employment Opportunity Commission (EEOC) and the Office of Civil Rights (OCR), *sexual harassment* includes, but is not limited to, unwanted talk or jokes about sex, sexualized pranks, uninvited physical contact, pressure for dates or sex, sexual abuse, and rape. This form of victimization can be categorized as *quid pro quo*, which refers to the exchange of sexual favors for special privileges (e.g., a promotion, a raise, a better grade) or *hostile environment* harassment, which results in an unpleasant work atmosphere that leaves women feeling demeaned or humiliated (O'Donohue, Downs, & Yeater, 1998). African American women have been sexually harassed in a variety of settings, including the church (Whitson, 1997), on the street (Davis, D. E., 1997), and in social settings (Wyatt & Riederle, 1995). However, most of the research has focused on sexual harassment in employment and academic settings.

Black women have a long history of sexual harassment in the workplace. During the antebellum period, both White and Black men raped enslaved women as they worked in the fields and in plantation households. After emancipation, employment discrimination limited Black women to jobs as domestic servants. Working conditions, such as low pay and isolation, left many Black women vulnerable to sexual harassment (Adams, 1997). This form of victimization continues to be a reality for African American women in the work force. Approximately one-third of Black women in a Los Angeles sample had been sexually harassed at work. In most cases, harassers made sexual propositions or offered job promotions in exchange for sexual favors (Wyatt & Riederle, 1995). Even more Black women, almost 75%, experienced workplace *gender harassment*, defined as degrading or insulting comments about women as a group (Piotrkowski, 1998).

Black women who are young, single, and work in low status jobs report the greatest frequency of sexual harassment (Mansfield, Koch, Henderson, & Vicary, 1991). However, supervisors and peers also sexually harass Black women who hold professional positions (Morrison, 1992; Smitherman, 1995). In addition, professional Black women often experience *contrapower* sexual harassment (e.g., a female professor being harassed by a male student). Black women may be especially vulnerable to harassment committed by male or White subordinates because their achieved status or formal organizational power does not mitigate their lower ascribed status as members of a marginalized group (Rospenda, Richman, & Nawyn, 1998).

A substantial number of Black women, more than 60%, are sexually harassed on college campuses (Cortina, Swan, Fitzgerald, & Waldo, 1998). Gender harassment, such as offensive jokes directed at women and the use of sexist teaching materials, was most commonly reported (Kalof, Eby, Matheson, & Kroska, 2001). Black college women were particularly offended by sexual propositions from White men or comments that characterized Black women as sexually promiscuous (Mecca & Rubin, 1999).

The limited research suggests that sexual and racial harassment may be combined in unique ways for African American women; however, few studies have investigated Black women's perceptions of sexual harassment (Shelton & Chavous, 1999). In this volume, Buchanan and

Ormerod (2002) used focus groups to explore racialized sexual harass-ment in the lives of professional Black women.

To summarize, this section was a literature review of violence, with a focus on prevalence rates, risk factors, and new directions for research. Although there are many unanswered questions, it is clear that child-hood sexual abuse, dating violence, intimate partner violence, sexual assault, and sexual harassment are common occurrences in the lives of African American women. The aim of this volume is to expand our knowledge in all of these areas.

PSYCHOLOGICAL SEQUELAE

I feel blue, I don't know what to do
Every woman in my fix is bound to feel blue, too

–Any Woman's Blues by Bessie Smith

Folks they think I'm crazy, I'm just a victim to the blues

–Victims to the Blues by Gertrude "Ma" Rainey
(as cited in Davis, A. Y., 1998, p. 252 & 260)

During the 1920s and 1930s, Blues women wrote songs about the sadness in their lives (Davis, A.Y., 1998). In the past few years, authors have written popular self-help books for Black women struggling with depression and the "blues" (Boyd, 1998), which some Black women de-scribe as dysphoria or a mild form of depression (Barbee, 1994). Many of the Black women interviewed in these self-help books (Mitchell & Herring, 1998) and memoirs (Danquah, 1998) attributed their depres-sion to the violence in their lives.

This section is a review of the most common psychological sequelae associated with violence in the lives of African American women. Be-fore this literature is discussed, the following caveats are offered. First, many researchers have focused on the experiences of low-income Black women, a population that is at risk for both victimization and mental health problems (U.S. Department of Health and Human Ser-vices, 2001). Black feminists (West, C. M., 2002) argue that future re-search should reflect the diverse backgrounds and experiences of African American women. Until this research can be conducted, read-ers should remember that the following results should not be general-ized to all victimized Black women. Second, many Black survivors are resilient and do not exhibit long-term negative consequences because of abuse (Hyman & Williams, 2001).

Black survivors of abuse may experience a variety of mental health problems, including dissociation (Banyard, Williams, & Siegel, 2001), low self-esteem (Banyard, 1999; Cecil & Matson, 2001; Russo, Denious, Keita, & Koss, 1997), and posttraumatic stress disorder (Hien & Bukszpan, 1999; Thompson, Kaslow, Lane, & Kingree, 2000). Many Black survivors of sexual abuse (Marcenko et al., 2000), partner violence (Hampton & Gelles, 1994), and gender harassment (Piotrkowski, 1998) also experience psychological distress, broadly defined as depression, anxiety, stress, and somatic complaints. In this section, I will discuss the association between Black women's victimization and increased rates of substance abuse, depression and suicide attempts. These mental health problems also increase the probability of physical health problems, which will also be discussed. Although these difficulties will be discussed separately, victimized Black women may experience multiple mental and physical health problems (Ross-Durow & Boyd, 2000).

Substance Abuse

When compared to their peers, Black survivors of childhood sexual abuse, domestic violence, and sexual assault consistently reported higher rates of use and abuse of various substances, including alcohol, marijuana, and crack cocaine (Curtis-Boles & Jenkins-Monroe, 2000; Davis, R. E., 1997; Marcenko et al., 2000). A history of repeated victimization appears to increase the likelihood of substance abuse. More specifically, multiple incidents of childhood sexual abuse predicted adult heavy drinking and binge drinking in one sample of African American women. Researchers speculate that binge drinking may be an effort to block memories of abuse, whereas heavy drinking may be an attempt to reduce generalized anxiety (Jasinski, Williams, & Siegel, 2000).

Although alcohol use does not cause domestic violence, drinking is often associated with violent interactions (Huang & Gunn, 2001). As evidence, two-thirds of the battered Black women in a shelter sample reported that their husbands were intoxicated during the assault (Joseph, 1997). A similar association was found in the National Alcohol Survey. Partner violence within Black couples, perpetrated by the man or woman, was more likely to occur if either partner had consumed large quantities of alcohol or had an alcohol problem (Cunradi, Caetano, Clark, & Schafer, 1999).

Depression

As expected, depression is a common experience for Black survivors of sexual assault (Rickert, Wiemann, & Berenson, 2000) and partner violence (Huang & Gunn, 2001; Russo et al., 1997). Certain groups are especially vulnerable to depression. They include Black battered women who reported multiple incidences of sexual victimization, such as marital rape or childhood sexual abuse (Campbell & Soeken, 1999a), Black adolescent girls who reported a long duration of childhood sexual abuse (Cecil & Matson, 2001), and sexually abused Black adolescent girls with a history of family conflict (Sanders-Phillips et al., 1995).

Of particular note, terminating a violent relationship may not reduce feelings of depression. Based on interviews with battered women over a three-year period, Campbell and Soeken (1999c) discovered that Black women's depression continued after they had terminated their violent relationships. In contrast, White women in this study reported a dramatic decline in depression when they ended their abusive relationships. Several factors may account for these findings. Ending an abusive relationship may not end the violence, particularly if there are children involved. In a shelter sample, one-third of the battered Black women continued to be abused by their partners after they ended the relationship (Sullivan & Rumptz, 1994). The inability to escape may lead to feelings of despair and depression. In addition, ending a violent relationship does not improve the marginalized status of most Black women. In fact, leaving an abusive partner may leave a survivor even more impoverished. Poor Black women with low educational attainment and less prestigious occupations, even if they have never been victimized, often report depression and other mental problems (Jackson & Mustillo, 2001).

Suicide Attempts

Black women in psychiatric facilities (Manetta, 1999) and substance abusing Black women (Hill, Boyd, & Kortge, 2000) were more likely to attempt suicide if they had a history of childhood physical or sexual abuse. The most comprehensive studies conducted on this topic are based on a sample of low-income African American women who visited a public health care hospital following a nonfatal suicide attempt. When compared to non-suicidal controls, suicide attempters were more likely to have had a childhood history of physical, emotional, and sexual abuse (Thompson et al., 2000) and a history of physical and emotional partner abuse. Distress, hopelessness, and drug use also accounted for the link between partner abuse and suicidal behavior (Kaslow et al., 1998).

Stark and Flitcraft (1995) contend that suicidality among battered women represents an effort to create "control in the context of no control" (p. 57). This may be true for some battered Black women. Mohr, Fantuzzo, and Abdul-Kabir (2001) interviewed a Black woman who overdosed on aspirin in response to being abused. This self-injurious behavior was a way of expressing frustration and anger at her abusive partner. The survivor stated, "I say what did he expect, he treat me and the kids like a doormat" (p. 83). According to the researchers, this suicidal gesture was a way of taking control by making her partner face the consequences of his abusive behavior. More research is required before we understand the factors that contribute to suicide attempts among victimized Black women.

Physical Health Problems

Mental and physical health problems are often interrelated. For example, battered Black women may experience psychological distress that is manifested as headaches (Hampton & Gelles, 1994) or hypertension (Lawson, Rodgers-Rose, & Rajaram, 1999). Furthermore, the combination of victimization and mental health problems increases the probability that African American women will experience physical and sexual health problems. For instance, physically and sexually abused Black women, particularly if they had experienced multiple victimizations, reported higher rates of unintended pregnancies and abortions (Wyatt et al., 1995) and reproductive health problems, such as decreased sexual desire, painful intercourse, genital irritation, repeated vaginal infections, and problems conceiving (Campbell & Soeken, 1999a; West, C. M. et al., 2000). High rates of sexually transmitted diseases (STDs) were also common among Black survivors of childhood sexual abuse (Wingood & DiClemente, 1997a), dating violence (Wingood, DiClemente, McCree, Harrington, & Davies, 2001), partner violence (Wingood & DiClemente, 1997b), and rape (Wingood & DiClemente, 1998).

In general, victimized Black women perceived less control over their sexuality (Wingood et al., 2001). Depression and substance abuse can make it especially difficult for Black survivors to make healthy sexual choices. These women may be at increased risk for STDs and reproductive health problems for several other reasons. First, the fear of a violent response may make many survivors reluctant to insist that their partners practice safe sex, such as condom use (Kalichman et al., 1998; Wingood &

DiClemente, 1997a). Second, some victimized Black women engage in risky sexual behaviors, including: prostitution (West, C. M. et al., 2000); anal sex, group sex, and partner swapping (Wyatt et al., 1995); sex with non-monogamous partners (Wingood et al., 2001); and sex with men who use drugs or men who have sex with other men (Kalichman et al., 1998).

In conclusion, some Black survivors are very resilient and do not exhibit long-term negative consequences as a result of their victimization (Hyman & Williams, 2001), whereas others experience a variety of mental health problems, including depression, substance abuse, suicide attempts, and physical health problems, such as sexually transmitted diseases. These difficulties may be exacerbated by poverty, racism, and sexism (Roosa, Reinholtz, & Angelini, 1999). Furthermore, their limited ability to practice self-care (Campbell & Soeken, 1999b) and their limited access to culturally sensitive medical care (McNutt, van Ryn, Clark, Fraiser, 2000; Russo et al., 1997) mean that many Black survivors will never receive treatment for their mental and physical health problems.

TOWARD HEALING

Once upon a time, I stood for all he did
Those days are gone, believe me kid
I've been mistreated and I don't like it, there's no use to say I do

–I've Been Mistreated and I Don't Like It by Bessie Smith
(as cited in Davis, A. Y., 1998, p. 300).

Although Blues women were often severely abused and depressed, they used music to actively resist their victimization. Contemporary Black women have even more options available to them. For example, they can benefit from therapy (West, C. M., 2002 [This volume]). Engaging in educational programs and activism can also promote healing.

African Americans welcome prevention efforts, particularly if practitioners use culturally sensitive intervention techniques (Fontes, Cruz, & Tabachnick, 2001). However, fear and mistrust of researchers have made many African American women reluctant to volunteer for research studies, especially studies which focus on sensitive topics (Earl & Penney, 2001). In this volume, Taylor (2002b) offers strategies that researchers, practitioners, and activists may use to create a research process which empowers Black women.

Based on her research with Black anti-rape activists, A. M. White (2001) concluded that, "activism should be encouraged as a healing modality just as individual and group therapy are encouraged" (p. 20). Violence against women must be perceived as a community problem. This requires Black activists, both women and men, to change the discourse surrounding rape and violence in the African American community (White, A. M., 2001). A pro-Black and pro-feminist dialogue requires us to acknowledge Black women's victimization and to acknowledge the oppression of Black men, while simultaneously holding them accountable for their violence. Tillet (2002 [This volume]) uses her experiences as a rape survivor and rape activist to begin such a Black feminist discourse.

The Black church has always been a site of Black feminist activism and a source of comfort for victimized Black women (West, T. C., 1999). Rev. Rosalyn Nichols (2002 [This volume]) explains how the murder of her childhood friend inspired her to challenge the sexism and silence surrounding domestic violence in her church and community. Black popular culture, including gospel music and media campaigns, also has been used as a source of education and activism (Oliver, 2000). In this volume, Aishah Simmons (2002), Black feminist film producer, rape survivor, and activist, describes her feature length documentary addressing sexual assault in the Black community.

In conclusion, this volume is a collection of articles written by feminist practitioners, scholars, and activists who are all deeply committed to addressing violence in the lives of Black women. Our goal is to identify the various forms of violence and to offer suggestions for intervention. Although there is much work to be done, it is important to remain optimistic. Mental health professionals and scholars should also be activists who work toward social change. Perhaps we should remember the advice offered by blues woman Ida Cox (cited in Davis, A. Y., 1998, p. 38):

> You never get nothing by being an angel child
> You'd better change your ways and get real wild
> Wild women are the only kind that really get by
> 'Cause wild women don't worry, wild women don't have the blues.

REFERENCES

Abney, V. D., & Priest, R. (1995). African Americans and sexual child abuse. In L. A. Fontes (Ed.), *Sexual abuse in nine North American cultures: Treatment and prevention* (pp. 11-30). Thousand Oaks, CA: Sage.

Abraham, M. (1999). Sexual abuse in South Asian immigrant marriages. *Violence Against Women, 5*, 591-618.

Adams, J. H. (1997). Sexual harassment and Black women: A historical perspective. In W. O'Donohue (Ed.), *Sexual harassment: Theory, research and treatment* (pp. 213-224). Boston: Allyn and Bacon.

Bachar, K., & Koss, M. P. (2001). From prevalence to prevention: Closing the gap between what we know about rape and what we do. In C. M. Renzetti, J. L. Edleson, & R. K. Bergen (Eds.), *Sourcebook on violence against women* (pp. 117-142). Thousand Oaks, CA: Sage.

Banks, M. E., & Ackerman, R. J. (2002). Head and brain injuries experienced by African American women victims of intimate partner violence. *Women & Therapy, 25* (3 & 4) 133-143.

Banyard, V. L. (1999). Childhood maltreatment and the mental health of low-income women. *American Journal of Orthopsychiatry, 69*, 161-171.

Banyard, V. L., Williams, L. M., & Siegel, J. A. (2001). Understanding links among childhood trauma, dissociation, and women's mental health. *American Journal of Orthopsychiatry, 71*, 311-321.

Banyard, V. L., Williams, L. M., Siegel, J. A., & West, C. M. (2002). Childhood sexual abuse in the lives of Black women: Risk and resilience in a longitudinal study. *Women & Therapy, 25* (3 & 4), 45-58.

Barbee, E. L. (1994). Healing time: The blues and African American women. *Health Care for Women International, 15*, 53-60.

Boyd, J. A. (1998). *Can I get a witness: For sisters, when the blues is more than a song.* New York: Dutton.

Brown, A. W., & Gourdine, R. M. (1998). Teenage Black girls and violence: Coming of age in an urban environment. In L. A. See (Ed.), *Human behavior in the social environment from an African American perspective* (pp. 105-124). Binghamton, NY: The Haworth Press, Inc.

Buchanan, N. T., & Ormerod, A. J. (2002). Racialized sexual harassment in the lives of African American women. *Women & Therapy, 25* (3 & 4), 107-124.

Burke, J. G., Gielen, A. G., McDonnell, K. A., O'Campo, P., & Maman, S. (2001). The process of ending abuse in intimate relationships: A qualitative exploration of the transtheoretical model. *Violence Against Women, 7*, 1144-1163.

Butler, L. (1999). African American lesbians experiencing partner violence. In J. C. McClennen & J. Gunther (Eds.), *A professional's guide to understanding gay and lesbian domestic violence: Understanding practice interventions* (pp. 50-57). Lewiston, NY: Edwin Mellen Press.

Campbell, J. C., & Soeken, K. L. (1999a). Forced sex and intimate partner violence: Effects of women's risk and women's health. *Violence Against Women, 5*, 1017-1035.

Campbell, J. C., & Soeken, K. L. (1999b). Women's responses to battering: A test of the model. *Research in Nursing & Health, 22*, 49-58.

Campbell, J. C., & Soeken, K. L. (1999c). Women's responses to battering over time: An analysis of change. *Journal of Interpersonal Violence, 14*, 21-40.

Carmody, D. C., & Washington, L. M. (2001). Rape myth acceptance among college women: The impact of race and prior victimization. *Journal of Interpersonal Violence, 16*, 424-436.

Cecil, H., & Matson, S. C. (2001). Psychological functioning and family discord among African American adolescent females with and without a history of childhood sexual abuse. *Child Abuse & Neglect, 25*, 973-988.

Clark, M. L., Beckett, J., Wells, M., & Dungee-Anderson, D. (1994). Courtship violence among African American college students. *Journal of Black Psychology, 20*, 264-281.

Coker, A. L., McKeown, R. E., Sanderson, M., Davis, K. E., Valois, R. F., & Huebner, E. S. (2000). Severe dating violence and quality of life among South Carolina high school students. *American Journal of Preventive Medicine, 19*, 220-227.

Cortina, L. M., Swan, S., Fitzgerald, L. F., & Waldo, C. (1998). Sexual harassment and assault: Chilling the climate for women in academia. *Psychology of Women Quarterly, 22*, 419-441.

Cunradi, C. B., Caetano, R., Clark, C. L., & Schafer, J. (1999). Alcohol-related problems and intimate partner violence among White, Black, and Hispanic couples in the U.S. *Alcoholism: Clinical and Experimental Research, 23*, 1492-1501.

Curtis-Boles, H., & Jenkins-Monroe, V. (2000). Substance abuse in African American women. *Journal of Black Psychology, 26*, 450-469.

Danquah, M. N. (1998). *Willow weep for me: A Black woman's journey through depression.* New York: W. W. Norton.

Davis, A. Y. (1998). *Blues legacies and Black feminism.* New York: Vintage.

Davis, D. E. (1997). The harm that has no name: Street harassment, embodiment, and African American women. In A. K. Wing (Ed.), *Critical race feminism: A reader* (pp. 192-202). New York: New York University Press.

Davis, R. E. (1997). Trauma and addiction experiences of African American women. *Western Journal of Nursing Research, 19*, 442-465.

DeMaris, A. (1990). The dynamics of generational transfer in courtship violence: A biracial exploration. *Journal of Marriage and the Family, 52*, 219-231.

Donovan, R., & Williams, M. (2002). Living at the intersection: The effects of racism and sexism on Black rape survivors. *Women & Therapy, 25* (3 & 4), 95-105.

Earl, C. E., & Penney, P. J. (2001). The significance of trust in the research consent process with African Americans. *Western Journal of Nursing Research, 23*, 753-762.

Fergusson, D. M., & Mullen, P. E. (1999). *Childhood sexual abuse: An evidence based perspective.* Thousand Oaks, CA: Sage.

Few, A. L., & Bell-Scott, P. (2002). Grounding our feet and hearts: Black women's coping strategies in psychologically abusive dating relationships. *Women & Therapy, 25* (3 & 4), 59-77.

Fontes, L. A., Cruz, M., & Tabachnick, J. (2001). Views of child sexual abuse in two cultural communities: An exploratory study among African Americans and Latinos. *Child Maltreatment, 6*, 103-117.

Geary, F. H., & Wingate, C. B. (1999). Domestic violence and physical abuse of women: The Grady Memorial Hospital experience. *American Journal of Obstetrics and Gynecology, 181*, S17-S21.

Hampton, R. L., & Gelles, R. J. (1994). Violence toward Black women in a nationally representative sample of Black families. *Journal of Comparative Family Studies, 25*, 105-119.

Hien, D., & Bukszpan, C. (1999). Interpersonal violence in a "normal" low-income control group. *Women & Health, 29*, 1-16.

Hill, E. M., Boyd, C. J., & Kortge, J. F. (2000). Variation in suicidality among substance-abusing women: The role of childhood adversity. *Journal of Substance Abuse Treatment, 19*, 339-345.

Honeycutt, T. C., Marshall, L. L., & Weston, R. (2001). Toward ethnically specific models of employment, public assistance, and victimization. *Violence Against Women, 7*, 126-140.

Huang, C. J., & Gunn, T. (2001). An examination of domestic violence in an African American community in North Carolina: Causes and consequences. *Journal of Black Studies, 31*, 790-811.

Hunt, G., & Joe-Laidler, K. (2001). Situations of violence in the lives of girl gang members. *Health Care for Women International, 22*, 363-384.

Huston, R. L., Prihoda, T. J., Parra, J. M., & Foulds, D. M. (1997). Factors associated with the report of penetration in child sexual abuse cases. *Journal of Child Sexual Abuse, 6*, 63-74.

Hyman, B., & Williams, L. (2001). Resilience among women survivors of child sexual abuse. *Affilia, 16*, 198-219.

Jackson, P. B., & Mustillo, S. (2001). I am woman: The impact of social identities on African American women's mental health. *Women & Health, 32*, 33-59.

Jasinski, J. L., Williams, L. M., & Siegel, J. (2000). Childhood physical and sexual abuse as risk factors for heavy drinking among African American women: A prospective study. *Child Abuse & Neglect, 24*, 1061-1071.

Jenkins, E. J. (2002). Black women and community violence: Trauma, grief, and coping. *Women & Therapy, 25* (3 & 4), 29-44.

Joseph, J. (1997). Woman battering: A comparative analysis of Black and White women. In G. Kaufman Kantor & J. L. Jasinski (Eds.), *Out of the darkness: Contemporary perspectives on family violence* (pp. 161-169). Thousand Oaks, CA: Sage.

Kalichman, S. C., Williams, E. A., Cherry, C., Belcher, L., & Nachimson, D. (1998). Sexual coercion, domestic violence, and negotiating condom use among low-income African American women. *Journal of Women's Health, 7*, 371-378.

Kalof, L., Eby, K. K., Matheson, J., & Kroska, R. J. (2001). The influence of race and gender on student self-reports of sexual harassment by college professors. *Gender & Society, 15*, 282-302.

Kaschak, E. (Ed.). (2001). Intimate betrayal: Domestic violence in lesbian relationships [Special issue]. *Women & Therapy, 23*(3).

Kaslow, N. J., Thompson, M. P., Meadows, L. A., Jacobs, D., Chance, S., Gibb, B., Bornstein, H. B., Hollins, L., Rashid, A., & Phillips, K. (1998). Factors that mediate and moderate the link between partner abuse and suicidal behavior in American women. *Journal of Consulting and Clinical Psychology, 66*, 533-540.

Kearney, M. H. (2001). Enduring love: A grounded formal theory of women's experience of domestic violence. *Research in Nursing & Health, 24,* 270-282.

Kenny, M. C., & McEachern, A. G. (2000). Prevalence and characteristics of childhood sexual abuse in multiethnic female college students. *Journal of Child Sexual Abuse, 9,* 57-70.

Kessler, R. C., Molnar, B. E., Feurer, I. D., & Appelbaum, M. (2001). Patterns and mental health predictors of domestic violence in the United States: Results from the National Comorbidity Survey. *International Journal of Law and Psychiatry, 24,* 487-508.

Lawson, E. J., Rodgers-Rose, L., & Rajaram, S. (1999). The psychosocial context of Black women's health. *Health Care for Women International, 20,* 279-289.

Leifer, M., & Shapiro, J. P. (1995). Longitudinal study of the psychological effects of sexual abuse in African American girls in foster care and those who remain home. *Journal of Child Sexual Abuse, 4,* 27-44.

Lewis, S. F., & Fremouw, W. (2001). Dating violence: A critical review of the literature. *Clinical Psychology Review, 21,* 105-127.

Mahoney, P., Williams, L. M., & West, C. M. (2001). Violence against women by intimate relationship partners. In C. M. Renzetti, J. L. Edleson, & R. K. Bergen (Eds.), *Sourcebook on violence against women* (pp. 143-178). Thousand Oaks, CA: Sage.

Malik, S., Sorenson, S. B., & Aneshensel, C. S. (1997). Community and dating violence among adolescents: Perpetration and victimization. *Journal of Adolescent Health, 21,* 291-302.

Manetta, A. A. (1999). Interpersonal violence and suicidal behavior in midlife African American women. *Journal of Black Studies, 29,* 510-522.

Mansfield, P. K., Koch, P. B., Henderson, J., & Vicary, J. R. (1991). The job climate for women in traditionally male blue-collar occupations. *Sex Roles, 25,* 63-79.

Marcenko, M. O., Kemp, S. P., & Larson, N. C. (2000). Childhood experiences of abuse, later substance use, and parenting outcomes among low-income mothers. *American Journal of Orthopsychiatry, 70,* 316-326.

McNutt, L., van Ryn, M., Clark, C., & Fraiser, I. (2000). Partner violence and medical encounters: African American women's perspectives. *American Journal of Preventive Medicine, 19,* 264-269.

Mecca, S. J., & Rubin, L. J. (1999). Definitional research on African American students and sexual harassment. *Psychology of Women Quarterly, 23,* 813-817.

Mitchell, A., & Herring, K. (1998). *What the blues is all about: Black women overcoming stress and depression.* New York: Perigee Books.

Mohr, W. K., Fantuzzo, J. W., & Abdul-Kabir, S. (2001). Safeguarding themselves and their children: Mothers share their strategies. *Journal of Family Violence, 16,* 75-92.

Molitor, F., Ruiz, J. D., Klausner, J. D., & McFarland, W. (2000). History of forced sex in association with drug use and sexual HIV risk behaviors, infection with STDs, and diagnostic medical care: Results from the Young Women Survey. *Journal of Interpersonal Violence, 15,* 262-278.

Morrison, T. (Ed.). (1992). *Race-ing justice, en-gendering power: Essays on Anita Hill, Clarence Thomas, and the construction of social reality*. New York: Pantheon.

National Center for Health Statistics (1997). *Vital statistic mortality data, underlying causes of death, 1979-1995*. Hyattsville, MD: Centers for Disease Control and Prevention.

National Center for Injury Prevention and Control (1997). Division of Violence Prevention, Center for Disease Control and Prevention. Atlanta, GA.

Neville, H. A., & Heppner, M. J. (1999). Contextualizing rape: Reviewing sequelae and proposing a culturally inclusive ecological model of sexual assault recovery. *Applied & Preventive Psychology, 8*, 41-62.

Neville, H. A., & Hamer, J. (2001). "We make freedom": An exploration of revolutionary Black feminism. *Journal of Black Studies, 31*, 437-461.

Nichols, R. R. (2002). Striving for a more excellent way. *Women & Therapy, 25* (3 & 4), 187-192.

O'Donohue, W., Downs, K., & Yeater, E. A. (1998). Sexual harassment: A review of the literature. *Aggression and Violent Behavior, 3*, 111-128.

O'Keefe, M. (1997). Predictors of dating violence among high school students. *Journal of Interpersonal Violence, 12*, 546-568.

Oliver, W. (2000). Preventing domestic violence in the African American community: The rationale for popular culture interventions. *Violence & Women, 6*, 533-549.

Pierce-Baker, C. (1998). *Surviving the silence: Black women's stories of rape*. New York: W. W. Norton & Company.

Piotrkowski, C. S. (1998). Gender harassment, job satisfaction, and distress among employed White and minority women. *Journal of Occupational Health Psychology, 3*, 33-43.

Rennison, C. M., & Welchans, S. (August, 2000). *Criminal victimization 1999: Changes 1998-99 with trends 1993-99*. Washington, DC: U. S. Department of Justice, Bureau of Justice Statistics.

Richie, B. E. (1994). *Compelled to crime: The gender entrapment of battered Black women*. New York: Routledge.

Rickert, V. I., Wiemann, C. M., & Berenson, A. B. (2000). Ethnic differences in depressive symptomatology among young women. *Obstetrics & Gynecology, 95*, 55-60.

Robinson, A. (2002). "There's a stranger in this house": African American lesbians and domestic violence. *Women & Therapy, 25* (3 & 4), 125-132.

Roosa, M. W., Reinholtz, C., & Angelini, P. J. (1999). The relation of child sexual abuse and depression in young women: Comparisons across four ethnic groups. *Journal of Abnormal Child Psychology, 27*, 65-76.

Rospenda, K. M., Richman, J. A., & Nawyn, S. J. (1998). Doing power: The confluence of gender, race, and class in contrapower sexual harassment. *Gender & Society, 12*, 40-60.

Ross-Durow, P. L., & Boyd, C. J. (2000). Sexual abuse, depression, and eating disorders in African American women who smoke cocaine. *Journal of Substance Abuse Treatment, 18*, 79-81.

Russo, N. F., Denious, J. E., Keita, G. P., & Koss, M. P. (1997). Intimate violence and Black women's health. *Women's Health: Research on Gender, Behavior, and Policy, 3*, 315-348.

Sanders-Phillips, K., Moisan, P. A., Wadlington, S., Morgan, S., & English, K. (1995). Ethnic differences in psychological functioning among Black and Latino sexually abused girls. *Child Abuse & Neglect, 19*, 691-706.

Shaw, J. A., Lewis, J. E., Loeb, A., Rosado, J., & Rodriguez, R. A. (2001). A comparison of Hispanic and African American sexually abused girls and their families. *Child Abuse & Neglect, 25*, 1363-1379.

Shelton, J. N., & Chavous, T. M. (1999). Black and White college women's perceptions of sexual harassment. *Sex Roles, 40*, 593-615.

Simmons, A. S. (2002). Using celluloid to break the silence about sexual violence in the Black community. *Women & Therapy, 25* (3 & 4), 179-185.

Smitherman, G. (Ed.). (1995). *African American women speak out on Anita Hill-Clarence Thomas.* Detroit, MI: Wayne State University Press.

Stark, E., & Flitcraft, A. (1995). Killing the beast within: Woman battering and female suicidality. *International Journal of Health Services, 25*, 43-64.

Sullivan, C. M., & Rumptz, M. H. (1994). Adjustment and needs of African American women who utilized a domestic violence shelter. *Violence and Victims, 9*, 275-286.

Taylor, J. Y. (2002a). "The straw that broke the camel's back": African American women's strategies for disengaging from abusive relationships. *Women & Therapy, 25* (3 & 4), 79-94.

Taylor, J. Y. (2002b). Talking back: Research as an act of resistance and healing for African American women survivors of intimate male partner violence. *Women & Therapy, 25* (3 & 4), 145-160.

Thompson, M. P., Kaslow, N. J., Lane, D. B., & Kingree, J. B. (2000). Child maltreatment, PTSD, and suicidal behavior among African American females. *Journal of Interpersonal Violence, 15*, 3-15.

Tillet, S. (2002). Fragmented silhouettes. *Women & Therapy, 25* (3 & 4), 161-177.

Tjaden, P., & Thoennes, N. (2000). *Extent, nature, and consequences of intimate partner violence: Findings from the National Violence Against Women Survey* (NCJ 181867). Washington, DC: U. S. Government Printing Office.

Urquiza, A. J., & Goodlin-Jones, B. L. (1994). Child sexual abuse and adult revictimization with women of color. *Violence and Victims, 9*, 223-232.

U. S. Department of Health and Human Services (2001). *Mental health: Culture, race, and ethnicity–A supplement to mental health: A report of the Surgeon General.* Rockville, MD: U. S. Department of Health and Human Services, Substance Abuse and Mental Health Services Administration, Center for Mental Health Services.

Valois, R. F., Oeltmann, J. E., Waller, J., & Hussey, J. R. (1999). Relationship between number of sexual intercourse partners and selected health risk behaviors among public high school adolescents. *Journal of Adolescent Health, 25*, 328-335.

Washington, P. A. (2001). Disclosure patterns of Black female sexual assault survivors. *Violence Against Women, 7*, 1254-1283.

Watson, J. M., Cascardi, M., Avery-Leaf, S., & O'Leary, K. D. (2001). High school students' responses to dating aggression. *Violence and Victims, 16*, 339-348.

West, C. M. (2002). Black battered women: New directions for research and Black feminist theory. In L. H. Collins, M. Dunlap, & J. Chrisler (Eds.), *Charting a new course: Psychology for a feminist future* (pp. 216-237). Westport, CT: Praeger.

West, C. M. (2002). "I find myself at therapy's doorstep": Summary and suggested readings on violence in the lives of Black women. *Women & Therapy, 25* (3 & 4), 193-201.

West, C. M., & Rose, S. (2000). Dating aggression among low income African American youth: An examination of gender differences and antagonistic beliefs. *Violence Against Women, 6,* 470-494.

West, C. M., Williams, L. M., & Siegel, J. A. (2000). Adult sexual revictimization among Black women sexually abused in childhood: A prospective examination of serious consequences of abuse. *Child Maltreatment, 5,* 49-57.

West, T. C. (1999). *Wounds of the spirit: Black women, violence, and resistance ethics.* New York: New York University Press.

White, A. M. (2001). I am because we are: Combined race and gender political consciousness among African American women and men anti-rape activists. *Women's Studies International Forum, 24,* 11-24.

Whitson, M. H. (1997). Sexism and sexual harassment: Concerns of African American women of the Christian Methodist Episcopal Church. *Violence Against Women, 3,* 382-400.

Wingood, G. M., & DiClemente, R. J. (1997a). Child sexual abuse, HIV sexual risk, and gender relations of African American women. *American Journal of Preventive Medicine, 13,* 380-384.

Wingood, G. M., & DiClemente, R. J. (1997b). Consequences of having a physically abusive partner on the condom use and sexual negotiation practices of young adult African American women. *American Journal of Public Health, 87,* 1016-1018.

Wingood, G. M., & DiClemente, R. J. (1998). Rape among African American women: Sexual, psychological, and social correlates predisposing survivors to risk of STD/HIV. *Journal of Women's Health, 7,* 77-84.

Wingood, G. M., DiClemente, R. J., McCree, D. H., Harrington, K., & Davies, S. L. (2001). Dating violence and the sexual health of Black adolescent females. *Pediatrics, 107.* Retrieved September 27, 2001, from *http://www.pediatrics.org/cgi/content/full/107/5/e72.*

Wyatt, G. E., Axelrod, J., Chin, D., Carmona, J. V., & Loeb, T. B. (2000). Examining patterns of vulnerability to domestic violence among African American women. *Violence Against Women, 6,* 495-514.

Wyatt, G. E., Loeb, T. B., Solis, B., Carmona, J. V., & Romero, G. (1999). The prevalence and circumstances of child sexual abuse: Changes across a decade. *Child Abuse & Neglect, 23,* 45-60.

Wyatt, G. E., Notgrass, C. M., & Gordon, G. (1995). The effects of African American women's sexual revictimization: Strategies for prevention. In C. F. Swift (Ed.), *Sexual assault and abuse: Sociocultural context of prevention* (pp. 111-134). Binghamton, NY: The Haworth Press, Inc.

Wyatt, G. E., & Riederle, M. (1995). The prevalence and context of sexual harassment among African American and White American women. *Journal of Interpersonal Violence, 10,* 309-321.

Black Women and Community Violence: Trauma, Grief, and Coping

Esther J. Jenkins

SUMMARY. The current article examines literature relevant to understanding the impact of community violence on African American women and children, with a focus on witnessing violence and injury, and the loss of close others. Survivors may report psychological distress, increased rates of aggression, diminished physical health, and additional challenges in their parental roles. Despite these challenges, they have developed a variety of coping strategies. Individual and community level interventions, based on the more successful coping mechanisms of violence survivors, are discussed. *[Article copies available for a fee from The Haworth Document Delivery Service: 1-800-HAWORTH. E-mail address: <getinfo@haworthpressinc.com> Website: <http://www.HaworthPress.com> © 2002 by The Haworth Press, Inc. All rights reserved.]*

KEYWORDS. Community violence, Blacks, violence, urban environments, aggression

Esther J. Jenkins, PhD, is Professor of Psychology at Chicago State University and Research Director at the Community Mental Health Council, Inc., a comprehensive community mental health center serving the south side of Chicago. She is also a member of the steering committee of the Institute on Domestic Violence in the African American Community. Her research interests include children's exposure to community violence, impact of sexual abuse on African American girls, and Black child mental health.

Address correspondence to: Esther J. Jenkins, PhD, Department of Psychology, Chicago State University, 9500 S. King Drive, Chicago, IL 60628 (E-mail: e-jenkins@csu.edu).

[Haworth co-indexing entry note]: "Black Women and Community Violence: Trauma, Grief, and Coping." Jenkins, Esther J. Co-published simultaneously in *Women & Therapy* (The Haworth Press, Inc.) Vol. 25, No. 3/4, 2002, pp. 29-44; and: *Violence in the Lives of Black Women: Battered, Black, and Blue* (ed: Carolyn M. West) The Haworth Press, Inc., 2002, pp. 29-44. Single or multiple copies of this article are available for a fee from The Haworth Document Delivery Service [1-800-HAWORTH, 9:00 a.m. - 5:00 p.m. (EST). E-mail address: getinfo@haworthpressinc.com].

For a 10-year period, beginning in the mid-1980s, there was a dramatic surge in violence in the United States. Reflecting the characteristics of those involved, research on this phenomenon has primarily focused on impoverished African American children and adolescents who live in urban communities. Researchers have examined a number of issues, including the prevalence and impact of violence exposure, particularly for youths who have lost friends or family members to violence (Horn & Trickett, 1998; Jenkins, 2001; Jenkins & Bell, 1997).

Surprisingly, little research on violence exposure has included adults' responses to living in such environments (Hill, Hawkins, Raposa, & Carr, 1995; Sanders-Phillips, 1996a, 1997; Wolfer, 2000). This oversight is significant because adults are greatly affected by these experiences of threat and loss. Moreover, this violence may be particularly distressing for women in these communities. Most of these women are mothers and mates, which has tremendous implications for loss, grief, fear, and worry by virtue of their relationships to the victims and their roles as protectors of their children. Mothers' responses to violence also have a profound effect on how successfully their children cope with the violence that they experience, and broader implications for effective child rearing practices and positive outcomes for their children (Mohr, Fantuzzo, & Abdul-Kabir, 2001; Sanders-Phillips, 1997).

This article examines literature relevant to understanding exposure to community violence among Black women, the implications of that exposure for the women and, where applicable, their children. Consistent with current practice, community violence is defined as aggression that occurs outside the home among non-family members; it may, and often does, involve known others and even family members as victims or perpetrators (Guterman, Cameron, & Staller, 2000). The current focus is primarily on witnessing violence and loss of intimates, rather than victimization. However, it is important to recognize that living in a violent milieu carries at least the threat, and often the reality, of being personally harmed.

EXPOSURE TO VIOLENCE

African American youth witness a substantial amount of community violence. According to a large literature review of selected studies, between 26% and 70% of inner city children have been exposed to severe violence, such as witnessing a shooting (Jenkins, 2001). A majority (70%) of these children saw a friend or relative being victimized

(Jenkins & Bell, 1994; Uehara, Chalmers, Jenkins, & Shakoor, 1996). In many cases, the child also knew the perpetrator (Richters & Martinez, 1993).

Among children and adolescents, research findings on the association between gender and witnessing community violence have been somewhat mixed and seem to be moderated by age. The findings generally show no gender differences in younger samples (Attar, Guerra, & Tolan, 1994; Farrell & Bruce, 1997; Uehara et al., 1996). Among older youths, some researchers found no gender differences (Giaconia et al., 1995), although others found that when compared to girls, boys witnessed more violence, particularly severe aggression against strangers (Jenkins & Bell, 1994; Schubiner, Scott, & Tzelepis, 1993; Singer, Anglin, Song, & Lunghofer, 1995). A more recent study found that girls experienced equally high rates of exposure. More than two-thirds of the urban girls, ages 12-20, and primarily African American clients at a community medical clinic, reported that at some point in their lives they had seen someone get shot (Lipschitz, Rasmusson, Anyan, Cromwell, & Southwick, 2000).

A substantial number of Black women have also witnessed violence in their communities. Similar to Black teenagers, they are equally likely to be familiar with the victim. Several years ago, several colleagues and I surveyed students at a predominately Black urban university. Reflecting the student body of the campus, the sample was primarily women and commuter students. Their average age was 27, and most participants were employed full- or part-time. Among the African American women in the sample, 30% had witnessed a murder, stabbing, or shooting (Jenkins, Kpo, & Barr, 1997). Likewise, using a sample of 136 African American mothers from Washington, D.C., Hill and her colleagues (1995) found that one-third reported being witnesses or victims of violence, with the majority reporting the latter.

Wolfer's (2000) study of 25 mothers in a violent Chicago public housing development provides rich data on Black women's exposure to violence. The women were recruited through word of mouth and, thus, may have been more distressed than nonparticipants. One is still struck by both the prevalence and severity of violence in their lives. All of the women had experienced violence as a witness, a victim, or both. This exposure was frequent and severe, with two-thirds of the incidents involving death or serious injury and 80% involving a gun. Furthermore, these women were exposed to much more violence than they recalled. This was discovered when Wolfer (1999) conducted in-depth interviews with six women from the sample. The women reported more violent encounters in a four-month period, when violence was reported on a weekly basis, than when they responded to the previous screening question regarding lifetime exposure. In addition to pointing out the pervasiveness of violence in these women's lives, such findings indicate that reports of lifetime exposure to violence may be an underestimate.

Loss of Significant Others

More prevalent than witnessing assault is the loss of an intimate because of violence. In high-risk environments, a majority of individuals have had a friend or family member severely injured or killed. In research at the Community Mental Health Council, more than 70% of the children reported the victimization of a family member or intimate (Jenkins & Bell, 1994; Uehara et al., 1996). In another study, almost all of the girls attending a community-based medical clinic reported that a friend or relative had been murdered, and 45% indicated that a "boyfriend, girlfriend, lover, or spouse" had died violently (Horowitz, Weine, & Jekel, 1995). Several years later, using clients from the same clinic, researchers discovered that two-thirds of the girls had lost a friend or family member to homicide (Lipschitz et al., 2000). These findings suggest that many Black girls will experience the death of an intimate.

Although adult women seem less likely than their youthful counterparts to report the violent death of an intimate, the prevalence is still quite high. In a sample of Los Angeles Head Start Mothers, 23% of the Black women in the sample had experienced the murder of a family member (Sanders-Phillips, 1996a). An even higher rate (55%) of Black college women had had an intimate murdered (Jenkins et al., 1997). These numbers are higher than those in a national sample of adult women, in which 13% reported the violent death of a close friend or family member, including deaths caused by drunk drivers (Resnick, Kilpatrick, Dansky, Saunders, & Best, 1993).

IMPACT OF VIOLENCE EXPOSURE

There is wide variation in the type and severity of reactions to violence exposure. Individual responses are a result of the incident and a constellation of individual, social risk, and protective factors (Mattis, Bell, Jagers, & Jenkins, 1999). However, few individuals are left untouched by these experiences, especially when violence exposure involves intimates. Reactions to witnessing violence, having close others victimized, or simply living in a violent milieu can include a host of traumatic stress reactions, including clinical disorders and subclinical reactions. These problems often manifest in poor work and school performance, and in impaired social relationships.

When close others are killed, trauma and grief reactions can complicate recovery. Trauma is often exacerbated by stressors that are secondary to the incident, such as involvement with the criminal justice system, loss of income, or changing residences. Physical health may deteriorate as a result of coping with chronic threat and frequent loss. Moreover, living in a violent environment can make keeping oneself and others safe a core concern around which much else is organized, sapping energy that could go toward more self-enhancing activities. For Black women, who are disproportionately poor and single heads of households, the violence occurs within the context of many other stressors, thus increasing the probability that it will have deleterious effects, including increased aggression, deteriorating physical health, and parenting problems.

Psychological Distress

Much of the research on trauma reactions has investigated Post-traumatic Stress Disorder (PTSD). First recognized in combat veterans, PTSD is a response to an extreme stressor that involves threat to the physical integrity of oneself or others. The event may have been experienced, witnessed, or happened to a family member or close other (American Psychiatric Association [APA], *Diagnostic and Statistical Manual of Mental Disorders, DSM-IV-TR*, 2000). Classic PTSD is characterized by behaviors that fall into the symptom categories of re-experiencing the event, avoidance of reminders, psychic numbing, and increased arousal and startle responses, with symptoms lasting at least one month. Similar symptoms that last less than one month are classified as Acute Stress Reaction (*DSM-IV-TR*, 2000). PTSD occurs in children (Pynoos, 1993; Terr, 1991) as well as adults. It is estimated that 20-25% of those exposed to criterion trauma actually develop PTSD (Kluft, Bloom, & Kinzie, 2000), although the percentages vary considerably by type of trauma (*DSM-IV-TR*, 2000). Almost an equal number of traumatized individuals develop partial or sub-syndromal PTSD in which they display some of the symptoms of PTSD without meeting all of the criteria. Traumatized individuals, with and without PTSD, have been found to have impairments in work and school performance, as well as in family and social functioning (Giaconia et al., 1995; Stein, Walker, Hazen, & Forde, 1997).

In addition to PTSD and Acute Stress Disorder, a number of other clinical disorders have been found in this population, including Panic, Major Depressive, Phobia, Somatization, and Substance Related disorders (*DSM-IV-TR*, 2000; Marmar, Foy, Kagan, & Pynoos, 1993), as well as subclinical levels of depression and anxiety. Traumatized individuals may engage in self-destructive behaviors or have feelings of shame, despair, hopelessness, altered beliefs about the nature of the world, impaired relationships, social withdrawal, hostility, and anger (*DSM-IV-TR*, 2000; Pynoos, 1993; Terr, 1991). All of these reactions have been found in children who reside in neighborhoods with high rates of violence (Jenkins, 2001; Horn & Trickett, 1998).

Although the victimization of an intimate is considered to be an "extreme traumatic stressor" in the assessment for PTSD (*DSM-IV-TR*, 2000), few researchers have used youth samples to investigate the effects of vicarious exposure. When examined, the victimization of a close other is associated with distress. To illustrate, in a sample of adolescent girls who were clients at an urban health clinic, 16% of those diagnosed with PTSD had experienced the homicide of a friend or intimate (Lipschitz et al., 2000).

In adult samples, the rate of PTSD owing to vicarious exposure is comparable to that of adolescent girls. In a nationally representative sample of women (11% African American), 22% of those reporting the homicide of a close friend or family member satisfied the criteria for PTSD (Resnick et al., 1993). In a Detroit area sample, 14% of those reporting the sudden death of a relative or friend satisfied the criteria (Breslau et al., 1998). Although females with histories of physical assault and sexual victimization are the most likely to report PTSD (Breslau, Kessler, Chilcoat, Peterson, & Lucia, 1999; Resnick et al., 1993), tragic or sudden death of a close other seems to be the most frequently occurring trauma (Breslau et al., 1998; Norris, 1992), thus accounting for the greatest number of PTSD cases.

One of the few studies that has specifically examined the impact of homicide of a family member used 150 survivors, primarily African American women, who were identified through the Atlanta Medical Examiners Office (Thompson, Norris, & Ruback, 1998). These survivors, half of whom were mothers, displayed more distress and PTSD symptoms than those suffering other types of trauma, including personal victimization. Of particular note, these homicide survivors' levels of distress, unlike the victims of other trauma, did not abate over time (Thompson et al., 1998).

Loss and Grief

Traumatic reactions, which result from the intended death or injury of a loved one, have distinct features. For example, it is common for survivors to report intense anger at the perpetrator, fantasies of retaliation, and a desire for retribution (Pynoos & Nader, 1988; Rinear, 1988; Rynearson, 1984). Many survivors also report a deep sense of loss. Not only have they lost their loved ones, they also may lose their assumptions about the safety of the world, their trust in others, and the belief that they can keep their families safe. Although some young Black women remain hopeful in the midst of death and community violence (Brown & Gourdine, 1998), many others have a difficult time adjusting to their losses. Survivors may develop a sense of hopelessness and loss of future orientation, with a belief that one will die young and violently (Temple, 2000).

Grief, characterized by feelings of sadness and depression, emotional pain and tearfulness, and intense longing for the person, is another common reaction. The trauma associated with the murder complicates and prolongs the grieving process, and may take precedence over grief resolution (Pynoos & Nader, 1988; Rinear, 1988; Rynearson, 1984, 1986). Although reminiscing about the loved one is necessary for grief resolution, thoughts of the deceased may also trigger anxiety about the manner of death. Trauma is associated with all forms of unnatural death and, to some extent, with natural death. However, trauma seems to be most intense in cases of homicidal death, which often involves mutilation and subsequent intrusive thoughts of the other's pain, horror, and helplessness (Rynearson, 1984, 1986).

The murder of a child is among the most difficult traumas to deal with. It represents "multiple losses of both a real and symbolic nature" (Rinear, 1988, p. 315). Some parents will lose another child to death or prison when he or she seeks to avenge the murder of a sibling; the same environmental factors that contributed to the death of one child have the potential for claiming other offspring. Grief and stress are prolonged by lengthy criminal justice proceedings and can be intensified by minimal sentences for perpetrators or a lack of police interest. When asked about the murder of her son, one Black woman dismissed the police investigation, saying ". . . to them it's just another Black mother's son" (Temple, 2000, p. 658).

Aggression

Exposure to community violence has been linked to increased levels of aggression across the life span. Children who grow up in violent communities exhibit substantial rates of aggression and delinquency, including fighting and carrying weapons (Jenkins, 2001). During adolescence, exposure to weapons and violent injury was a strong predictor of involvement in both community violence and dating aggression among Black high school students (Gorman-Smith, Tolan, Sheidow, & Henry, 2001). Additionally, increasing numbers of Black adolescent girls are using aggressive behaviors to protect themselves from perceived threats in dangerous environments (Brown & Gourdine, 1998; Pugh-Lilly, Neville, & Poulin, 2001).

This pattern of aggression may continue into adulthood. Siegel (2000) discovered this in her longitudinal sample of 136 urban, low-income, predominately Black women (78%) who had documented cases of childhood sexual abuse. Those who had witnessed violent episodes in which someone was killed or seriously injured were at significantly greater odds of fighting during their teenage years, while those who reported the murder of a close friend or relative were at significantly higher odds of fighting as adults and using aggression against a romantic partner.

Physical Health

Along with its mental health implications, violence exposure can compromise physical health, directly and indirectly. It is fairly well documented that acute and chronic stress, irrespective of source, decreases immune system functioning and increases vulnerability to disease and infection (Cohen & Williamson, 1991). Less directly, stress from exposure to violence can compromise health by decreasing the individual's motivation to engage in those behaviors that promote health. In a sample of 243 low-income Latinas and Black women, Sanders-Phillips (1996a, 1996b) found the murder of a family member was associated with a variety of unhealthy behaviors. In addition to being more likely to drink and smoke, frequently noted responses to trauma, these women were less likely to eat breakfast or get adequate sleep or exercise. This lack of self-care was believed to be a direct consequence of the survivors' mental statuses following the violence exposure, and included depression, anxiety, hopelessness, and powerlessness. Poverty and racism may certainly exacerbate these health problems (Clark, Andersen, Clark, & Williams, 1999).

Parenting

Community violence can have a profound impact on Black women's ability to effectively parent their children. As Hill and colleagues (1995) noted:

> ... the impact of community violence can shake the very foundation of the basic relationships between parents, children, and families. For the first time in their lives, mothers in our study are facing the reality that they are not able to fulfill a fundamental responsibility of parenting in most societies, that is, ensure the protection of their children. (p. 67)

Not surprisingly, when compared to Whites, Blacks reported higher levels of anomie about parenthood as measured by the item, "It is not fair to bring a child into this world" (Hussain & Smith, 1996).

After a child is born, parents continue to be concerned about safety. Researchers asked 400 low-income African American mothers from Los Angeles about their biggest fear for their infants as they grew up. Some new mothers (10%) were concerned about their children growing up in their community, which is understandable because 14% of these women had been robbed and 6% had witnessed a violent crime in the year prior to the survey. Even more mothers (39%), regardless of their victimization status, were fearful that their children would be exposed to gangs or violence (Schuster, Halfon, & Wood, 1998).

Black mothers in impoverished and violent areas often modify their child rearing practices in order to protect their children. For example, some parents use corporal punishment to control and discipline their children, reasoning that it will prevent them from getting into more serious trouble in the streets. These punitive measures may be effective with some children. For other children, however, physical punishment is associated with increased levels of aggression and delinquency, the very problems that parents are seeking to avoid (Kaljee, Stanton, Ricardo, & Whitehead, 1995; Sanders-Phillips, 1997). After making futile attempts to control or protect their child, some parents may give up in despair and relinquish the child to the streets.

In contrast, other parents become overprotective, employing excessive restrictions on the child's activities and peers. In particularly dangerous situations, mothers and their children stay indoors; in essence, they become prisoners in their own homes. Although reducing exposure to violence, this lack of social interaction may impede the child's normal developmental needs to be autonomous, to explore their world, and to establish peer relationships. For the mothers, such inactivity and boredom can result in less exercise and more overeating, factors that contribute to common illnesses among Black women, including obesity, diabetes, and hypertension. This self-imposed isolation also may cut the family off from vital support systems (Sanders-Phillips, 1997; Wolfer, 2000).

On a more positive note, many Black women have developed ways to safeguard their children. By using positive parenting methods, mothers have helped their children to circumvent community danger and to grow into healthy, productive, nonviolent youths. Effective methods included maintaining open lines of communication and involving the child in church or recreational activities. Parents also used neighborhood resources (e.g., schools, religious organizations, local community leaders) (Kaljee et al., 1995; Mohr et al., 2001).

In addition to affecting parenting styles, pervasive community violence can affect a mother's ability to parent. Parents who are suffering traumatic stress from violence exposure are often less effective in helping children deal with dangerous situations, as parental behavior provides cues to children regarding the nature and extent of threat. When adult care-givers are appropriately calm and effective in the face of danger, while not minimizing the seriousness of the situation, the outcome for the child is much better than if the parent is either not present (accessible) or is overwhelmed by the situation (Dulmus & Wodarski, 2000; Pynoos, 1993). For example, in a large sample of Black South African children, researchers found that community violence was less likely to be associated with academic and psychological problems when the mothers reported relatively low levels of distress (Barbarin, Richter, & deWet, 2001).

COPING

Few researchers have explored the techniques that Black women (or children) use to cope with the violence in their communities. However, the existing literature indicates that they use a variety of coping techniques, which appear to vary based on the women's demographics. For example, Hill and colleagues (1995) discovered that poor, less educated, Black mothers who lived in high crime areas coped by praying and instituting safety measures, such as avoiding dangerous people and situations. Residents of low crime areas, predominately Black mothers with more education and income, avoided violence by keeping to themselves, practicing safety measures, and using political activism (e.g., participating in a neighborhood watch program, or organizing the community around violence prevention activities).

Similar coping methods were discovered when Wolfer (2000) conducted a series of repeated in-depth interviews with Black women residents of a Chicago housing project. Specifically, the women used three methods for coping with community violence. *Getting away* was a common strategy that included staying indoors or leaving the neighborhood on day trips or overnight visits. When interacting with community members, the women developed ways of *getting along*. For example, they learned to identify and minimize their interactions with dangerous people or situations. When this was not possible, the women tried to resolve or avert conflict in an attempt to avoid future problems with the person. If necessary, they used resistance strategies, such as physically fighting back or calling the police. Comforting their children and seeking support from relatives and close friends also helped the women to tolerate their circumstances. Despite their best efforts, the women could not completely prevent violence from touching their lives; thus, they developed ways of *getting through*. A few women used drugs or alcohol to manage their distress. More common methods of coping included praying, blocking thoughts about traumatic events, engaging in self-soothing behaviors, such as listening to gospel music, and using spiritual concepts of fate to make sense of the violence (e.g., the murder of a friend was God's will). Low-income Black mothers of young children enrolled in a Head Start Program used similar coping strategies (Mohr et al., 2001).

SUGGESTIONS FOR INTERVENTION

To summarize, community violence is a sad reality for many Black women. They are victims, witnesses, and grief stricken wives, girlfriends, and mothers of murder victims. Even for those who do not sustain direct loss, which is rare in high violence areas, the constant threat of injury and death shapes the psychological functioning of survivors. They report psychological distress, including PTSD, increased rates of aggression, diminished physical health, and additional challenges in performing their role as parents. These problems are exacerbated by poverty, racism, sexism, and limited support systems. Despite this adversity, many Black women develop effective coping strategies.

Therapists need to know more about community violence in the lives of their clients (Guterman & Cameron, 1999). Based on the research, individual and community level interventions are suggested.

Individual Level

- *Conduct a comprehensive assessment.* It is important to determine the level of community violence experienced by the client. In addition, the therapist should ask the client about her experience with parental violence and child abuse, as a witness or victim, and about her experiences with violence in her adult intimate relationships.
- *Address parenting concerns.* Service providers should be attuned to parental fears, which are realistic in the context of their violent environment (Schuster et al., 1998). Parents should not minimize the impact of community violence or underestimate the violence seen by their children. Parental denial may eliminate the possibility of adult-child interaction and support (Hill & Jones, 1997). Instead, service providers should help parents develop nonviolent, positive parenting techniques that strike a balance between protecting the child and allowing the child to meet normal developmental needs.
- *Draw on the strengths of the client.* The service provider should assume a competence orientation that acknowledges successful strategies used by survivors. For example, service providers should acknowledge the clients' need to rely on prayer or social support systems (Mohr et al., 2001).

Community Level

- *Work with community strength.* Service providers can work with schools, churches, and community groups to implement violence prevention programs, such as conflict resolution or peer mediation programs. These programs should be located at safe, easily accessible locations.
- *Encourage activism.* Clients should be encouraged to participate in various forms of activism, including contacting government leaders, organizing neighborhood watch groups, and demanding cultural sensitivity training for police officers. Service providers should actively work to eliminate violence in these communities as a primary prevention of mental health disorders.

In conclusion, recent reports indicate that violence in this country is declining, particularly in urban areas (Bureau of Justice Statistics, 2001). This is good news for everyone, especially for women and children who live in high-risk environments. However, until violence and poverty are eradicated, we must work to effectively intervene with individuals in these communities, many of whom have already been scarred by fear and trauma.

REFERENCES

American Psychiatric Association (APA). (2000). *Diagnostic and statistical manual of mental disorders* (4th ed., Text Revision [DSM-IV-TR]). Washington, DC: Author.

Attar, B. K., Guerra, N. C., & Tolan, P. H. (1994). Neighborhood disadvantage, stressful life events, and adjustment in urban elementary school children. *Journal of Clinical Child Psychology, 23*, 391-400.

Barbarin, O., Richter, L., & deWet, T. (2001). Exposure to violence, coping, resources and psychological adjustment of South African children. *American Journal of Orthopsychiatry, 71*, 16-25.

Breslau, N., Kessler, R. C., Chilcoat, H. D., Peterson, E. L., & Lucia, V. C. (1999). Vulnerability to assaultive violence: Further specification of sex differences in post-traumatic stress disorder. *Psychological Medicine, 29*, 813-821.

Breslau, N., Kessler, R. C., Chilcoat, H. D., Schultz, L. R., Davis, G. C., & Andreski, P. (1998). Traumatic and posttraumatic stress disorder in the community: The 1996 Detroit area survey of trauma. *Archives of General Psychiatry, 55*, 626-632.

Brown, A. W., & Gourdine, R. M. (1998). Teenage Black girls and violence: Coming to age in an urban environment. *Journal of Human Behavior in the Social Environment, 1*, 105-124.

Bureau of Justice Statistics (May, 2001). *Criminal victimization 2000: Changes 1999-2000 with trends 1993-2000* (NCJ 187007). Washington, DC: Office of Justice Programs, U. S. Department of Justice.

Clark, R., Andersen, N. B., Clark, V. R., & Williams, D. R. (1999). Racism as a stressor for African Americans. *American Psychologist, 54*, 805-816.

Cohen, S., & Williamson, G. M. (1991). Stress and infectious disease in humans. *Psychological Bulletin, 109*, 5-24.

Dulmus, C. N., & Wodarski, J. S. (2000). Trauma-related symptomatology among children of parents victimized by urban community violence. *American Journal of Orthopsychiatry, 70*, 272-277.

Farrell, A. D., & Bruce, S. E. (1997). Impact of exposure to community violence on violent behavior and emotional distress among urban adolescents. *Journal of Clinical Child Psychology, 26*, 2-14.

Giaconia, R. M., Reinherz, H. Z., Silverman, A. B., Paktz, B., Frost, A. K., & Cohen, E. (1995). Traumas and posttraumatic stress disorder in a community population of older adolescents. *Journal of the American Academy of Child and Adolescent Psychiatry, 34*, 1369-1380.

Gorman-Smith, D., Tolan, P. H., Sheidow, A. J., & Henry, D. B. (2001). Partner violence among urban adolescents: Do the same family factors relate? *Journal of Research on Adolescence, 11*, 273-295.

Guterman, N. B., & Cameron, M. (1999). Young clients' exposure to community violence: How much do their therapists know? *American Journal of Orthopsychiatry, 69*, 382-391.

Guterman, N. B., Cameron, M., & Staller, K. (2000). Definitional and measurement issues in the study of community violence among children and youths. *Journal of Community Psychology, 28*, 571-587.

Hill, H., Hawkins, S., Raposa, M., & Carr, P. (1995). Relationship between multiple exposure to violence and coping strategies among African American mothers. *Violence and Victims, 10*, 55-71.

Hill, H. M., & Jones, L. P. (1997). Children's and parents' perceptions of children's exposure to violence in urban neighborhoods. *Journal of the National Medical Association, 89*, 270-276.

Horn, J. L., & Trickett, P. K. (1998). Community violence and child development: A review of research. In P. K. Trickett & C. J. Schellenback (Eds.), *Violence against children in the family and the community* (pp. 103-138). Washington, DC: American Psychological Association.

Horowitz, K., Weine, S., & Jekel, J. (1995). PTSD symptoms in urban adolescent girls: Compounded community trauma. *Journal of the American Academy of Child and Adolescent Psychiatry, 34*, 1353-1361.

Hussain, M. A., & Smith, J. C. (1996). Assessing the impact of violence on motivation for parenthood among Blacks and Whites. *Journal of Negro Education, 65*, 424-433.

Jenkins, E. J. (2001). Violence and trauma in the lives of African American children. In A. M. Neal-Barnett, J. M. Contreras, & K. A. Kerns (Eds.), *Forging links: African American children clinical developmental perspectives* (pp. 107-128). Westport, CT: Praeger.

Jenkins, E. J., & Bell, C. C. (1994). Violence exposure, psychological distress, and high risk behaviors among inner-city high school students. In S. Friedman (Ed.), *Anxiety disorders in African Americans* (pp. 76-88). New York: Springer Publishing.

Jenkins, E. J., & Bell, C. C. (1997). Exposure and response to community violence among children and adolescents. In J. Osofsky (Ed.), *Children in a violent society* (pp. 9-31). New York: Guilford.

Jenkins, E. J., Kpo, W., & Barr, M. (1997, October). *Violence exposure and substance use among students at a predominately Black urban university.* Paper presented at the Third National Conference on Family and Community Violence Prevention, New Orleans, LA.

Kaljee, L. M., Stanton, B., Ricardo, I., & Whitehead, T. L. (1995). Urban African American adolescents and their parents: Perceptions of violence within and against their communities. *Human Organization, 54*, 373-382.

Kluft, R. P., Bloom, S. L., & Kinzie, D. (2000). Treating traumatized patients and victims of violence. In C. C. Bell (Ed.), *Psychiatric aspects of violence: Issues in prevention and treatment* (pp. 79-102). San Francisco: Jossey-Bass.

Lipschitz, D. S., Rasmusson, A. M., Anyan, W., Cromwell, P., & Southwick, S. M. (2000). Clinical and functional correlates of posttraumatic stress disorder in urban adolescent girls in a primary care clinic. *Journal of the American Academy of Child and Adolescent Psychiatry, 39*, 1104-1111.

Marmar, C., Foy, D., Kagan, B., & Pynoos, R. (1993). An integrated approach for treating posttraumatic stress. In J. M. Oldham, M. B. Riba, & A. Tasman (Eds.), *Review of Psychiatry, 12*, Washington, DC: American Psychiatric Press.

Mattis, J., Bell, C. C., Jagers, R., & Jenkins, E. J. (1999). Towards a critical approach to stress-related disorders in African Americans. *Journal of the National Medical Association, 91*, 80-85.

Mohr, W. K., Fantuzzo, J. W., & Abdul-Kabir, S. (2001). Safeguarding themselves and their children: Mothers share their strategies. *Journal of Family Violence, 16*, 75-92.

Norris, F. H. (1992). Epidemiology of trauma: Frequency and impact of different potentially traumatic events on different demographic groups. *Journal of Consulting and Clinical Psychology, 60*, 409-418.

Pugh-Lilly, A. O., Neville, H. A., & Poulin, K. L. (2001). In protection of ourselves: Black girls' perceptions of self-reported delinquent behaviors. *Psychology of Women Quarterly, 25*, 145-154.

Pynoos, R. S. (1993). Traumatic stress and developmental psychopathology in children and adolescents. In J. M. Oldham, M. B. Riba, & A.Tasman (Eds.), *Review of Psychiatry, 12*(205-237). Washington, DC: American Psychiatric Press.

Pynoos, R. S., & Nader, K. (1988). Psychological first aid and treatment approach to children exposed to community violence: Research implications. *Journal of Traumatic Stress, 1*, 445-473.

Resnick, H. S., Kilpatrick, D. G., Dansky, B. S., Saunders, B. E., & Best, C. L. (1993). Prevalence of civilian trauma and posttraumatic stress disorder in a representative national sample of women. *Journal of Consulting and Clinical Psychology, 61*, 984-991.

Richters, J., & Martinez, P. (1993). The NIMH community violence project: I. Children as victims of and witnesses to violence. *Psychiatry, 56*, 984-991.

Rinear, E. E. (1988). Psychosocial aspects of parental response patterns to the death of a child by homicide. *Journal of Traumatic Stress, 1*, 305-322.

Rynearson, E. K. (1984). Bereavement after homicide: A descriptive study. *Journal of Psychiatry, 141*, 507-510.

Rynearson, E. K. (1986). Psychological effects of unnatural dying on bereavement. *Psychiatry Annals, 62*, 272-275.

Sanders-Phillips, K. (1996a). The ecology of urban violence: Its relationship to health promotion behaviors in low income Black and Latino communities. *American Journal of Health Promotion, 10*, 308-317.

Sanders-Phillips, K. (1996b). Correlates of health promotion behaviors in low-income Black women and Latinas. *American Journal of Preventive Medicine, 12*, 450-458.

Sanders-Phillips, K. (1997). Assaultive violence in the community: Psychological responses of adolescent victims and their parents. *Journal of Adolescent Health, 21*, 356-365.

Schubiner, H., Scott, R., & Tzelepis, A. (1993). Exposure to violence among inner-city youth. *Journal of Adolescent Health, 14*, 214-219.

Schuster, M. A., Halfon, N., & Wood, D. L. (1998). African American mothers in South Central Los Angeles. *Archives of Pediatrics and Adolescent Medicine, 152*, 264-268.

Siegel, J. A. (2000). Aggressive behavior among women sexually abused as children. *Violence and Victims, 15*, 235-255.

Singer, M. D., Anglin, T., Song, L., & Lunghofer, L. (1995). Adolescents' exposure to violence and associated symptoms of psychological trauma. *Journal of the American Medical Association, 273*, 477-482.

Stein, M., Walker, J., Hazen, A., & Forde, D. (1997). Full and partial post traumatic stress disorder: Findings from a community study. *American Journal of Psychiatry, 154*, 114-119.

Temple, S. D. (2000). A clinical perspective on inner-city youths' exposure to homicide: Community and policy implications. *Journal of Community Psychology, 28*, 655-667.

Terr, L. (1991). Childhood traumas: An outline and overview. *American Journal of Psychiatry, 48*, 10-20.

Thompson, M. P., Norris, F., & Ruback, R. B. (1998). Comparative distress levels of inner-city family members of homicide victims. *Journal of Traumatic Stress, 11*, 223-242.

Uehara, E. S., Chalmers, D., Jenkins, E. J., & Shakoor, B. H. (1996). African American youth encounters with violence: Results from the community mental health council violence screening project. *Journal of Black Studies, 26*, 768-781.

Wolfer, T. A. (1999). "It happens all the time": Overcoming the limits of memory and method for chronic community violence experience. *Journal of Interpersonal Violence, 14*, 1070-1094.

Wolfer, T. A. (2000). Coping with chronic community violence: The variety and implications of women's efforts. *Violence and Victims, 15*, 283-302.

TYPES OF VIOLENCE

Childhood Sexual Abuse in the Lives of Black Women: Risk and Resilience in a Longitudinal Study

Victoria L. Banyard
Linda M. Williams
Jane A. Siegel
Carolyn M. West

Victoria L. Banyard, PhD, is affiliated with the Department of Psychology, University of New Hampshire. Linda M. Williams, PhD, is affiliated with The Stone Center at Wellesley College. Jane A. Siegel, PhD, is affiliated with the Department of Sociology, Anthropology, and Criminal Justice at Rutgers University, Camden. Carolyn M. West, PhD, is affiliated with the Department of Interdisciplinary Arts and Sciences, University of Washington, Tacoma.

The research was supported by National Center on Child Abuse and Neglect (90-CA-1406) and Recovery from Sexual Abuse (90-CA-1552).

Address correspondence to: Victoria L. Banyard, PhD, Department of Psychology, University of New Hampshire, Conant Hall, 10 Library Way, Durham, NH 03824 (E-mail: vlbcisunix.unh.edu).

[Haworth co-indexing entry note]: "Childhood Sexual Abuse in the Lives of Black Women: Risk and Resilience in a Longitudinal Study." Banyard, Victoria L. et al. Co-published simultaneously in *Women & Therapy* (The Haworth Press, Inc.) Vol. 25, No. 3/4, 2002, pp. 45-58; and: *Violence in the Lives of Black Women: Battered, Black, and Blue* (ed: Carolyn M. West) The Haworth Press, Inc., 2002, pp. 45-58. Single or multiple copies of this article are available for a fee from The Haworth Document Delivery Service [1-800-HAWORTH, 9:00 a.m. - 5:00 p.m. (EST). E-mail address: getinfo@haworthpressinc.com].

SUMMARY. Childhood sexual abuse (CSA) is associated with long-term mental health consequences. This article reviews the results of one longitudinal study, whose sample consisted primarily of African American women. The purpose is to give voice to an understudied group of CSA survivors and to highlight the variability in risk and protective factors. Key findings related to mental health consequences, re-traumatization, and resilience are reviewed and set within the broader context of research on African American women and child sexual abuse. Implications for future research and clinical practice are discussed. *[Article copies available for a fee from The Haworth Document Delivery Service: 1-800-HAWORTH. E-mail address: <getinfo@haworthpressinc.com> Website: <http://www.HaworthPress.com> © 2002 by The Haworth Press, Inc. All rights reserved.]*

KEYWORDS. Blacks, trauma, mental health, re-victimization

Childhood sexual abuse (CSA) has been documented in all segments of society (e.g., Finkelhor, Hotaling, Lewis, & Smith, 1990) with documented long-term consequences for women's psychological functioning and well-being (e.g., Fergusson & Mullen, 1999). Black feminist survivors (Wilson, 1994) have documented many painful personal accounts of childhood sexual abuse. Empirical researchers have also discovered child sexual abuse in this population. For example, Wyatt, Loeb, Solis, and Carmona (1999) reported a 10-year comparison of prevalence rates of child sexual abuse in a community sample of African American and European American women. There were no significant changes in reported rates of abuse over 10 years and no racial differences in the characteristics of the abuse experience. However, 29% of the African American women in the sample reported child sexual abuse in the 1994 survey. Although this was lower than the 39% prevalence rate for European American women, it is still a substantial rate of victimization. Research has also documented the wide-ranging negative mental health consequences associated with experiencing child sexual abuse (e.g., Beitchman et al., 1992). These findings suggest that CSA is an important element in understanding Black women's health (Lawson, Rodgers-Rose, & Rajaram, 1999).

Kenny and McEachern (2000) reviewed findings related to ethnicity and child sexual abuse, including patterns of prevalence, disclosure, and consequences. They called for further research that explores the experiences of ethnically diverse individuals. Feminist scholars, particularly Black feminist researchers, have asserted the need to reexamine notions of difference and to move beyond treating all women as a homogenous group (Collins, 2000; Hare-Mustin & Marecek, 1990; West, 2002). Such critiques have important implications for the study of child sexual abuse, calling for greater attention to how child sexual abuse is experienced in the lives of understudied groups of women. Moreover, in order to understand variability among survivors, researchers need to move beyond simply comparing survivors to non-survivors (West, Williams, & Siegel, 2000).

In response to such feminist critiques, this article will describe the findings of a longitudinal study of women, primarily African American, as a focal point for examining patterns of risk and resilience in the lives of CSA survivors. The study's findings have been discussed in detail elsewhere (McCahill, Meyer, & Fischman, 1979; Banyard & Williams, 1996; Banyard, Williams, & Siegel, 2000c). The purpose of this article is to summarize and review these findings in the context of other studies of child sexual abuse, particularly studies that focus on African American survivors.

THE WOMEN'S STUDY

Participants

The Women's Study, which began in the early 1970s, has followed a group of female childhood sexual abuse survivors and a comparison sample for more than 25 years. Participants were drawn from a sample of 206 victims of child sexual abuse who were examined in the emergency room of a large city hospital from 1973 to 1975. They and/or family members were interviewed at the time as part of a larger study on the consequences of sexual assault (McCahill et al., 1979). The sample was composed primarily of African American girls (84%) who ranged in age from 10 months to 12 years at the time of the abuse. The reported sexual abuse involved sexual contact by force, threat of force, misuse of authority, or by a person who was five or more years older than the child, whether or not force was used.

The abuse ranged from genital fondling to sexual intercourse and was perpetrated by a wide range of individuals–fathers, stepfathers, other family members, friends, acquaintances, and strangers (all males). Soon after each girl was seen in the hospital, consent to participate in the study was obtained from the children and/or their caregivers, and then the child and caregiver were interviewed.

An average of 17 years after the abuse, 136 women (66% of the original sample) were located through phone directories, official and government records, and neighborhood canvassing. The survivors were reinterviewed in 1990 or 1991 as part of a follow-up study on the consequences of child sexual abuse. The mean age for the sample at the time of reinterview was 25.5 years. Most (86%) were African American, and most (61%) had never been married. Fifty percent of the women had a high school diploma or GED equivalent. Although 29% were working full- or part-time, the majority of women were unemployed (64%). Their median personal income was less than $8,000 in the year before the interview.

In 1997, which was 23 years after the abuse, 87 of the original 206 girls were recontacted and reinterviewed. In order to make comparisons, we also contacted 87 women who were seen, but not for sexual abuse, at the same city hospital in the early 1970s. On average, the women were 31.6 years old at this time, and 89% identified themselves as African American. Women interviewed at wave 2 were more likely to have been sexually abused by a family member than non-interviewed women and, at wave 3, a greater proportion of interviewed women were African American. Overall, however, interviewed and non-interviewed women did not differ on demographic variables or characteristics of their abuse.

Procedures

Institutional review board procedures were followed for obtaining consent. Before each interview, informed consent was obtained, which included a description of the sensitive nature of the interview material. Participants were advised that they could stop the interview at any time. The caregivers who were interviewed in the early 1970s were not reinterviewed.

All waves of the data were collected through face-to-face interviews. The interviewers were two women, one European American and one African American, who had received training and supervision to ensure that they were able to establish rapport with the women and conduct interviews with sensitive and potentially upsetting personal topics. Although the interviewers knew the purpose of the study, they were blind to the details of the women's histories of victimization.

Although a few participants were interviewed in their own homes, almost all were interviewed in a private office. Each interview began with questions about more neutral aspects of the woman's life, such as education and employment status. After sufficient rapport had been established, the interviewers asked questions about other topics such as relationships in her family of origin, drug and alcohol use, sexual history, psychological functioning, and detailed questions about sexual victimization.

On average, the interviews lasted three hours and were followed by a debriefing period, which gave the women an opportunity to ask questions. There was also a discussion of how she was feeling about the interview. Interviews were suspended if the interviewer determined that the participant was in any distress. Counseling services from a local sexual abuse treatment center were made available to participants if they were interested.

REVIEW OF THE RESEARCH

The participants' voices in the Women's Study revealed the negative consequences associated with child sexual abuse, including a variety of mental health problems, difficulties functioning as a parent, and elevated rates of aggressive behavior. The women also demonstrated how responses to trauma might vary based on the number and types of traumatic experiences. Equally as important, the Women's Study discovered that survivors, despite their trauma, could be very resilient.

Consequences of Child Sexual Abuse

Several articles, based on data from The Women's Study, point to the negative impact of child sexual abuse on the health and well-being of African American women. Banyard, Williams, and Siegel (2001b) used wave 3 of the study to investigate the adult mental health functioning of CSA survivors and the comparison group. When compared to the non-abused group, survivors of child sexual abuse experienced higher levels of anxiety, depression, dissociation, sexual concerns, intrusive symptoms, and an impaired sense of self.

The size of the sample in the Women's Study also permitted the examination of variations among survivors. Banyard, Williams, and Siegel (2001d) discovered that some survivors experienced negative reactions when they disclosed their abuse. For example, the person they told was unsupportive, blamed the survivor, called the survivor a liar, or punished the survivor. These survivors reported higher levels of dissociative symptoms.

Other analyses examined the association between mental health functioning and characteristics of the child sexual abuse, such as the use of force, the survivor's relationship with the perpetrator, and level of invasiveness (Banyard & Williams, 1996; Jasinski, Williams, & Siegel, 2000). Survivors who had experienced force reported higher levels of such problems as depressive symptoms, anxiety, and sleep disturbance. Women who were abused by a family member, when compared to survivors who were victims of extrafamilial abuse, were more likely to report an array of mental health symptoms. Higher levels of anxiety and heavy drinking in adulthood also were found among survivors who were older at the time of the abuse and among survivors who had experienced multiple instances of CSA. These findings fit with both the broader literature on the negative effects of child sexual abuse and its links to a broad array of mental health effects across the life span (see Jumper, 1995; Kendall-Tackett, Williams, & Finkelhor, 1993; Neumann, Houskamp, Pollock, & Briere, 1996; Polusny & Follette, 1995 for reviews) and studies that specifically examine the experiences of African American women (e.g., Rhodes, Ebert, & Meyers, 1993; Russo, Denious, Keita, & Koss, 1997; Thompson, Kaslow, Lane, & Kingree, 2000; Wyatt & Newcomb, 1990; West, 2002).

Measures used in the Women's Study also permitted examination of the impact of child sexual abuse on specific behaviors, including the ability to function as a parent and adult aggressive behavior. Banyard, Williams and Siegel (2001a) discovered that adult sexual assault and partner violence, but not CSA, were associated with more negative parenting outcomes. This differs from other studies that found links between child sexual abuse and parenting difficulties, such as negative perceptions of one's self as a parent and greater use of physical punishment (Banyard, 1997; DiLillo, 2001). Future research should explore the impact of CSA on African American women's family roles.

Other areas of behavior examined in the Women's Study included criminality and aggression. Several feminist scholars have posited that child sexual abuse is an important factor in the onset of delinquency because it can lead girls to run away, which, in turn, forces them to engage in criminal behavior for survival (Belknap, Holsinger, & Dunn, 1997; Chesney-Lind, 1997). Richie (1996) has shown that victimization plays an important role in what she has referred to as the *gender entrapment* of African American women in which women's criminal behavior is inextricably tied with their involvement in violent relationships with their partners. In addition, sexual victimization has been associated with aggression in children (Kendall-Tackett et al., 1993); however, before the Women's Study, there had been few attempts to determine if this relationship persisted beyond childhood.

Analyses of official arrest records by Siegel and Williams (2001) found that the child sexual abuse victims were at higher risk of arrest than were the women in the comparison group as adults, but not as juveniles. However, the victims of abuse were significantly more likely to have been arrested for violent offenses in both adolescence and adulthood. African Americans were no more likely to have been arrested than White women, either as juveniles or adults, except for violent offenses; in that case, the African American women faced a substantially higher risk of arrest than the White women.

The increased risk of violence faced by victims of sexual abuse was reflected as well in self-reports of extensive aggressive behavior in the form of physical fighting, with both intimate partners and others (Siegel, 2000). Women with a history of repeated sexual victimization and exposure to other forms of violence, such as witnessing violence, experiencing beatings in childhood, and having family members or close friends who were murdered, were at significantly greater risk of perpetrating violence. Those who were victims of violence at the hands of their intimate partners were also more likely to report engaging in physical fighting. Thus, the women's own violence was coupled with another troubling aspect of their lives: vulnerability to repeat victimization.

Re-Victimization

Linkages between a history of child sexual abuse and re-victimization in adulthood, defined as the occurrence of at least one incident of sexual abuse during childhood followed by a subsequent incident of adult physical or sexual victimization, have been reported in several studies, including those with samples of African American women (e.g., Roodman & Clum, 2001; Wyatt, Notgrass, & Gordon, 1995). Almost all of these studies, however, have been based on retrospective reports by adults. In addition to experiencing violence in intimate relationships, many Black women are exposed to a broad array of traumatic experiences, including community violence (Jenkins, 2002). Re-victimized Black survivors are especially vulnerable to mental health problems (Russo et al., 1997). For example, almost one-quarter of the re-traumatized women surveyed by Hien and Bukszpan (1999) met diagnostic criteria for lifetime posttraumatic stress disorder.

The Women's Study extends our knowledge of re-victimization because it assessed for various forms of trauma in adulthood, including witnessing violence, experiencing a serious accident, the traumatic loss of a friend or family member, and various forms of physical and sexual assaults over the life span. Siegel and Williams (2001) found that the risk of adult re-victmization was not shared equally among all those in the Women's Study who experienced child sexual abuse. Women whose only experience of youthful sexual victimization occurred when they were under age 13 were not at increased risk of adult sexual re-victimization compared to those who experienced no child sexual abuse. However, a small group of women were at extremely high risk of adult sexual and physical victimization if they had been victimized as young children (i.e., under age 13) and again in adolescence. In addition, West, Williams, and Siegel (2000) found that survivors who had experienced sexual abuse in both childhood and adulthood were also at increased risk for partner violence in their adult intimate relationships.

Furthermore, sexual re-victimzation had an adverse impact on Black women's reproductive and sexual health. Specifically, when compared to women sexually abused in childhood only, re-victimized women experienced more problems with conceiving, repeated vaginal infections, sexually transmitted diseases, and painful intercourse (West et al., 2000). Banyard, Williams, and Siegel (2001b) found that exposure to multiple traumatic events (broadened beyond exposure to sexual re-victimization) across the life span were associated with higher levels of psychological distress. Furthermore, the relationship between child sexual abuse and such outcomes as depressive symptoms, anxiety, and negative feelings about self was mediated by reports of exposure to this variety of other traumatic events. Thus, for some symptoms, the links between child sexual abuse and adult mental health symptoms are explained by links between child sexual abuse and re-traumatization. Taken together, with the aforementioned risk of self-reported aggression for those exposed to other forms of violence, these findings underscore the need for careful additional attention to the links between child sexual abuse and a web of other traumatic events.

The longitudinal nature of the Women's Study also permitted examination of risk and protective factors for repeated trauma exposure within the sample of child sexual abuse survivors. West et al. (2000) found that child sexual abuse survivors whose abuse involved physical force were at greater risk for reexperiencing abuse in the form of adult sexual assault. Banyard, Williams, and Siegel (2001c) found increased risk for a wide range of trauma re-exposure in adulthood for women who also experienced extreme poverty, family-of-origin difficulties, depression and dissociation, and substance abuse. Social support was a protective factor. These findings fit with earlier work on risk factors by researchers, such as Koss and Dinero (1989), but extend the findings to a community sample of women, most of whom were African American. These findings further support the need to attend to important differences among women–not only differences between Black women and other survivors, but also variability in the experiences of African American women themselves.

Resilience

In addition to documenting the ways in which child sexual abuse places African American women at risk for re-traumatization and psychological distress, the Women's Study also sought to examine the complex phenomenon of resilience. Despite having experienced childhood sexual abuse, resilient women are functioning relatively well in many aspects of their lives. Hyman and Williams (2001) defined resilience as "physical health, mental health, interpersonal relationships, adherence to community standards, and economic well being" (p. 203).

However, 40 survivors (29% of the sample) had high scores on the resilience scale, and 25 women (18% of the sample) demonstrated what the researchers referred to as *excellent resilience*, which was characterized by competent functioning in nearly all areas assessed. The highly resilient women were less likely to have experienced incest or severe child physical abuse. In addition, they were more likely to have been reared in stable homes, which meant that they experienced fewer moves or foster care placements and less parental drug abuse. Income level of family of origin was not related to resilience. Receiving abuse-specific therapy was not significantly related to resilience, though it should be noted that a relatively small portion of the sample of women received this type of professional intervention. Graduation from high school was also predictive of resilience for this sample.

For this group of women, social support in the form of receiving support from someone special and significant in their lives was an important protective factor characteristic of the more resilient women. In a similar vein, Siegel (2000) found that women who reported a strong feeling of attachment to their mothers were less likely to be in abusive relationships, which, in turn, lowered the risk that they themselves would engage in violence. These results suggest the need to attend not only to strengths within the survivor, but also to building strengths and supports around the survivor–including stabilizing the family of the abused child and strengthening informal support networks.

These findings fit with the broader literature on understanding competent outcomes following child sexual abuse (e.g., Spaccarelli & Kim, 1995; Valentine & Feinauer, 1993). Harvey (1996), for example, discusses the importance of understanding a variety of ecological factors that may predict recovery from sexual abuse. She highlights the fact that many survivors do not seek professional help but may find other paths to recovery. The Women's Study supports this notion in that only a minority of the study's participants was in psychotherapy, yet many were able to find paths toward healing through other connections. This study extends discussions of resilience that have more often focused on European American women's experiences, and illustrates the important strengths of African American female survivors.

SUGGESTIONS FOR INTERVENTION

In summary, a variety of research points to the importance of understanding child sexual abuse in the lives of African American women. The voices of participants in the Women's Study remind us of the negative consequences of CSA, including the ways in which it places survivors at greater risk for mental health concerns, such as depression, anxiety, traumatic intrusions, and impaired views of the self, as well as increased contact with the criminal justice system and concerns in relationships with others. These women also tell us of the variability in survivors' responses to trauma as not all women experienced the same constellation of effects. Furthermore, these survivors remind us of the strengths of survivors of child sexual abuse, and of Black women in particular. Furthermore, although a relatively small portion of the women used therapy to address their history of abuse (Hyman & Williams, 2001), practitioners should be prepared to assist African American survivors of childhood sexual abuse. The following suggestions are made for clinical practice:

Establish competence. Therapists should become familiar with a variety of topics, including the psychobiology of trauma; research on memories for trauma, dissociation, and posttraumatic stress disorder; and variables associated with resilience and coping (Enns et al., 1998).

Conduct a thorough assessment. Service providers should consider using self-report measures, such as the Trauma History Screen, which is designed to enable clinicians to gather information about a broad range of traumatic experiences (Allen, Huntoon, & Evans, 1999). Black women are also at risk for community violence and racial trauma, such as racial profiling by the police (Daniel, 2000; Jenkins, 2002). These forms of trauma should not be overlooked. Assessment and treatment strategies need to consider the complex web of trauma exposure that may characterize the experiences of some survivors.

Treatment plan. It is especially important to be attentive to how the experience of child sexual abuse is influenced by the client's race, social class, and sexual orientation (Enns, 1996). A culturally sensitive treatment plan for African American survivors may involve addressing such topics as spirituality or stereotypes about Black women's sexuality (Robinson, 2000; Wilson, 1994). Future work should focus on merging the growing fields of culturally sensitive therapeutic intervention and trauma treatment, work that is being done by Black feminist scholars (Daniel, 2000).

Develop a support system. A strong support system has been shown to improve the psychological functioning of victimized Black women and to reduce their likelihood of suicidal behavior (Young, Twomey, & Kaslow, 2000). If necessary or appropriate, the service provider may need to educate relatives, friends, and community members about the risk factors and symptoms associated with childhood sexual abuse (Fontes, Cruz, & Tabachnick, 2001). Tully (1999) encourages practitioners to recognize the ways in which traditional strengths of African American communities may help the survivor cope in the aftermath of victimization.

In conclusion, the Women's Study provides further evidence of the importance of understanding child sexual abuse in the lives of African American survivors. The Women's Study helps document both the long-term negative effects of CSA as well as the fact that despite these life challenges, many survivors are resilient and develop effective coping strategies. The voices of participants from the Women's Study encourage us to continue to develop interventions that appreciate the complex differences among women and to support research that gives voices to the perspectives of various survivors of child sexual abuse.

REFERENCES

Allen, J. G., Huntoon, J., & Evans, R. B. (1999). A self-report measure to screen for trauma history and its application to women in inpatient treatment for trauma-related disorders. *Bulletin of the Menninger Clinic, 63,* 422-429.

Banyard, V. L. (1997). The impact of childhood sexual abuse and family functioning on four dimensions of women's later parenting. *Child Abuse & Neglect, 21,* 1095-1107.

Banyard, V. L., & Williams, L. M. (1996). Characteristics of child sexual abuse as correlates of women's adjustment: A prospective study. *Journal of Marriage and the Family, 58*, 853-865.

Banyard, V. L., Williams, L. M., & Siegel, J. A. (2001a). *The impact of trauma and depression on parenting: An exploration of mediating risk and protective factors.* Unpublished manuscript.

Banyard, V. L., Williams, L. M., & Siegel, J. A. (2001b). The long-term mental health consequences of child sexual abuse: An exploratory study of the impact of multiple traumas in a sample of women. *Journal of Traumatic Stress, 14*, 697-715.

Banyard, V. L., Williams, L. M., & Siegel, J. A. (2001c). *Retraumatization among adult women sexually abused in childhood: Exploratory analyses in a prospective study of predominantly African American women.* Unpublished manuscript.

Banyard, V. L., Williams, L. M., & Siegel, J. A. (2001d). Understanding links among childhood trauma, dissociation, and women's mental health. *American Journal of Orthopsychiatry, 71*, 311-321.

Beitchman, J. H., Zucker, K. J., Hood, J. E., DaCosta, G. A., Akman, D., & Cassavia, E. (1992). A review of the long-term effects of child sexual abuse. *Child Abuse & Neglect, 16*, 101-118.

Belknap, J., Holsinger, K., & Dunn, M. (1997). Understanding incarcerated girls: The results of a focus group study. *Prison Journal, 77*, 381-404.

Chesney-Lind, M. (1997). *The female offender: Girls, women, and crime.* Thousand Oaks, CA: Sage.

Collins, P. H. (2000). *Black feminist thought: Knowledge, consciousness, and the politics of empowerment.* New York: Routledge.

Daniel, J. H. (2000). The courage to hear: African American women's memories of racial trauma. In L. C. Jackson & B. Greene (Eds.), *Psychotherapy with African American women: Innovations in psychodynamic perspectives and practice* (pp. 126-144). New York: Guilford Press.

DiLillo, D. (2001). Interpersonal functioning among women reporting a history of childhood sexual abuse: Empirical findings and methodological issues. *Clinical Psychology Review, 21*, 553-576.

Enns, C. Z. (1996). The Feminist Therapy Institute code of ethics: Implications for working with survivors of child sexual abuse. *Women & Therapy, 19*, 79-91.

Enns, C. Z., Campbell, J., Courtois, C. A., Gottlieb, M. C., Lese, K. P., Gilbert, M. S., & Forrest, L. (1998). Working with adult clients who may have experienced childhood abuse: Recommendations for assessment and practice. *Professional Psychology: Research and Practice, 29*, 245-256.

Fergusson, D. M., & Mullen, P. E. (1999). *Childhood sexual abuse: An evidence based perspective.* Thousand Oaks, CA: Sage.

Finkelhor, D., Hotaling, G., Lewis, I. A., & Smith, C. (1990). Sexual abuse in a national survey of adult men and women: Prevalence, characteristics, and risk factors. *Child Abuse & Neglect, 14*, 19-28.

Fontes, L. A., Cruz, M., & Tabachnick, J. (2001). Views of child sexual abuse in two cultural communities: An exploratory study among African Americans and Latinos. *Child Maltreatment, 6*, 103-117.

Hare-Mustin, R. T., & Marecek, J. (1990). *Making a difference: Psychology and the construction of gender.* New Haven: Yale University Press.

Havey, M. R. (1996). An ecological view of psychological trauma and trauma recovery. *Journal of Traumatic Stress, 9,* 3-23.

Hien, D., & Bukszpan, C. (1999). Interpersonal violence in a "normal" low-income control group. *Women & Health, 29,* 1-16.

Hyman, B., & Williams, L. (2001). Resilience among women survivors of child sexual abuse. *Affilia, 16,* 198-219.

Jasinski, J. L., Williams, L. M., & Siegel, J. (2000). Childhood physical and sexual abuse as risk factors for heavy drinking among African American women: A prospective study. *Child Abuse & Neglect, 24,* 1061-1071.

Jenkins, E. J. (2002). Black women and community violence: Trauma, grief, and coping. *Women & Therapy, 25* (3 & 4), 29-44.

Jumper, S. A. (1995). A meta-analysis of the relationship of child sexual abuse to adult psychological adjustment. *Child Abuse & Neglect, 19,* 715-728.

Kendall-Tackett, K. A., Williams, L. M., & Finkelhor, D. (1993). Impact of sexual abuse on children: A review and synthesis. *Psychological Bulletin, 113,* 164-180.

Kenny, M. C., & McEachern, A. G. (2000). Racial, ethnic, and cultural factors of childhood sexual abuse: A selected review of the literature. *Clinical Psychology Review, 20,* 905-922.

Koss, M. P., & Dinero, T. E. (1989). Discriminant analysis of risk factors for sexual victimization among a national sample of college women. *Journal of Consulting and Clinical Psychology, 57,* 242-250.

Lawson, E. J., Rodgers-Rose, L., & Rajaram, S. (1999). The psychosocial context of Black women's health. *Health Care for Women International, 20,* 279-289.

McCahill, T., Meyer, L. C., & Fischman, A. (1979). *The aftermath of rape.* Lexington, MA: Lexington Books.

Neumann, D. A., Houskamp, B. M., Pollock, V. E., & Briere, J. (1996). The long-term sequelae of childhood sexual abuse in women: A meta-analytic review. *Child Maltreatment, 1,* 6-16.

Polusny, M. A., & Follette, V. M. (1995). Long-term correlates of child sexual abuse: Theory and review of the empirical literature. *Applied and Preventive Psychology, 4,* 143-166.

Rhodes, J. E., Ebert, L., & Meyers, A. B. (1993). Sexual victimization in young, pregnant and parenting, African American women: Psychological and social outcomes. *Violence and Victims, 8,* 153-163.

Richie, B. E. (1996). *Compelled to crime: The gender entrapment of battered Black women.* New York: Routledge.

Robinson, T. L. (2000). Making the hurt go away: Psychological and spiritual healing for African American women survivors of childhood incest. *Journal of Multicultural Counseling and Development, 28,* 160-176.

Roodman, A. A., & Clum, G. A. (2001). Revictimization rates and method variance: A meta-analysis. *Clinical Psychology Review, 21,* 183-204.

Russo, N. F., Denious, J. E., Keita, G. P., & Koss, M. P. (1997). Intimate violence and
Black women's health. *Women's Health: Research on Gender, Behavior, and Policy, 3*, 315-348.

Siegel, J. A. (2000). Aggressive behavior among women sexually abused as children.
Violence and Victims, 15, 235-255.

Siegel, J. A., & Williams, L. M. (2001). *The relationship between child sexual abuse
and female delinquency and crime: A prospective study.* Unpublished manuscript.

Spaccarelli, S., & Kim, S. (1995). Resilience criteria and factors associated with resilience in sexually abused girls. *Child Abuse & Neglect, 9*, 1171-1182.

Thompson, M. P., Kaslow, N. J., Lane, D. B., & Kingree, J. B. (2000). Childhood maltreatment, PTSD, and suicidal behavior among African American females. *Journal
of Interpersonal Violence, 15*, 3-15.

Tully, M. A. (1999). Lifting our voices: African American cultural responses to trauma
and loss. In K. Nader, N. Dubrow, & B. H. Stamm (Eds.), *Honoring differences:
Cultural issues in the treatment of trauma and loss* (pp. 23-48). Philadelphia, PA: Brun-
ner/Mazel.

Valentine, L., & Feinauer, L. L. (1993). Resilience factors associated with female survivors
of childhood sexual abuse. *The American Journal of Family Therapy, 21*, 216-224.

West, C. M. (2002). Black battered women: New directions for research and Black
feminist theory. In L. H. Collins, M. Dunlap, & J. Chrisler (Eds.), *Charting a new
course: Psychology for a feminist future.* (pp. 216-237) Westport, CT: Praeger.

West, C. M., Williams, L. M., & Siegel, J. A. (2000). Adult sexual revictimization
among Black women sexually abused in childhood: A prospective examination of
serious consequences of abuse. *Child Maltreatment, 5*, 49-57.

West, C. M. (2002). Battered, Black, and blue: An overview of violence in the lives of
Black women. *Women & Therapy, 25* (3 & 4), 5-27.

Wilson, M. (1994). *Crossing the boundary: Black women survive incest.* Seattle, WA:
Seal Press.

Wyatt, G. E., & Newcomb, M. (1990). Internal and external mediators of women's
sexual abuse in childhood. *Journal of Consulting and Clinical Psychology, 58*,
758-767.

Wyatt, G. E., Loeb, T. B., Solis, B., Carmona, J. V., & Romero, G. (1999). The prevalence and circumstances of child sexual abuse: Changes across a decade. *Child
Abuse & Neglect, 23*, 45-60.

Wyatt, G. E., Notgrass, C. M., & Gordon, G. (1995). The effects of African American
women's sexual revictimization: Strategies for prevention. In C. F. Swift (Ed.), *Sexual assault and abuse: Sociocultural context of prevention* (pp. 111-134).
Binghamton, NY: The Haworth Press, Inc.

Young, S., Twomey, H., & Kaslow, N. J. (2000). Suicidal behavior in African Ameri-
can women with a history of childhood maltreatment. In T. Joiner & M. D. Rudd
(Eds.), *Suicide science: Expanding the boundaries* (pp. 221-230). Boston: Kluwer
Academic Publishers.

Grounding Our Feet and Hearts:
Black Women's Coping Strategies
in Psychologically Abusive Dating Relationships

April L. Few
Patricia Bell-Scott

SUMMARY. This qualitative study investigated the decision-making processes and coping strategies that six heterosexual Black college women used to terminate psychologically abusive dating relationships. Leaving was a four-stage process: (a) assessment of the relationship; (b) separation from the abusive partner; (c) reestablishment of social networks; and (d) declaration of self-empowerment. Coping strategies included self-healing resources. Intervention strategies are provided. *[Article copies available for a fee from The Haworth Document Delivery Service: 1-800-HAWORTH. E-mail address: <getinfo@haworthpressinc.com> Website: <http://www.HaworthPress.com> © 2002 by The Haworth Press, Inc. All rights reserved.]*

April L. Few, PhD, is Assistant Professor, Department of Human Development, Virginia Polytechnic Institute and State University. Her current research interests include psychological abuse in dating relationships, rural battered women, Black women's sexuality, and mother-daughter relationships. She has presented her research at national and international conferences. Patricia Bell-Scott, PhD, is Professor of Family Development and Women's Studies and Adjunct Professor of Psychology at the University of Georgia, Athens. She has taught and written about Black women's narratives for 20 years. Her award winning books include, *Life notes: Personal writing by contemporary Black women* (1994) and *Flat-footed truths: Telling Black women's lives* (1998). She is also a contributing editor to *Ms.* magazine.

Address correspondence to: April L. Few, Department of Human Development, Virginia Polytechnic Institute and State University, Blacksburg, VA 24061 (E-mail: alfew@vt.edu).

[Haworth co-indexing entry note]: "Grounding Our Feet and Hearts: Black Women's Coping Strategies in Psychologically Abusive Dating Relationships." Few, April L., and Patricia Bell-Scott. Co-published simultaneously in *Women & Therapy* (The Haworth Press, Inc.) Vol. 25, No. 3/4, 2002, pp. 59-77; and: *Violence in the Lives of Black Women: Battered, Black, and Blue* (ed: Carolyn M. West) The Haworth Press, Inc., 2002, pp. 59-77. Single or multiple copies of this article are available for a fee from The Haworth Document Delivery Service [1-800-HAWORTH, 9:00 a.m. - 5:00 p.m. (EST). E-mail address: getinfo@haworthpressinc.com].

KEYWORDS. Blacks, dating violence, emotional abuse, coping, relationship termination

Research on intimate partner violence among Blacks has focused primarily on married couples (Hampton & Gelles, 1994). Consequently, less is known about dating violence among Black college students (Clark, Beckett, Wells, & Dungee-Anderson, 1994; West & Rose, 2000). In particular, we need to understand how Black college women assign meaning to their experiences of psychological abuse and how they recover and heal. Their experiences can best be explained by using a Black feminist approach, which takes into account race, class, and gender oppression (Neville & Hamer, 2001). Thus, this qualitative study is a Black feminist analysis of the decision-making processes and coping strategies that heterosexual Black college women use to terminate psychologically abusive dating relationships.

DATING VIOLENCE AMONG BLACK COUPLES

Psychological abuse is a broad term that describes various behaviors including verbal abuse (e.g., name calling, insulting), emotional abuse (e.g., humiliation, degradation), and intimidation/threats (e.g., attempts to frighten, threats of harm to self or others). After an extensive review of the research, O'Leary (1999) defined psychological abuse as:

> . . . acts of recurring criticism and/or verbal aggression toward a partner, and/or acts of isolation and domination of a partner. Generally, such actions cause the partner to be fearful of the other or lead the partner to have very low self-esteem . . . (p. 19)

Substantial rates of emotional abuse have been reported among Black college students. Rouse (1988) found that psychological aggression, defined as possessiveness and rejection, was reported by more than 80% of the Black college students in her sample. Similarly, Clark and colleagues (1994) found that 92% of men and 94% of women participants admitted to using some form of verbal abuse, for example, insulting or swearing at a dating partner. They concluded that psychological aggression ". . . appears so frequently that it seems to be normative" (p. 277). The cumulative evidence reveals that psychological abuse occurs far more often than physical abuse in dating relationships.

Approximately 30% of college students reported physical dating violence (Lewis & Fremouw, 2001). Although most of the research has been conducted on White college students, similar rates of physical abuse have been found among Black undergraduates. About one-third of Black college students had sustained or inflicted physical aggression in a dating relationship, with pushing, slapping, and hitting being reported most often (Clark et al., 1994).

According to rape researchers, approximately 25% of women have been victims of attempted or completed rape, and most of these rapes occurred in the context of a dating relationship (Marx, Van Wie, & Gross, 1996). Few studies have focused on Black women's experiences with date rape; however, sexual assault is also a frequent occurrence in this population. Although both Black female and male undergraduates had been pressured to have sex, more women experienced forced intercourse and sexual injury (Rouse, 1988). More recently, researchers discovered that women were more likely to be victims of attempted rape than their male counterparts in a sample of low-income African American youth (West & Rose, 2000).

To conclude, substantial rates of psychological, physical, and sexual abuse appear to occur across ethnic groups. However, it is important to consider the unique experiences of Black women. When confronting abuse in dating relationships, Black women must devise strategies that allow them to escape a culture of violence that encourages the subjugation of their bodies, sanity, and spirit.

BLACK WOMEN'S STRATEGIES FOR COPING WITH INTIMATE VIOLENCE

Black survivors of dating violence are active help-seekers (Mahlstedt & Keeny, 1993). In the following section, we will review the research on the termination process and coping strategies used by battered women.

The Leaving Process

Although researchers have used different terms to identify stages of the leaving process, the pattern is generally the same. Survivors of abuse, similar to their non-abused counterparts, enter their relationships with great hope. Landenburger (1998) referred to the initial development of an abusive relationship as the "binding phase." During this time, some survivors may minimize the abuse, while others cope by using various methods to counteract the abuse, such as relinquishing parts of themselves in an effort to please the abuser (Wuest & Merritt-Gray, 1999).

The leaving process begins when the survivor realizes that she cannot control her partner's violent behavior. The first stage has been identified as the *turning point*, a pivotal event that causes the woman to reassess her relationship and characterize it as abusive. An escalation in violence, property damage, and serious injury are commonly identified turning points (Campbell, J., Rose, Kub, & Nedd, 1998). During the second stage, the survivor separates from her abuser. *Breaking free* (Wuest & Merritt-Gray, 1999) or *disengaging* (Landenburger, 1998) may be accomplished in a variety of ways, such as spending longer periods away from home, leaving town, and emotionally withdrawing. *Not going back* is the stage when the survivor has terminated the relationship and is actively working to sustain the separation. Reestablishing social networks and activities is crucial during this time. The survivor may seek assistance from therapists, friends, or relatives. With support, she can move toward a life without the abuser (Wuest & Merritt-Gray, 1999). During *recovery* (Landenburger, 1998), the final stage of the leaving process, the survivor continues to work toward healing and empowerment.

Although the termination process appears to be similar across racial groups, Black battered women confront multiple oppressions when they attempt to extract themselves from abusive relationships (Campbell, J. et al., 1998; Moss, Pitula, Campbell, & Halstead, 1997; Taylor (2002 [This volume]). For instance, institutional racism and sexism may pull Black women in two directions. On the one hand, they may be at increased risk for abuse because Black men (not all) have been privileged and socialized by a Western patriarchal system that keeps them economically and politically disempowered, while simultaneously encouraging them to project their anger toward Black women without fear of legal sanctions. On the other hand, racial loyalty dictates that Black women protect Black men from a discriminatory legal system, even at the risk of their own physical and mental health (Few, 1999; McNair & Neville, 1996).

Coping Strategies

Black women have used a variety of coping strategies to survive intimate partner violence, such as attending support groups (Taylor, 2000) and seeking emotional support from friends, sisters, and mothers (Mahlstedt & Keeny, 1993). In addition, Black women have used personal writings to document their emotional, physical, and sexual abuse (Adisa, 1997; Bell-Scott, 1994). An investigation of this literature reveals that Black women have used nonfictional and fictional writing as a vehicle for solace, empowerment, and resistance to abusive relationships.

Spirituality as a coping strategy deserves special attention. Many theologians, social scientists, and laypersons describe spirituality as a consciousness of a divine presence within oneself, and as a force that gives life meaning and direction. What is distinct about Black spirituality is that its roots are African and grounded in African slavery, in Black religious music and traditions, and in Black cultural responses to personal and communal suffering (Smith, 1999). Black women may express this spirituality in a variety of ways, including dance, art, music, cooking, personal adornment (e.g., clothing or hair care rituals), poetry, activism, journaling, or reading the stories of Black women. Given the importance of spirituality, it is not surprising that battered women have used faith and prayer to cope with the violence in their lives (Short et al., 2000).

Goals of the Study

In order to help these survivors, service providers need to understand how Black women terminate abusive dating relationships and the strategies they use to cope in the aftermath of their victimization. Accordingly, this qualitative study used a Black feminist approach to: (a) investigate the process used by Black college women to terminate emotionally abusive dating relationships; (b) identify effective coping strategies used to heal from the abuse; and (c) offer suggestions for intervention.

METHOD

Sample

The participants were six heterosexual Black women enrolled in a southeastern university. The study was advertised in electronic and paper announcements, including a contact number, and on student listserves and in student centers. The selection criteria included: (a) were self-identified as a survivor of emotional abuse; (b) were single; (c) were between the ages of 18-30; (d) were enrolled in college; (e) had been involved in an emotionally abusive relationship for at least two months; and (f) had terminated the emotionally abusive relationship at least six months prior to the study.

Data Collection

Data were collected with two semistructured interviews. Pseud-onyms were used to maintain confidentiality. We defined psychological abuse as any coercive and manipulative behavior that was perpetrated with the malicious intent of destabilization, disempowerment, and/or destruction of the physical, psychological, and emotional well-being of another for a perceived increase in personal gain (O'Leary, 1999; Tolman, 1992). The women were screened for psychological abuse us-ing the Psychological Maltreatment of Women Inventory (PMWI) de-veloped by Tolman (1989). Other data sources included journals, poetry, unmailed letters, and other forms of creative art that docu-mented the abusive relationship. Upon completion of the interviews, the women were given a contact list of local therapists and crisis lines, an information leaflet on dating violence, and a reading list of books about Black women, dating violence, self-esteem, and self-help tech-niques that were approved by a clinical psychologist.

Data Analysis

The constant-comparative method (Lincoln & Guba, 1985), Reissman's (1993) representational model, and Alexander's (1988) *principles of sa-lience* were used in the interpretation and analysis. The four stages in the constant-comparative method include: (a) simultaneous data col-lecting and analysis by the researcher; (b) sorting and creating catego-ries (axial and focused coding) based on researcher interpretation of emerging patterns and themes from the data; (c) generating hypotheses from the data and testing hypotheses with further data collection; and (d) using theoretical memos in the analysis, integration, and delineation of existing multiple relationships between categories in order to write the theory grounded in the experience of the informants.

There are five levels of Reissman's (1993) representational model that reflect interactive steps of qualitative inquiry. First, the researcher "attends to the experience" as the participant reframes her experience. The meaning of narrative that a participant assigns to a particular phe-nomenon is dynamic, shifting from one interpretation to another as she "tells her experience." Finally, the researcher "transcribes the experi-ence" while simultaneously "analyzing the data" in order to produce a hybrid narrative (i.e., "reading the experience"). The resulting hybrid narrative (Behar, 1993) is a combination of both the woman's interpre-tations of her experience and the researcher's interpretation of the woman's narrative. Alexander's (1988) principles of salience include: primacy, frequency, uniqueness, negation, emphasis, omission, error or distortion, isolation, and incompletion. This technique aids in the development of core categories and the focused coding of the data.

A computer-assisted textual analysis enhanced the dependability and credibility of the coding and allowed the auditor to follow all procedures closely. Individual computer files on each woman were created, collapsed, and combined into a single database in order to illuminate similarities and dissimilarities across the narratives. Multiple sources of data were used to triangulate the data and to confirm emergent themes and inconsistencies. An auditor reviewed the research journals and notes, coded transcripts, and additional materials (e.g., journal, poetry).

RESULTS

Participants

As illustrated in Table 1, the women in our sample had experienced a substantial amount of violence in their lives. All of the participants reported violence in their families of origin. With the exception of one woman, Patricia, all of the survivors experienced multiple forms of dating violence. Each woman reported that violence had occurred in her first significant adult relationship.

LEAVING AS A PROCESS

We identified four stages in the termination process (Table 2).

Assessment of the Relationship

During this stage, the survivor reached a personal threshold that made it impossible to ignore or deny the psychological abuse. This acknowledgement was often precipitated by a turning point, such as a traumatic event that caused the woman to reevaluate her relationship. An escalation in the level of violence, sexual assault, or a life-threatening event were pivotal episodes that resulted in the women redefining their relationships as dangerous and abusive.

Escalating levels of violence. Turning points for two participants occurred when the relationship moved from psychological to physical

TABLE 1 Participants' Profiles

NAME (Age during relationship)	Family-of-Origin	Dating Relationship History	Social Networks	Type of Abuse	Psychological Symptoms	Coping Strategies	Turning Points	Decision to Leave
Christina (19-21)	Divorce Violence	First adult relationship First abusive Older partner	Isolated Small circle Friends, no help	Psychological Physical	Depression Eating disorder Isolation	Journaling Spirituality Self-help books Talked to mother Therapy	Fight in bar	Left immediately Personal threshold
Faith (15-20)	Separated Violence	First adult relationship First abusive Older partner	Isolated Small circle Friends, no help	Psychological Physical Sexual	Depression Isolation	Journaling Spirituality Self-help books	Car accident	Left immediately Personal threshold
Lisa (25)	Divorce Violence	Previous partners Second abusive Older partner	Isolated Small circle Friends, no help	Psychological Physical Sexual	Depression Isolation	Journaling Spirituality Talked Self-help books	Physical fight	Left immediately Personal threshold
Patricia (26-28)	Married Violence	First adult relationship First abusive Older partner	Isolated Small circle Friends, no help	Psychological	Depression Eating disorder Isolation Suicidation	Journaling Spirituality Self-help books Talked Therapy	Abandoned at airport	Left 2-3 months Personal threshold
Shawnté (20-21)	Divorce Sexual abuse	First adult relationship First abusive Older partner	Isolated Small circle Friends, no help	Psychological Physical Sexual	Depression Isolation Suicidation "Zoning"	Spirituality Talked Therapy	Attempted rape	Left 3 months Personal threshold
Tamika (21-25)	Divorce Violence	First adult relationship Older partner	Isolated Small circle Friends, no help	Psychological Physical Sexual	Depression Eating disorder Isolation Suicidation	Journaling Spirituality Self-help books Talked Therapy	Attempted rape	Left 1 year Personal threshold

66

TABLE 2. Stages in the Decision to Leave

ASSESSMENT OF RELATIONSHIP	SEPARATION FROM PARTNER	REESTABLISHMENT OF SOCIAL NETWORKS	DECLARATION OF SELF-EMPOWERMENT
• Recognizes psychological abuse • Conducts cost-benefit analysis of relationship through ruminative coping strategies • Evaluates turning points • Reframes experiences in the relationship • Ends "splitting process" to define abuse and to eliminate self-blame • Defines personal threshold for abuse • Makes the decision to leave the abusive partner	• Begins emotional separation from abusive partner • Stops talking to abusive partner • Creates geographic distance from abusive partner • Divests completely from relationship	• (Re)connects to established social networks • Builds new positive social networks • (Re)engages in favorite social activities	• Reclaims self through spirituality • Rebuilds self-esteem • Validates personal needs and desires • Processes life lessons from relationship • Leaves abusive partner completely

Note: Processes within each stage are not necessarily in a prioritized order because each process may occur simultaneously or in a variety of combinations.

abuse. Both women reported that the first physical assault occurred in a public setting. Lisa was assaulted in a car when she attempted to collect the rent money from her boyfriend. Although she was screaming and fighting for her life, witnesses ignored the "spectacle." Lisa escaped from the car, bloodied, angry, and in a state of disbelief. Christina's struggle with her abusive partner occurred in a local bar. Angered by her refusal to acknowledge him, Christina's partner manhandled her and prevented her from leaving the premises. Rather than intervening on her behalf, his policemen friends restrained her.

It is significant that Lisa and Christina were assaulted in public settings. Other women in this study also reported a lack of public intervention during altercations with abusive Black partners. Their stories are indicative of how violence between Black intimates in public settings may be dismissed or even perceived as socially acceptable (Barbee, 1992).

Sexual assault. Shawnté, a devout Baptist who felt tremendous guilt about engaging in premarital sex, was repeatedly raped by her boyfriend. During sex, she often dissociated, or "zoned out." Tamika's turning point was an attempted rape:

> We were fighting. I was trying to hit him and keep my clothes on. This went on for three hours. It was exhausting. He ripped my shirt off and pushed me to the floor and was trying to hold me down. And I fought and fought him. Screaming. And I know someone must have heard me, but no one ever came to help me. We went through this for a few hours. And at some point I stopped fighting. I was so tired. And he was on top of me, holding me down. And then he stopped. Got up and went to his bedroom. Closed the door. And I just laid there on the floor. Too exhausted to move . . .

Although their turning points involved sexual violation, Tamika and Shawnté did not immediately leave their abusive partners. Like other survivors, their initial reactions were shock, fear, confusion, and anger (Neville & Heppner, 1999). Their abusive partners apologized profusely and promised never to hurt them again. Assessing the relationship was a difficult undertaking. However, after ruminating about the sexual assault, the women began to break the emotional bond with their abusers.

Life-threatening events. Surviving a dangerous situation compelled one woman to reevaluate her relationship. Faith reached her turning point after a car accident. Following an argument with her boyfriend, her car skidded off the road when she fell asleep at the wheel. Faith interpreted the incident as a message from a divine spirit to leave the relationship. "The relationship could have destroyed me if I would have stayed in it. . . . For all I know, I could have died in that car accident over that. It just wasn't healthy."

Many women reported an assessment period that was triggered by a turning point or the cumulative effects of emotional abuse. During this period, the women reframed their experiences and defined a personal threshold for abuse. For instance, after reflecting on her friends' relationships, Shawnté concluded that healthy relationships should not involve the violations and betrayals that characterized her relationship:

> After the rape in the car, I was just like . . . I can't deal . . . I can't keep dealing with it, and then I started to look back on it. You know, other things that had happened in the relationship in the past, and that's when I started to realize . . . And I understand that you don't know everything that goes on in other people's relationship but you . . . They ain't going through stuff like this! You know! And then that's when I realized that it wasn't healthy.

The assessment period varied in length from one day to several months. Three of the women, Tamika, Patricia, and Shawnté, remained in the relationship at least two months after making the decision to leave. They struggled to resist old patterns of intimidation and excessive displays of affection by abusive partners and to establish new patterns of self-empowerment. By contrast, Lisa, Faith, and Christina assessed the incident, made the decision to leave, and left the relationship the same day. The shock of the physical abuse and concerns about their safety compelled them to act quickly.

Separation from Partner

In order to regain control over their lives, the participants emotionally and physically distanced themselves from their abusive partners. A variety of methods were used to maintain this separation. All of the women stopped talking to their partners. Some women changed their daily routines, which made them inaccessible. Severing their ties with the abusers enabled the women to follow through on their decisions to leave.

Reestablishing Social Networks and Activities

After the women had successfully terminated the relationships, they used their energy to connect with others. For example, Tamika rejoined her college dance troupe. Patricia reconnected with women in her sister circle. Lisa chose her friends more carefully and focused on succeeding in graduate school. Faith became a leader in various college organizations, and Shawnté got involved in intramural sports and church activities. Christina directed her energies toward completing her college degree.

Declaration of Self-Empowerment

In the final stage, the women felt more powerful and autonomous. Instead of immediately becoming involved in new dating relationships, the survivors focused their energies on rebuilding their self-esteem, reconnecting with their spiritual selves, validating personal needs and desires, and processing the lessons learned from their abusive relationships. Christina articulated her feelings in this stage:

> Because of being with him, I didn't think much about myself. I didn't think much about what my abilities were, what my strengths were. I focused more on my weaknesses and what I couldn't do . . . Coming out of that relationship, I was able to realize that I was a strong person and realized that I was important . . . And that I needed to surround myself with people who felt the same about themselves.

COPING STRATEGIES

For the women in this study, their victimization was associated with mental and physical health problems. A review of Table 1 reveals that most survivors felt depressed, suicidal, and isolated. One woman reported dissociating ("zoning") after being sexually assaulted. Patricia described her feelings as:

> In a daze. Spent entire weekend in bed and did nothing. I want him back but I know I can't. He's been too disrespectful to forgive or forget. I am physically worn. Want to go home and die. What is wrong? . . . Why can't I go back to the way it was. I'm absolutely crazy! . . . Admit looked at vomit pills carefully today. Not functioning well.

The women used a variety of ways to cope with their distress. They wrote in their journals, sought comfort in their spirituality and religion, and read self-help books written by Black women. Some women used their social support networks. However, few survivors sought help from a therapist; instead, they disclosed the abuse to their mothers or peers.

Journals

The women used various creative ways to express their heartbreak, anger, confusion, and frustration. Tamika kept a notebook full of mailed and unmailed letters to her abusive partner. Lisa wrote poetry. Faith documented her pain in coloring books and imaginary scenarios of things that she wanted to happen. During her abusive relationship, Christina filled three journals:

> Because of everything that I was feeling, I wrote, I had to. You know, I was angry and I was upset. I was mad and I was sad. At least in my journal, it was something that I could write and it would be there . . . There was just so much going through my head and a lot of it. I was just so overwhelmed and I needed to get it out somewhere. I journaled out things that I had discussed with people. Some things that I hadn't discussed with people. And I wrote about what I had hoped or wished would be different.

At times, she kept a checklist of the costs and benefits of the relationship, noting and rereading the concessions she had made. When she felt helpless, journal writing gave her power from an internal source.

Self-Help Books

Other survivors drew strength from other women's words and experiences. Inspirational self-help books written by Black women were especially important. According to the survivors, the books helped them to identify positive characteristics in themselves and to question the abusers' behavior. Five of the women purchased books on self-healing and empowerment written by Iyanla Vanzant (1998), a Yoruba priestess. The words of Black women "had a very special meaning" to Lisa:

> It's hard for me to pick up books by White authors. Because their stories, I just don't relate to at all. The message and the story may be the same but the finer details, they're not the same. I needed to connect to other Black women to cope and survive.

Spirituality

Most of the women in this study identified spirituality as a major influence in their decisions to terminate their relationships. Lisa's sense of spirituality reminded her that the situation was temporary. It reassured Faith that she did not deserve to be mistreated and could find healthy, fulfilling relationships among family and friends. Spirituality helped Tamika regain the power she thought she had lost to her abusive partner. Similarly, a sense of spirituality helped Christina develop a new perspective on her life and create positive goals. She concluded, "God had a better plan for me."

In order to reignite her sense of spirituality and escape the misery of her abusive relationship, Patricia returned to church. Although raised as a Catholic, she discovered that a Black Baptist church met her spiritual needs:

> . . . going in there, hearing people talk and hearing the music . . . It was such a release for me. It's something you have to feel. And I think it's very unique to Black people. Especially Black women. Sometimes, I just want[ed] to cry because I felt so at peace.

The music, the communal feeling of belonging, and the messages of courage she heard in church allowed her to reclaim and empower herself. Although Patricia distinguished spirituality from organized religion, she found that the church was the place to begin listening to her spirit again.

Social Support Network

Five of the participants disclosed the abuse to close friends. Although this provided some solace, many of their female friends also were involved in abusive dating relationships, which made it difficult for them to offer problem-focused coping strategies. In addition, some male friends were unhelpful. After learning of the abuse, many positioned themselves to be future dating partners.

All of the women reported a need to connect to a community of women. For instance, after making the decision to leave, Patricia sought affirmation from members of her "sister circle," an informal support group of women who helped her avoid returning to her abusive partner. She explained, "In my sister circle, . . . my girlfriends acknowledge[d] that my feelings were right. It's what got me through." It was especially important to connect with Black women who shared similar cultural and interpersonal experiences. According to the participants, as Black women in emotionally abusive dating relationships with Black men, their experiences were unique. For example, all of the women expressed a concern that Black female-male intimate relationships were perceived as inherently dysfunctional and adversarial. This made the leaving process especially difficult because, as stated by Lisa and echoed by the other women, ". . . there was a responsibility to prove that old stereotype wrong."

Therapy

In conjunction with other coping strategies, four of the survivors turned to therapists for support. However, there were several reasons why therapy was not considered as the survivors' first choice. First, the women claimed that it was too expensive to maintain over time. Second, three survivors felt that therapists were culturally insensitive to the experiences of Black women. Patricia reported that one therapist told her to try dating White men because "White men would find her [Patricia] attractive." Third, similar to victimized Black women in previous studies (Neville & Pugh, 1997), one survivor believed that Black women should be "able to handle their own affairs" and should not "air dirty laundry to White folks."

DISCUSSION

In this qualitative study, a Black feminist analysis was used to explore dating violence in the lives of six Black college women. The women in our sample had experienced a substantial amount of violence in their young lives. Consistent with previous research (DeMaris, 1990), all of the women reported violence in their families of origin. Although psychological abuse was the focus of this study, similar to Black women in other studies (Clark et al., 1994; West & Rose, 2001), some survivors were physically assaulted in public and others were repeatedly raped.

This study also confirmed that leaving was a process that occurred in stages. After a turning point, the survivors assessed their relationships, separated from their abusive partners, reestablished social networks, and worked toward self-empowerment. As the survivors worked toward healing, they used a variety of coping strategies, which were based on Black women's experiences and culture. For instance, they documented their feelings in journals, read self-help books written by Black women, and relied on spirituality and faith.

Equally as important, the women sought help from members of their social support system. In previous studies, Black college women were generally satisfied when they disclosed their victimization (Mahlstedt & Keeny, 1993; Neville & Pugh, 1997). In contrast, when our survivors sought help, they discovered that female friends were struggling with their own abusive dating relationships, while male friends positioned themselves to be future dating partners. This is unfortunate because social reactions perceived as hurtful by survivors have been associated with increased distress, depression, and health problems (Campbell, R., Ahrens, Sefl, Wasco, & Barnes, 2001).

Suggestions for Intervention

Although standardized scales were not used in this study, it is clear that dating violence took a toll on the survivors' physical and mental health functioning. The women in our study felt depressed, suicidal, and isolated, which are feelings commonly reported by survivors of dating aggression (Harned, 2001). However, similar to Black victimized college women in other studies (Neville & Pugh, 1997), they were reluctant to seek therapy. Based on our findings, we offer the following suggestions for intervention:

Community outreach. Service providers need to find creative ways to extend themselves to the Black community. Information can be disseminated through community leaders, religious institutions, gospel music shows, and ethnic events (Oliver, 2000). A well-drafted, culturally sensitive statement concerning dating aggression could be published in Black newspapers. This technique has been used successfully to raise awareness concerning rape in the Black community (White, 1999).

Culturally appropriate education. Once a community connection has been established, service providers should provide culturally appropriate educational services. For example, facilitators can discuss the double bind faced by Black women: How do survivors report Black batterers without appearing to be racially disloyal? Black female and male antirape activists have been inspired by a strong race and gender consciousness. Thus, a Black feminist framework, which emphasizes how abuse is influenced by race and gender oppression, can be used to shape educational programs (White, Potgieter, Strube, Fisher, & Umana, 1997; White, Strube, & Fisher, 1998). Survivors also should be educated about the potential benefits of therapy (Neville & Pugh, 1997).

Therapeutic techniques. Service providers should conduct a thorough assessment. Survivors should be asked about violence in their family of origin and about the types of dating aggression they have experienced, including psychological, physical, and sexual abuse. If appropriate, the therapist can discuss the termination process with the survivor. For Black women who minimize their victimization or embrace the image of the "strong" Black woman, it may be especially important to give them permission to be vulnerable (Donovan & Williams, 2002 [This volume]). Support groups can be used to reduce feelings of social isolation (Taylor, 2000). Finally, service providers should explore the therapeutic impact of writing, and of inspirational literature written by Black women who have survived abusive relationships. Having resources that reflect the experiences and the challenges faced by Black women may also alleviate feelings of cultural alienation.

In conclusion, this study is further documentation that psychological, physical, and sexual dating aggression is a serious problem among Black college women. Although terminating these relationships can sometimes be a difficult process, Black women are able to develop effective coping strategies.

REFERENCES

Adisa, O. P. (1997). Undeclared war: African American women writers explicating rape. *Women's Studies International Forum, 15*, 363-374.

Alexander, I. (1988). Personality, psychological assessment, and psychobiography. In D. McAdams & R. Ochberg (Eds.), *Psychobiography and life narratives* (pp. 265-294). Durham, NC: Duke University Press.

Barbee, E. L. (1992). Ethnicity and woman abuse in the United States. In C. M. Sampselle (Ed.), *Violence against women: Nursing research, education, and practice issues* (pp. 153-166). New York: Hemisphere Publishing Corporation.

Behar, R. (1993). *Translated woman: Crossing the border with Esperanza's story.* Boston: Beacon Press.

Bell-Scott, P. (Ed.) (1994). *Life notes: Personal writings by contemporary Black women.* New York: W. W. Norton.

Campbell, J., Rose, L., Kub, J., & Nedd, D. (1998). Voices of strength and resistance: A contextual and longitudinal analysis of women's responses to battering. *Journal of Interpersonal Violence, 13*, 743-762.

Campbell, R., Ahrens, C. E., Sefl, T., Wasco, S. M., & Barnes, H. E. (2001). Social reactions to rape victims: Healing and hurtful effects on psychological and physical health outcomes. *Violence and Victims, 16*, 287-302.

Clark, M., Beckett, J., Wells, M., & Dungee-Anderson, D. (1994). Courtship violence among African American college students. *Journal of Black Psychology, 20*, 264-281.

DeMaris, A. (1990). The dynamics of generational transfer in courtship violence: A biracial exploration. *Journal of Marriage and Family, 52*, 219-231.

Donovan, R., & Williams, M. (2002). Living at the intersection: The effects of racism and sexism on Black rape survivors. *Women & Therapy, 25* (3 & 4), 95-105.

Few, A. L. (1999). The (un)making of martyrs: Black mothers, daughters, and intimate violence. *The Journal of the Association for Research on Mothering, 1*, 68-75.

Hampton, R., & Gelles, R. (1994). Violence toward Black women in a nationally representative sample of Black families. *Journal of Comparative Family Studies, 25*, 105-119.

Harned, M. S. (2001). Abused women or abused men? An examination of the context and outcomes of dating violence. *Violence and Victims, 16*, 269-285.

Landenburger, K. M. (1998). Exploration of women's identity: Clinical approaches with abused women. In J. C. Campbell (Ed.), *Empowering survivors of abuse: Health care for battered women and their children* (pp. 61-69). Thousand Oaks, CA: Sage.

Lewis, S. F., & Fremouw, W. (2001). Dating violence: A critical review of the literature. *Clinical Psychology Review, 21*, 105-127.

Lincoln, Y., & Guba, E. (1985). *Naturalistic inquiry.* Beverly Hills, CA: Sage.

Mahlstedt, D., & Keeny, L. (1993). Female survivors of dating violence and their social networks. *Feminism & Psychology, 3*, 319-333.

Marx, B. P., Van Wie, V., & Gross, A. M. (1996). Date rape risk factors: A review and methodological critique of the literature. *Aggression and Violent Behavior, 1*, 27-45.

McNair, L., & Neville, H. (1996). African American women survivors of sexual assault: The intersection of race and class. *Women & Therapy, 18*, 107-118.

Moss, V. A., Pitula, C. R., Campbell, J. C., & Halstead, L. (1997). The experience of terminating an abusive relationship from an Anglo and African American perspective: A qualitative descriptive study. *Issues in Mental Health Nursing, 18*, 433-454.

Neville, H. A., & Hamer, J. (2001). "We make freedom": An exploration of revolutionary Black feminism. *Journal of Black Studies, 31*, 437-461.

Neville, H. A., & Heppner, M. J. (1999). Contextualizing rape: Reviewing sequelae and proposing a culturally inclusive ecological model of sexual assault recovery. *Applied and Preventive Psychology, 8*, 41-62.

Neville, H. A., & Pugh, A. O. (1997). General and specific factors influencing African American women's reporting patterns and perceived social support following sexual assault: An exploratory investigation. *Violence Against Women, 3*, 361-381.

O'Leary, K. D. (1999). Psychological abuse: A variable deserving critical attention in domestic violence. *Violence and Victims, 14*, 3-23.

Oliver, W. (2000). Preventing domestic violence in the African American community: The rationale for popular culture interventions. *Violence Against Women, 6*, 533-549.

Reissman, C. (1993). *Narrative analysis.* Newbury Park, CA: Sage.

Rouse, L. (1988). Abuse in dating relationships: A comparison of Blacks, Whites, and Hispanics. *Journal of College Student Personnel, 29*, 312-319.

Short, L. M., McMahon, P. M., Chervin, D. D., Shelley, G. A., Lezin, N., Sloop, K. S., & Dawkins, N. (2000). Survivors' identification of protective factors and early warning signs for intimate partner violence. *Violence Against Women, 6*, 272-285.

Smith, A. (1999). Reaching back and pushing forward: A perspective on African spirituality. *Theology Today, 56*, 44-58.

Taylor, J. Y. (2000). Sisters of the yam: African American women's healing and self-recovery from intimate male partner violence. *Issues in Mental Health Nursing, 21*, 515-531.

Taylor, J. Y. (2002). "The straw that broke the camel's back": African American women's strategies for disengaging from abusive relationships. *Women & Therapy*, *25* (3 & 4), 79-94.

Tolman, R. (1989). The initial development of a measure of psychological maltreatment of women by their male partners. *Violence and Victims*, *4*, 159-178.

Tolman, R. (1992). Psychological abuse of women. In R. Ammerman & M. Hersen (Eds.), *Assessment of family violence: A clinical and legal sourcebook* (pp. 291-310). New York: Wiley.

Vanzant, I. (1998). *One day my soul just opened up.* New York: Fireside Books.

West, C. M., & Rose, S. (2000). Dating aggression among low income African American youth: An examination of gender differences and antagonistic beliefs. *Violence Against Women*, *6*, 470-494.

White, A. M. (1999). Talking feminist, talking Black: Micromobilization processes in a collective protest against rape. *Gender & Society*, *13*, 71-100.

White, A. M., Potgieter, C. A., Strube, M. J., Fisher, S., & Umana, E. (1997). An African-centered, Black feminist approach to understanding attitudes that counter social dominance. *Journal of Black Psychology*, *23*, 398-420.

White, A. M., Strube, M. J., & Fisher, S. (1998). A Black feminist model of rape myth acceptance: Implications for research and antirape advocacy in Black communities. *Psychology of Women Quarterly*, *22*, 157-175.

Wuest, J., & Merritt-Gray, M. (1999). Not going back: Sustaining the separation in leaving abusive relationships. *Violence Against Women*, *5*, 110-133.

"The Straw That Broke the Camel's Back": African American Women's Strategies for Disengaging from Abusive Relationships

Janette Y. Taylor

SUMMARY. In this ethnographic study, a womanist framework was used to investigate the disengaging-terminating process used by Black women ($N = 21$) who had survived intimate male partner abuse. Data interpretation revealed three stages of disengaging described by the survivors: (a) defining moments: rejecting the violence and exiting the relationship; (b) moving away: distancing the self; and (c) moving on: finding affirmation and support. This process is representative of individual and collective acts of resistance. Suggestions for therapeutic interventions are offered for each stage of the disengagement process. *[Article copies available for a fee from The Haworth Document Delivery Service: 1-800-HAWORTH. E-mail address: <getinfo@haworthpressinc.com> Website:*

Janette Y. Taylor is Assistant Professor in the College of Nursing, University of Iowa. She received both her PhD in Nursing Science and the graduate certificate in Women's Studies from the University of Washington, Seattle. Dr. Taylor is certified as a Women's Health Care Nurse Practitioner. Her research interests are in women's health. Her current research focuses on resilience and recovering among African American women survivors of intimate male partner abuse, as well as on incarcerated abused women.

This research was supported by Women's Health Nursing Research Training Grant NINR T3NR07039, NRSA from NINR 5F31NR0718702, Nurses Educational Fund, Inc., Sigma Theta Tau, Psi Chapter-at-Large and Hester McLaws Award, University of Washington School of Nursing, Seattle, WA. Special thanks to the women who shared their testimonies.

Address correspondence to: Janette Y. Taylor, College of Nursing, The University of Iowa, Iowa City, IA 52242 (E-mail: janette-taylor@uiowa.edu).

[Haworth co-indexing entry note]: "The Straw That Broke the Camel's Back: African American Women's Strategies for Disengaging from Abusive Relationships." Taylor, Janette Y. Co-published simultaneously in *Women & Therapy* (The Haworth Press, Inc.) Vol. 25, No. 3/4, 2002, pp. 79-94; and: *Violence in the Lives of Black Women: Battered, Black, and Blue* (ed: Carolyn M. West) The Haworth Press, Inc., 2002, pp. 79-94. Single or multiple copies of this article are available for a fee from The Haworth Document Delivery Service [1-800-HAWORTH, 9:00 a.m. - 5:00 p.m. (EST). E-mail address: getinfo@haworthpressinc.com].

KEYWORDS. Blacks, battered women, violence, relationship termination

There is a growing body of literature on the process used by battered women to terminate their abusive partnerships. Researchers have focused on how these women survive in the relationship, prepare to leave, and how they cope with the initial crisis after leaving (Landenburger, 1998; Merritt-Gray & Wuest, 1995). More recently, researchers have explored how battered women sustain the separation from their partners and how they develop effective strategies for moving on with their lives (Wuest & Merritt-Gray, 1999, 2001). With few exceptions (Few & Bell-Scott, 2002 [This volume]; Moss, Pitula, Campbell, & Halstead, 1997), most studies have used White American participants. As a result, little is known about how Black women disengage and terminate abusive relationships with male partners. Accordingly, in this ethnographic study, I have used a womanist framework to investigate the termination process used by African American survivors of domestic violence.

BLACK WOMEN AND THE LEAVING PROCESS

Researchers have begun to investigate racial differences in the termination process. Similar to other researchers (e.g., Landenburger, 1998), Moss and colleagues (1997) discovered a three stage leaving process in their sample of formerly battered women (15 Black and 15 White). During the *being in* stage the survivors learned to endure the violence. They used a variety of coping mechanisms, including denial, contemplating or attempting suicide, and drinking in order to self-medicate. Eventually, they recognized the extent of the abuse and moved toward *getting out*. Usually, there was a catalyst for leaving the relationship, such as seeing the effect of abuse on their children. As the survivor worked to escape the violence, she often received negative and unhelpful responses from relatives, police, and the clergy. Many survivors, as they moved toward *going on*, experienced a mourning period, during which they grieved the loss of their idealized relationship, their sense of identity, and their trust in others. Women with children also realized that a complete separation from their abusive partners might never be possible.

The termination process appears to be similar across racial groups (Campbell et al., 1998). However, battered Black women often face additional challenges. It is common for them to have negative interactions with social service agencies. For example, some women feel disrespected, mistreated and, in some cases, sexually harassed by medical providers (McNutt, van Ryn, Clark, & Fraiser, 2000; Russo, Denious, Keita, & Koss, 1997). Police officers have a history of being unresponsive to Black women when they call for assistance, even when children are present (Robinson & Chandek, 2000). Battered women's shelters may be culturally insensitive and unwelcoming environments (Donnelly, Cook, & Wilson, 1999), and the welfare system can make it more difficult for Black women to make the transition from public assistance to jobs that pay a living wage (Brush, 2001). Certainly, some social service agencies and providers are becoming more responsive to the needs of diverse populations. Furthermore, battered Black women are active help seekers. However, the lack of support from these important agencies can create additional barriers to leaving.

Cultural expectations can also complicate the termination process for some Black women. For example, they may be trapped in abusive relationships by a community code of silence and the façade of the strong Black woman who should be able to survive without assistance. In addition, survivors may experience social pressure to maintain their families. Black women, like many other community members, are well aware of Black men's plight. Many are prospering; however, elevated rates of drug abuse, homicide, unemployment, and incarceration create a scarcity of marriageable Black men in some communities. Although they may face disapproval or accusations of racial disloyalty, many battered Black women protect themselves and their children by leaving. In contrast, the decision to leave is more complex for other Black women. Family and community pressure, the perceived scarcity of future partners, or an unwillingness to turn their partners over to an overcrowded, oppressive penal system makes some survivors reluctant to report the abuse or to leave the relationship (Moss et al., 1997; Richie, 1996).

To summarize, women's efforts to terminate abusive relationships often occur in stages: learning to survive the abuse, preparing to leave, coping with the initial crisis of leaving, and sustaining the separation (Landenburger, 1998; Wuest & Merritt-Gray, 1999). With few exceptions (Few & Bell-Scott, 2002 [This volume]), researchers have neglected to study the termination process used by battered Black women. This is an oversight in the research. Accordingly, this study uses a womanist framework to investigate the leaving process used by 21 battered Black women.

METHOD

Design

For this study, I used a qualitative descriptive approach modeled after Spradley's (1979) ethnographic research methodology. Ethnography is both the art and the science of describing a group or culture. This research methodology is a search for themes or patterns through studying the parts of a culture, the relationship of the parts to each other, and the relationship of parts to the whole cultural context (Fetterman, 1989; Germain, 1986). Traditional ethnography does not specify a framework congruent with Black women's lives. Therefore, this method was expanded to include a Black feminist or *womanist* analysis, which seeks to (a) discover the cultural knowledge that African American women use to organize their behavior and interpret their experiences, and (b) consider how race, class, and gender oppression shape the lives of African American women (Collins, 2000).

A womanist ethnography engages the same theory building practice as ethnography. However, there is an additional task embedded within the reflective process of conventional ethnography. Similar to critical ethnography (Thomas, 1993), a womanist ethnographic approach examines the hidden agendas, power imbalances, power centers, and assumptions that inhibit, repress, and constrain African American individuals, families, and communities. Because of the theoretical underpinnings of the methodology and the appropriateness of its application to the health experiences of Black women (Banks-Wallace, 2000; Taylor, 1998), a womanist ethnography was selected as the method for exploring the termination-disengaging strategies used by African American women survivors of intimate male partner abuse.

Sample

After Institutional Review Board approval, a purposive sample was recruited. In order to be included, participants had to be African American women who identified themselves as individuals who had survived and successfully disengaged from an abusive intimate relationship with an African American male partner or male partner of color. Additional selection criteria included: (a) age 18 or older; (b) ability to speak and read English; (c) at least six months since terminating their abusive relationship and not currently involved in an abusive relationship; (d) perceived self as thriving, for example, provided for herself and family and was an active community member.

Informants were obtained through flyers placed at local African American beauty salons and other organizations frequented by African American women. I also asked members of professional organizations, such as Mary Mahoney Professional Nurses' Organization and Washington State Association of Black Professionals in Health Care, to distribute flyers in sites that were frequented by potential participants. Several women were recruited after I gave a brief presentation about the project at several support group meetings. In addition, other informants and community advocates referred participants to the study.

Data Collection

The interviews were scheduled for a time and place that was convenient and safe for each woman. Data was collected via semistructured interviews (Spradley, 1979; Yow, 1994). Women were asked broad open-ended questions: What was the relationship with your husband or partner like? Describe the relationship to me. Why and how did you terminate the relationship? Can you tell me when and why you decided to leave for good? What happened between the time you left the relationship and now? What has your life been like since you left the abusive relationship? Each woman was offered an opportunity to be interviewed over two sessions. The first interview was used to gather data, and the second interview was an opportunity to collect additional information and to have informants verify and validate my interpretation of their testimonies and emerging themes. The interviews lasted between 45 minutes and 1.5 hours. The women received $20.00 each in compensation for their time. The women also were offered a copy of the interview transcripts, a final copy of the dissertation, and an invitation to attend the dissertation defense. This research methodology was empowering and healing for many participants (Taylor, 2002 [This volume]).

Data Analysis

All interviews were audiotaped and transcribed verbatim onto computer diskette. Field notes and notes taken during the interview or field observation/witnessing were also transcribed onto computer diskette. Computerized information was entered into HyperRESEARCH, which is a data management software program that allows segments of the transcripts to be coded for the content analysis and comparative analysis (Hesse-Biber, Kinder, Dupuis, Dupuis, & Tornabene, 1999). The data was retrieved and systematically organized according to patterns and themes.

Themes were carefully extracted through the process of logical analysis of content from all data sources. The themes were verified with the women at the second interview session. In addition to informant verification, random segments of the interviews were independently coded to determine the reliability of level one codes. The overall approach to data analysis was to examine the interviewees' narratives, which were personal testimonies, and to frame them within a larger social context. First person narratives illustrate the themes.

RESULTS

Participants

The sample was comprised of 21 African American women, who were residents of Snohomish, King, and Pierce Counties in the state of Washington. They ranged in age from 24 to 70 years old ($M = 39.4$). Seventeen of the women had a minimum of a high school diploma or GED. A majority of the women (81%) were employed outside the home. The gross annual income ranged from $4,068 to $52,000, with an average income of $20,523. Sixteen of the women were mothers and all but one were single parents. The women reported a broad range of physical, sexual, and psychological abuse.

STRATEGIES FOR DISENGAGING FROM ABUSIVE RELATIONSHIPS

As illustrated in Table 1, the women described a three-phase process for disengaging from abusive relationships.

Defining Moments

Defining moments were memorable and pivotal times that marked the women's lives. Life altering decisions were made after these events. In response to the question, "Can you tell me when or why you decided to leave for good?" women began their testimonies with a similar metaphor: "Oh you want to know the straw that broke the camel's back?" or "The straw that broke the camel's back was when . . ." The *straw* repre-

TABLE 1. Strategies for Disengaging from Abusive Relationships

Defining Moments: Rejecting the Violence and Exiting the Relationship
  Listening to other women's stories of abuse
  Witnessing the abuser's violence toward others
  Observing the impact on children
  Accepting partner's rejection
  Encouragement from other women
Moving Away: Distancing the Self
  Seeking shelter and safety
  Negotiating nonsupportive networks
Moving On: Finding Affirmation and Support
  Valuing the wisdom of community elders
  Listening to supportive friends and family

sented an unbearable strain or stressor that occurred–one that "broke their backs" or pierced through their defenses and denial, shifted their consciousness, and eventually moved them to action. A variety of events prompted the women to psychologically or physically disengage from their abusive partners.

Listening to other women's stories of abuse. Defining moments were profoundly impactful and indicated a time when women moved to a new level of consciousness or awareness about themselves and their relationships. One woman, who was a domestic violence advocate, explained her interaction with another survivor:

> This one woman comes in, she's in exam room number 1. I don't remember what her face looks like, but I'll never forget our conversation. She starts telling me her story and she's telling me my story to me . . . And I think at that moment the light bulb went on [and] that's when I began to disengage from him. (age 49, recovering 1 year and 3 months)

This seems to be a common pattern. Women who have been assaulted are sometimes reluctant to label themselves victims, battered, or abused. In contrast, they are more willing to label the same behavior abusive if it is inflicted on another woman. When the level of commitment to her abusive partner starts to decline, a woman becomes more willing to self-identify as battered (Hamby & Gray-Little, 2000).

Witnessing the abuser's violence toward others. For some women, the seriousness of their abuse became evident when they witnessed the abuser's anger and physical violence directed toward others. This violence was symbolic of the abuse that the survivor had endured. At this point, women could no longer disregard the significance of abuse in their lives. One participant described the consequences to a neighbor, who attempted to intervene and stop the violence directed at her:

> My ex [boyfriend] clicked, and he beat this guy up so bad. Broke his jaw, broke his hand . . . knocked his head into the wall and knocked a hole in the wall . . . And basically I saw that beating as for me. . . . That's when it dawned on me. (age 25, recovering 1 year and 5 months)

When violence is made visible to victim-survivors, the decision to leave the relationship is often difficult because women value their intimate relationships and their families. Women want the violence to end, not the relationship (Landenberger, 1998).

Observing the impact on children. Children are frequently involved in episodes of domestic violence, either as witnesses, victims, or participants when they intervene to protect their mothers. This form of family violence can have a profound impact on children (Anderson & Cramer-Benjamin, 1999). Similar to battered women in other samples (Campbell et al., 1998; Moss et al., 1997), the survivors in the current study were mobilized to action when they saw the influence of the violence on their children. One woman became alarmed when she observed her children imitating the violence:

> I started watching my children and I thought, oh my God! They were just totally into the [abusive] behavior they see [between] their parents. [T]hat really became the force for me to say, "This is not right and you need to get your act together, woman." (age 32, recovering 6 months)

She ended the relationship in order to interrupt the intergenerational cycle of violence and to provide better role models for her children. Another woman expressed concern about her children's safety when she said,

> What caused me to finally realize that I needed to leave was the fact that he started to abuse my children . . . He started abusing my

then 4-year-old-daughter; I knew that I had to protect her and to get out of the marriage. (age 47, recovering 14 years)

Accepting partner's rejection. In several cases, the abusers were incarcerated. This facilitated the women's ability to terminate these relationships. In other cases, the defining moment occurred when the abuser initiated actions to dissolve the relationship. For example, one woman coped with the violence by physically and sexually withdrawing from her husband. In response, he said:

> You're starting to make me feel really bad. You make me feel like a rapist. I'm not able to feel like I'm a good husband; I'm not able to feel like a good father. And you're stripping me of my manhood. You should just leave me. You should just divorce me. It's obvious you don't want me. You should just leave. (age 32, recovering 6 months)

Although this survivor had experienced serious violence and marital rape, she had not considered leaving the relationship prior to the abuser's suggestion. Regardless of which person initiated the break-up, the moment was memorable and often marked with relief. One woman recalled, "When he made up his mind to leave, I didn't try to stop him 'cause I figured I could do better without him. And I did" (age 70, recovering 17 years).

Encouragement from other women. Finally, some women initiated the separation process after drawing strength from other women. These confidants affirmed the survivors' worth and reinforced their desire to live a life that was free of violence. One participant was simply told, "You don't have to let anybody abuse you like that" (age 38, recovering 8 years). This message was particularly powerful because it came from a trusted outside source, rather than a family member or friend. Other women needed a community of supportive friends and associates before they could make the break. As one woman explained, "I left a community that sanctioned the behavior of my ex-husband and moved to an area where [independent and strong] women were reinforcing that I didn't have to stay. And that's when I started preparing to leave" (age 47, recovering 12 years).

Consistent with previous research (Campbell et al., 1998), some women were able to quickly exit the relationship after the defining moment, while other women had to negotiate their way out of the home over a period of several years. These survivors had to maneuver and skillfully manage complex, and often dangerous, dynamics as they attempted to escape and reclaim their lives.

Moving Away

The women developed strategies to emotionally and physically distance themselves from their abusive partners. Leaving town was one obvious way to accomplish this goal. One woman explained the importance of relocating: "He could see that I was moving away. So he would do more crazy things . . . I left town. I couldn't stay in town with him because wherever I moved he'd find me" (age 46, recovering 9 years). Eventually, survivors had to establish some stability in their lives, which meant finding shelter and safety, often without the help of strong social support networks.

Seeking shelter and safety. Women prioritized shelter and safety as vital in their efforts to move toward autonomy. In general, the women were reluctant to go into a shelter with their children. However, the lack of economic resources forced them to turn to other social services, such as welfare, food banks, and low-income housing. Although using these services conflicted with their highly valued notions of self-sufficiency, the women viewed this as a temporary solution that helped them achieve greater independence. One woman described the stigmatization as, "The children and I had to be on welfare for awhile you know and that was really a demoralizing and dehumanizing experience . . . I had to take a step back in order to take a step forward" (age 47, recovering 14 years).

Once the survivors had established permanent residences, they wanted to feel safe in their new environments. In some cases, developing a sense of security was not possible because some abusers continued to harass and intimidate the women, even after they had formally terminated the relationships:

> My husband continued to stalk me for the next 5 years . . . harass me by phone . . . I had to get my phone number changed 4 or 5 times . . . he would drive by the apartment, he slashed my tires, he wrote threatening notes to me, even though I had a protection order against him. (age 47, recovering 14 years)

Unfortunately, ending the relationship does not always end the abuse (Campbell et al., 1998). Consequently, some women had to work, sometimes for years, to keep themselves and their children safe from the perpetrators.

Although they feared retaliation from their abusive partners, many women were reluctant to seek help from the legal system. Some survivors grew up in communities where there was a deeply entrenched code of silence, which was difficult to breach, even when they were being victimized. According to one survivor, the violence had to be life threatening before she would consider calling the police, "You just don't do it. I mean unless you're dying, you just don't do it" (age 28, recovering 1 year). Distrust and fear about the maltreatment of their partner made some women limit their contact with the criminal justice system:

> There were times where I didn't want to utilize the police or courts because I didn't trust that the system would work for me like it might work for someone else. Not so much for me, but just for [abuser's name] because of the fairness to him as a man of color . . . It's like I'm still looking out for him. (age 32, recovering 6 months)

This put the survivor in a precarious situation. She had to keep herself safe, while simultaneously protecting her abuser from a discriminatory legal system. Other women made themselves and the safety of their children a priority. Although it was sometimes challenging, they sought help from various social service agencies.

Negotiating nonsupportive networks. At a time when support was crucial, some survivors were criticized for terminating the relationship. According to some family and community members, there is a shortage of "good" men who were economically stable and available for long-term relationships. Consequently, a high value was placed on "getting a man" or "having a man." When some participants left their abusers, they were blamed for cutting themselves off from resources and disrupting the public presentation of family cohesiveness. The message was very clear. Despite the personal cost to the woman, she was expected to maintain the relationship, even if it meant living with violence. One survivor gave an example of this social pressure:

> She [her mother] wanted me to stay there because he had a good job, and he was a good person as far as she was concerned. Even though he pulled a gun on her . . . he was a good person . . . like today she feels that way. (age 50, recovering 19 years)

Another woman's family was openly hostile and rejected her when she ended the abusive relationship. (After about a year, her family members returned and apologized.) Some members of the faith community also were unsupportive. A minister instructed one survivor to "Go home and be a good wife" (age 47, recovering 14 years). In general, the women developed strategies to avoid these discouraging messages.

Moving On

The survivors were determined to sustain the separation from their abusive partners. Receiving positive support from people who reinforced their decisions to leave and valued them as individuals helped them to move on with their lives. One participant simply stated, "You have to be true to yourself first before you can move on" (age 46, recovering 9 years). This affirmation came from a variety of sources, including community agencies, support groups, and individual psychotherapy. Women also coped by relying on their faith, religion, and spirituality.

Valuing the wisdom of community elders. Older women in the community provided strength, guidance, and encouragement. One survivor described this feeling of support:

> There were 5 African American women who were elder women in my life who I really looked up to as role models and they understood what was happening in terms of abuse. They told me that I was going through a storm and that one day, that storm would pass, and I would be able to help someone else. They were there for me emotionally, financially, and spiritually. (age 47, recovering 14 years)

Community elders were valuable sources of support. Their wisdom and guidance were viewed as essential for the emotional survival of many survivors. This support from older women was welcomed and received with respect.

Listening to supportive friends and family. Supportive family members and friends also helped the women work toward healing and self-recovery. Some survivors discovered that their fathers and male confidants could be very sensitive as they tried to rebuild their lives. For example, one woman noted the role of her father when she said: "One of the other things I wanted to mention that really helped me at the time that the relationships ended was my father's support" (age 47, recovering 12 years). However, most women relied on support from female friends. Regardless of the level of support from others, the women had to find personal ways to manage the loss of their relationships. This involved creating an identity that was separate from their abusive partners, as well as managing the emotional hurt and sense of failure.

CLINICAL IMPLICATIONS

Consistent with previous research (Moss et al., 1997), the battered Black women in this study faced a variety of barriers and challenges as they moved through the three-stage process of disengaging from their abusive partners. Therapists and service providers should be prepared to assist women at each stage. Accordingly, the following suggestions are offered.

Defining Moments

Defining moments were pivotal events that prompted the survivor to consider leaving her abuser. For example, hearing another woman's story of abuse helped them to identify the abuse in their own lives. Regardless of ethnicity, women are sometimes reluctant to see themselves as victims, particularly when they are emotionally invested in their abusive relationships (Hamby & Gray-Little, 2000). Embracing the image of the strong Black woman can make some African American women especially resistant to adopting this label. It is important to help the woman name the violence in her life, while helping her to understand that it is possible to simultaneously be both a victim and a survivor (West, 1999).

Several women became concerned when the violence was directed at others, such as their neighbors or children. A woman is at increased risk for homicide if her partner has a history of assaulting nonfamily members. The therapist should consider conducting a danger assessment (Campbell, 1998). Women should not be blamed for the violence in their homes. However, it might be helpful to educate them about the possible negative emotional, academic, and social consequences for children who witness family violence (Anderson & Cramer-Benjamin, 1999).

Moving Away

During this stage, the survivors developed strategies to emotionally and physically distance themselves from their abusers. The biggest challenge was finding shelter and safety. Ending the relationship does not always end the violence. Consequently, therapists should emphasize safety planning. Although some survivors were reluctant to use the legal system, they were active help seekers, even when they were forced to interact with hostile and unsupportive social service agencies. Advocates can help survivors negotiate these systems and obtain necessary services (Sullivan & Rumptz, 1994). All service providers should keep a list of culturally sensitive services in their area.

Many survivors encounter family or community disapproval when they leave abusive partners. However, some Black survivors are influenced by a community code of silence, racial loyalty, and a desire to maintain their relationships in order to disprove stereotypes that characterize Black families as dysfunctional. The scarcity of suitable partners and fear of reporting Black men to an overburdened legal system are also genuine concerns for some Black women (Richie, 1996). Therapy can be a supportive environment to sort out these dual loyalties and to role-play assertive responses to community or family members who disapprove of their decisions to terminate these relationships.

Moving On

With the help of supportive relatives and friends, survivors can rebuild their lives (Rose, Campbell, & Kub, 2000). According to Black feminists, African American women have a long legacy of seeking support from their *other-mothers*. These older women welcome an opportunity to share their life experiences (Few, 1999). Consistent with this history, survivors in this study turned to community elders for financial and spiritual support. If other-mothers are not available or are not an appropriate option, therapists should consider referring the survivor to a culturally sensitive support group (Taylor, 2000).

In conclusion, terminating an abusive relationship can be challenging for many women. It is important that therapists understand the process of disengaging and the barriers faced by battered, Black women. They should also understand the resilience that these survivors possess. With this knowledge, therapists can better support the survivor during this difficult time.

REFERENCES

Anderson, S. A., & Cramer-Benjamin, D. B. (1999). The impact of couple violence on parenting and children: An overview and clinical implications. *The American Journal of Family Therapy, 27*, 1-19.

Banks-Wallace, J. (2000). Womanist ways of knowing: Theoretical considerations for research with African American women. *Advances in Nursing Science, 22*, 33-45.

Brush, L. D. (2001). Poverty, battering, race, and welfare reform: Black-White differences in women's welfare-to-work transitions. *Journal of Poverty, 5*, 67-89.

Campbell, J. C. (Ed.) (1998). *Empowering survivors of abuse: Health care for battered women and their children.* Thousand Oaks, CA: Sage.

Campbell, J., Rose, L., Kub, J., & Nedd, D. (1998). Voices of strength and resistance: A contextual and longitudinal analysis of women's responses to battering. *Journal of Interpersonal Violence, 13*, 743-762.

Collins, P. H. (2000). *Black feminist thought: Knowledge, consciousness, and the politics of empowerment.* New York: Routledge.

Donnelly, D. A., Cook, K. J., & Wilson, L. A. (1999). Provision and exclusion: The dual face of services to battered women in three deep south states. *Violence Against Women, 5*, 710-741.

Fetterman, D. M. (1989). *Ethnography: Step by step.* Newbury Park, CA: Sage.

Few, A. L. (1999). The (un)making of martyrs: Black mothers, daughters, and intimate violence. *Journal of the Association for Research on Mothering, 1*, 68-75.

Few, A. L., & Bell-Scott, P. (2002). Grounding our feet and hearts: Black women's coping strategies in psychologically abusive dating relationships. *Women & Therapy, 25* (3 & 4), 59-77.

Germain, C. (1986). Ethnography: The method. In P. M. Munhall & C. J. Oiler (Eds.), *Nursing research: A qualitative perspective* (pp. 147-162). Norwalk, CT: Appleton-Century-Crofts.

Hamby, S. L., & Gray-Little, B. (2000). Labeling partner violence: When do victims differentiate among acts? *Violence and Victims, 15*, 173-186.

Hesse-Biber, S., Kinder, T. S., Dupuis, P. R., Dupuis, A., & Tornabene, E. (1999). *HyperRESEARCH: A content analysis tool for the qualitative researcher.* Randolph, MA: Research Ware, Inc.

Landenburger, K. M. (1998). Exploration of women's identity: Clinical approaches with abused women. In J. Campbell (Ed.), *Empowering survivors of abuse: Health care for battered women and their children* (pp. 61-69). Thousand Oaks, CA: Sage.

McNutt, L., van Ryn, M., Clark, C., & Fraiser, I. (2000). Partner violence and medical encounters: African American women's perspectives. *American Journal of Preventive Medicine, 19*, 264-269.

Merritt-Gray, M., & Wuest, J. (1995). Counteracting abuse and breaking free: The process of leaving revealed through women's voices. *Health Care for Women International, 16*, 399-412.

Moss, V. A., Pitula, C. R., Campbell, J. C., & Halstead, L. (1997). The experience of terminating an abusive relationship from an Anglo and African American perspective: A qualitative descriptive study. *Issues in Mental Health Nursing, 18*, 433-454.

Richie, B. E. (1996). *Compelled to crime: The gender entrapment of battered Black women.* New York: Routledge.

Robinson, A. L., & Chandek, M. S. (2000). Differential police response to Black battered women. *Women & Criminal Justice, 12*, 29-61.

Rose, L. E., Campbell, J., & Kub, J. (2000). The role of social support and family relationships in women's responses to battering. *Health Care for Women International, 21*, 27-39.

Russo, N. F., Denious, J. E., Keita, G. P., & Koss, M. P. (1997). Intimate violence and Black women's health. *Women's Health: Research on Gender, Behavior, and Policy, 3*, 315-348.

Spradley, J. P. (1979). *The ethnographic interview.* New York: Holt, Reinhart, & Winston.

Sullivan, C. M., & Rumptz, M. H. (1994). Adjustment and needs of African American women who utilized a domestic violence shelter. *Violence and Victims, 9*, 275-286.

Taylor, J. Y. (1998). Womanism: A methodologic framework for African American women. *Advances in Nursing Science, 21*, 53-64.

Taylor, J. Y. (2000). Sisters of the yam: African American women's healing and recovery from intimate male partner violence. *Issues in Mental Health Nursing, 21*, 515-531.

Taylor, J. Y. (2002). Talking back: Research as an act of resistance and healing for African American women survivors of intimate male partner violence. *Women & Therapy, 25* (3 & 4), 145-160.

Thomas, J. (1993). *Doing critical ethnography.* Newbury Park, CA: Sage.

West, T. C. (1999). *Wounds of the spirit: Black women, violence, and the resistance ethics.* New York: New York University Press.

Wuest, J., & Merritt-Gray, M. (1999). Not going back: Sustaining the separation in the process of leaving abusive relationships. *Violence Against Women, 5*, 110-133.

Wuest, J., & Merritt-Gray, M. (2001). Beyond survival: Reclaiming self after leaving an abusive male partner. *Canadian Journal of Nursing Research, 32*, 79-94.

Yow, V. R. (1994). *Recording oral history: A practical guide for social scientists.* Thousand Oaks, CA: Sage.

Living at the Intersection:
The Effects of Racism and Sexism
on Black Rape Survivors

Roxanne Donovan
Michelle Williams

SUMMARY. Empirical and clinical data indicate that Black rape survivors are blamed more and are less likely to disclose their assaults than other women. We propose that these differences are, in large part, due to how Black women are perceived and evaluated. Specifically, we link two historical images of Black women, Jezebel and Matriarch, to the contemporary experience of Black rape survivors. The paradoxical and destructive implications of these images on Black rape survivors' decisions to disclose and report their rapes are discussed. Racially sensitive intervention strategies are also provided. *[Article copies available for a fee from The Haworth Document Delivery Service: 1-800-HAWORTH. E-mail address:*

Roxanne Donovan is currently a PhD candidate in Clinical Psychology at the University of Connecticut. She has also received several academic awards including a University of Connecticut Pre-Doctoral Graduate Fellowship and a citation for academic excellence from the Connecticut General Assembly. Her research interests include perceptions of Black women and perceived gender and ethnic differences in communication. Michelle Williams, PhD, is Assistant Professor at the University of Connecticut with a joint appointment in the Department of Psychology and the Institute of African American Studies. Her research focuses on ethnic identity development, multicultural psychology, domestic violence, and sexual coercion.

Address correspondence to: Michelle Williams, PhD, University of Connecticut, Psychology Department, 406 Babbidge Road, Unit 1020, Storrs, CT 06269-3515 (E-mail: mwilliams@psych.psy.uconn.edu).

[Haworth co-indexing entry note]: "Living at the Intersection: The Effects of Racism and Sexism on Black Rape Survivors." Donovan, Roxanne, and Michelle Williams. Co-published simultaneously in *Women & Therapy* (The Haworth Press, Inc.) Vol. 25, No. 3/4, 2002, pp. 95-105; and: *Violence in the Lives of Black Women: Battered, Black, and Blue* (ed: Carolyn M. West) The Haworth Press, Inc., 2002, pp. 95-105. Single or multiple copies of this article are available for a fee from The Haworth Document Delivery Service [1-800-HAWORTH, 9:00 a.m. - 5:00 p.m. (EST). E-mail address: getinfo@haworthpressinc.com].

95

KEYWORDS. Blacks, rape, sexual assault, counseling, self-disclosure, images

Living at the intersection of race, class, and gender oppression can further complicate Black women's rape experiences (Holzman, 1996; McNair & Neville, 1996). As evidence, some Black women are reluctant to disclose their sexual assaults (McNair & Neville, 1996; Washington, 2001), report the crime to the police (Feldman-Summers & Ashworth, 1981; Holzman, 1996; Wyatt, 1992), or seek counseling (Neville & Pugh, 1997). Regardless of ethnicity, women remain silent about sexual assault for a variety of reasons. For example, victim blaming may play a role in women's unwillingness to come forward with traumatic accounts of victimization. This may be particularly problematic for Black women because historically, and even today, their claims of rape have not been taken seriously (Wyatt, 1992). In addition, Black feminists argue that the combination of racism and sexism has created oppressive images of Black women, which may influence their disclosure and reporting patterns (Collins, 2000; West, 2000). Accordingly, we explore the historical origins of two stereotypical images, Jezebel and the Matriarch, and discuss how they contribute to the marginalization of Black rape survivors. We also offer suggestions for intervention.

HISTORICAL OVERVIEW

Black women have a long history of sexual victimization in the United States. In the antebellum South, they were objectified and subjected to numerous indignities and atrocities. Before being sold, they were stripped naked and examined on the auction block. This exploitation was a daily occurrence on the plantation. When federal laws prohibited the importation of Africans, Black women were required to reproduce in order to replenish the enslaved work force. Some slave owners used various incentives to encourage reproduction, such as increased food and clothing allotments. However, many enslaved women were victims of forced breeding and rape, committed by both slave owners and enslaved men. Sadly, the laws did not protect African American women from these abuses. In fact, there were no legal consequences for sexually assaulting Black women (Roberts, 1997; White, D. G., 1985).

The belief that Black women are unrapeable continues to exist. For example, in several studies, researchers asked college students to respond to hypothetical scenarios that involved sexual assault (Varelas & Foley, 1998; Willis, 1992). When the victim was a Black woman, students were less likely to define the incident as date rape, to believe the crime should be reported to the police, and to hold the perpetrator accountable (Foley, Evanic, Karnik, King, & Parks, 1995). In addition, students rated a Black date rape victim, when compared to her White equivalent, as less truthful and more responsible for her sexual assault (Willis, 1992). It also appeared that Black rape survivors were held more responsible for their victimization, regardless of the perpetrator's race (Varelas & Foley, 1998). These data suggest that Black women's long history of sexual victimization, coupled with racial stereotypes, exacerbated their rape experiences. Overall, Black survivors may receive less empathy, consideration, and judicial support than their White counterparts.

OPPRESSIVE IMAGES

According to Foley and colleagues (1995), "[R]acial history and rape myths... make African American women more vulnerable to forced sexual encounters while simultaneously making accusations of rape more difficult for them" (p. 15). Certainly, rape survivors of all ethnic backgrounds may be stigmatized by rape myths, which are "attitudes and beliefs that are generally false but are widely and persistently held, and that serve to deny and justify male sexual aggression against women" (Lonsway & Fitzgerald, 1994, p. 134). However, Black women have the added burden of oppressive stereotypes, such as the Jezebel and Matriarch images, which serve to reinforce these rape myths. Below we will discuss the historic origins of these images and illustrate how they influence the disclosure patterns of Black rape survivors.

Jezebel

The Jezebel image is typically projected onto women who are perceived to be sexually promiscuous, lustful, and immoral. This stereotype can potentially be applied to women of all ethnic backgrounds; however, when race is considered, this image is often associated with

Black women. According to Collins (2000), Jezebel was a powerful rationalization for the sexual atrocities perpetrated against enslaved African women. This image was necessary in order to justify the rape and forced breeding of Black women. As Christensen (1988) pointed out, it is paradoxical that "the only women to ever suffer socially sanctioned and induced sexual abuse were branded 'loose and immoral'" (p. 192). Because Black women were portrayed as Jezebels, they became sexual temptresses who led men astray, rather than victims of abuse (Collins, 2000; West, 2000).

Contemporary Jezebels are referred to as *welfare queens*, *hoochies*, *freaks*, and *hoodrats*. Although the names have changed, the message is the same: Black women are sexually available and sexually deviant. This image is reinforced in the media, in the form of music videos, rap songs, magazines, movies, and pornography (Collins, 2000). Because these images are so pervasive, they get projected onto all Black women. For example, after viewing sexually seductive rap videos featuring Black women, college students were more likely to describe Black women as *indecent*, *sleazy*, and *sluttish* (Gan, Zillmann, & Mitrook, 1997). The researchers concluded that the "perceived traits and conduct of a rather small number of female Black rappers were generalized to other members of the population, namely Black women" (p. 397).

The Jezebel image is particularly destructive for Black rape survivors. As it did during slavery, this image continues to portray African American victims as responsible for their assaults, no matter what the circumstances. This reinforces rape myths, which promote the idea that a survivor's behavior somehow contributed to her victimization, or that a perpetrator is less responsible for his actions. Research has shown that women, in general, are more likely to be blamed for their sexual assault if they were drinking, dressed in revealing clothing, or went to a man's apartment (Marx, Wie, & Gross, 1996). Although Black women are susceptible to these rape myths, they are also burdened with the additional stereotype of Black women as promiscuous. In other words, Black women get a *double dose* of rape myths, those that target all survivors and those that claim Black women are especially deserving of sexual assault. If Black women are perceived as inherently promiscuous, then regardless of the situation, they are at greater risk of being blamed when they are raped. Fear of being blamed and reinforcing the Jezebel stereotype may also hinder the likelihood that Black women will disclose or report their rapes.

Matriarch

Although the implications of the Jezebel image are clear, the Matriarch image is subtler, but equally as damaging to Black rape survivors. This image comes out of a 1960s government report which claimed that slavery had destroyed Black families by reversing the roles for men and women (Moynihan, 1965). Thus, the Matriarch image was created. She was a super-strong, aggressive Black woman who had emasculated Black men by taking their leadership role in the family (Collins, 2000; Moynihan, 1965). According to this report, her unwillingness to conform to traditional female roles, for example, being a stay-at-home mother and wife, resulted in lower moral values and single-parenthood. As a result, Black women are seen as the major contributor to inner city poverty and all its associated problems, including the poor academic performance and high incarceration of Black youths. This image made it easier to ignore how poverty, underfunded schools, employment discrimination, and institutionalized racism created these social problems (Collins, 2000).

As a form of resistance, some Black women have embraced the strength that characterizes the Matriarch image. They have taken on the persona of the *Strong Black Woman,* who is self-sufficient, independent, and able to survive life's difficulties without assistance. Many women who embrace this icon also feel obligated to take on the problems of family and community members (Romero, 2000). This resilience can be a source of pride and an effective survival strategy; however, as noted by Thompson (2000), this behavior can be detrimental "when there is too much of a good thing" (p. 239). Without an appropriate balance between self-care and care for others, many Black women develop mental and physical health problems, including depression, anxiety, substance abuse, high blood pressure, and obesity.

Like the Jezebel image, the Matriarch image is deeply rooted in history and can be especially harmful for Black rape survivors. Darlene Clark Hine (1989), an African American historian, unearthed this history and explained:

> I suggest that rape and the threat of rape influenced the development of a culture of dissemblance among Black women. By dissemblance I mean the behavior and attitudes of Black women that created the appearance of openness and disclosure but actually shielded the truth of their inner lives and selves from their oppressors. (p. 912)

In other words, Black women developed a culture of silence around sexual assault. Although stories of victimization were passed down through the generations as a way of preparing Black girls to protect themselves (Wyatt, 1992), in general, Black women were reluctant to speak publicly or privately about their assaults (McNair & Neville, 1996). Unfortunately, this silence makes it difficult for Black rape survivors to seek and receive emotional support. According to researchers, "Approximately half of the women who did not seek counseling identified what we conceptualized as inner strength and minimization as a significant contributor to this decision" (Neville & Pugh, 1997, p. 375).

Even when Black rape survivors disclose their trauma, the Matriarch image can affect how they are perceived. If it is assumed that Black women are inherently strong and resilient, then Black rape survivors may be viewed as less traumatized than other victims of assault. Although not specific to Black women, there is some evidence to indicate that perceiving rape survivors as more resilient results in increased victim blame (Donovan, 2001). Thus, Black women face a double bind. Remaining silent may hinder their recovery, but disclosing their rapes makes them more susceptible to being blamed, questioned, and stereotyped at a time when they are most in need of empathy and intervention.

THERAPEUTIC INTERVENTIONS

Black women need a safe therapeutic environment to discuss their victimization. Although some therapists receive training in this area, all therapists need to be sensitive to cultural differences when counseling rape survivors (Holzman, 1994, 1996). The following suggestions are offered:

Take a Supportive Therapeutic Stance

In general, rape survivors who considered it helpful to discuss their assault or had someone believe their account of the assault experienced fewer emotional and physical health problems than survivors who did not find their support to be healing or who received neutral reactions (Campbell, Ahrens, Sefl, Wasco, & Barnes, 2001). In fact, negative or hurtful reactions can be more detrimental than receiving no support at all. Therefore, family and friends should be instructed to be supportive in a way that the survivor *perceives* to be supportive. For example, a friend may find it healing to express revenge fantasies; however, this may not be experienced as healing to the survivor. If support is not forthcoming, it may be necessary to encourage the survivor to use selective disclosure.

Before working with this population, service providers should become aware of their own internalized rape myths and negative images of abuse victims. Because the manifestation of oppressive images and rape myths can be subtle, it is important that therapists and service providers do not become complacent when relying on general therapeutic skills; otherwise, they may re-victimize the survivor. It might be helpful for therapists to seek additional support or, if appropriate, therapy for their own victimization.

Address Oppressive Images

Both survivors and therapists may internalize oppressive images. For example, societal rape myths, coupled with the Jezebel image, may shape the sexual decision-making patterns of some Black rape survivors. Specifically, sexually victimized women may have multiple partners, which increases their risk of re-victimization, unwanted pregnancy, and sexually transmitted diseases. These reproductive health problems should not be attributed to Black women's promiscuity and immorality. Instead, the therapist should suspect a history of sexual abuse or other trauma experiences (West, 2000; West, Williams, & Siegel, 2000).

Similarly, the Matriarch image can further complicate the therapy experience for Black women. Endorsing the image of the strong Black woman can make many survivors reluctant to seek counseling (Neville & Pugh, 1997). This image, along with the culture of silence, may make survivors reluctant to disclose the abuse in the initial stages of therapy. Even when disclosure takes place, clients may minimize their symptomatology, dismiss the need to focus on the sexual assault, or divert attention to other issues such as child care needs, work issues, or life stressors. These issues are pertinent and need to be addressed in order to prevent a premature termination of therapy; however, therapists should be cognizant that, even though a safe therapeutic environment is important for all rape survivors, the additional influence of racial stereotypes makes it a particularly salient issue for Black rape survivors (Romero, 2000; Thompson, 2000).

If an African American man victimized the survivor, she may fear that her disclosure will reinforce the stereotype of Black men as sexual predators. She may also be fearful of turning another Black man over to an oppressive criminal justice system. Because these fears may silence many Black rape survivors, therapists should neither ignore nor minimize these feelings of disloyalty or fear. Pierce-Baker (1998) candidly expressed this dilemma when she wrote:

> I felt responsible for upholding the image of the strong black man for our young son, *and* for the white world with whom I had contact . . . I didn't want to confirm the white belief that all black men rape. Better not to talk about it . . . so I'd kept silent about what happened to me. (p. 64)

As a result of this situation, it may be helpful to explore how race, class, and gender intersect to affect the disclosure patterns of Black rape survivors. Moreover, therapists can point out that the oppression of Black men does not excuse the victimization of Black women (Pierce-Baker, 1998).

Encourage Social Support and Activism

For some survivors, being able to speak openly and honestly about their rapes in the company of other Black women can be a very powerful, healing experience. However, other survivors, depending on their comfort level or racial identity, may prefer to receive support from a mixed-race group (Taylor, 2000). Regardless of the group composition, many rape survivors can benefit from developing a strong social support network.

Activism, for example, participating in protest actions, can empower rape survivors. It is particularly helpful if activism takes place in a Black feminist environment in which participants are working to eliminate race, class, and gender oppression. This collective action makes rape a Black community problem and reduces the culture of silence and the self-blame rape survivors may experience. Activism also mobilizes the Black community to address and challenge the images and myths that continue to impact the lives of African Americans. In addition, it is an opportunity for Black women to work together toward a solution (White, A.M., 1999, 2001).

CONCLUSION

Black women's experiences of rape are inextricably linked to gender and race. Our culture's views of Black women affect how Black rape survivors are evaluated and how they respond to their trauma. For example, compared to other women, Black rape survivors are judged as less truthful and more to blame for their rapes. Black rape survivors are also less likely to seek supportive interventions and to disclose or report their rapes. In this article, we have discussed how racist images of Black women contribute to the silence and overall marginalization of Black rape survivors. Specifically, we have looked at the influences of the Jezebel and Matriarch images and discussed how both negatively affect the disclosure patterns and perceptions of Black rape survivors.

Finally, it should be noted that the relevance of oppressive images for individual Black women will be influenced by their racial identity, cultural affiliation, access to support, and comfort with traditional interventions. As such, it is recommended that research be undertaken to evaluate how these images interact with other variables to impact Black rape survivors.

REFERENCES

Campbell, R., Ahrens, C. E., Sefl, T., Wasco, S. M., & Barnes, H. E. (2001). Social reactions to rape victims: Healing and hurtful effects on psychological and physical health outcomes. *Violence and Victims, 16,* 287-302.

Christensen, C. P. (1988). Issues in sex therapy with ethnic and racial minority women. *Women & Therapy, 7,* 187-205.

Collins, P. H. (2000). *Black feminist thought: Knowledge, consciousness, and the politics of empowerment.* New York: Routledge.

Donovan, R. A. (2001, August). *How promiscuity, resilience, and race affect rape blame attribution.* Poster session presented at the annual convention of the American Psychological Association, San Francisco, CA.

Feldman-Summers, S., & Ashworth, C. D. (1981). Factors related to intentions to report a rape. *Journal of Social Issues, 37,* 53-70.

Foley, L. A., Evanic, C., Karnik, K., King, J., & Parks, A. (1995). Date rape: Effects of race and assailant and victim and gender on subjects on perceptions. *Journal of Black Psychology, 21,* 6-18.

Gan, S., Zillmann, D., & Mitrook, M. (1997). Stereotyping effect of Black women's sexual rap on White audiences. *Basic and Applied Social Psychology, 19,* 381-391.

Hine, D. C. (1989). Rape and the inner lives of Black women in the Middle West: Preliminary thoughts on the culture of dissemblance. *Signs: Journal of Women in Culture and Society, 14,* 912-920.

Holzman, C. G. (1994). Multicultural perspectives on counseling survivors of rape. *Journal of Social Distress and the Homeless, 3,* 81-97.

Holzman, C. G. (1996). Counseling adult women rape survivors: Issues of race, ethnicity, and class. *Women & Therapy, 19*, 47-62.

Lonsway, K. A., & Fitzgerald, L. F. (1994). Rape myths: In review. *Psychology of Women Quarterly, 18*, 133-164.

Marx, B. P., Wie, V. V., & Gross, A. M. (1996). Date rape risk factors: A review and methodological critique of the literature. *Aggression and Violent Behavior, 1*, 27-45.

McNair, L. D., & Neville, H. A. (1996). African American women survivors of sexual assault: The intersection of race and class. *Women & Therapy, 18*, 107-118.

Moynihan, D. P. (1965). *The Negro family: The case for national action.* Washington, DC: Government Printing Office.

Neville, H., & Pugh, A. O. (1997). General and culture-specific factors influencing African American women's reporting patterns and perceived social support following sexual assault: An exploratory investigation. *Violence Against Women, 3*, 361-381.

Pierce-Baker, C. (1998). *Surviving the silence: Black women's stories of rape.* New York: W. W. Norton & Company.

Roberts, D. (1997). *Killing the Black body: Race, reproduction, and the meaning of liberty.* New York: Pantheon Books.

Romero, R. E. (2000). The icon of the strong Black women: The paradox of strength. In L. C. Jackson & B. Greene (Eds.), *Psychotherapy with African American women: Innovations in psychodynamic perspectives and practice* (pp. 225-238). New York: Guilford Press.

Taylor, J. Y. (2000). Sisters of the yam: African American women's healing and self-recovery from intimate male partner violence. *Issues in Mental Health Nursing, 21*, 515-531.

Thompson, C. L. (2000). African American women and moral masochism: When there is too much of a good thing. In L. C. Jackson & B. Greene (Eds.), *Psychotherapy with African American women: Innovations in psychodynamic perspectives and practice* (pp. 239-231). New York: Guilford Press.

Varelas, N., & Foley, L. A. (1998). Blacks' and Whites' perceptions of interracial and intraracial date rape. *The Journal of Social Psychology, 138*, 392-400.

Washington, P. A. (2001). Disclosure patterns of Black female sexual assault survivors. *Violence Against Women, 7*, 1254-1283.

West, C. M. (2000). Developing an "oppositional gaze" toward the image of Black women. In J. C. Chrisler, C. Golden, & P. D. Rozee (Eds.), *Lectures on the psychology of women* (pp. 220-233). New York: McGraw Hill.

West, C. M., Williams, L. M., & Siegel, J. A. (2000). Adult sexual revictimization among Black women sexually abused in childhood: A prospective examination of serious consequences of abuse. *Child Maltreatment, 5*, 49-57.

White, A. M. (1999). Talking feminist, talking Black: Micromobilization process in a collective protest against rape. *Gender & Society, 13*, 77-100.

White, A. M. (2001). I am because we are: Combined race and gender political consciousness among African American women and men anti-rape activists. *Women's Studies International Forum, 24*, 11-24.

White, D. G. (1985). *Ar'n't I a woman? Female slaves in the plantation south.* New York: W. W. Norton and Company.

Willis, C. E. (1992). The effect of sex role stereotype, victim and defendant race, and prior relationship on race culpability attributions. *Sex Roles, 26,* 213-226.

Wyatt, G. E. (1992). The sociocultural context of African American and White American women's rape. *Journal of Social Issues, 48,* 77-91.

Racialized Sexual Harassment in the Lives of African American Women

NiCole T. Buchanan
Alayne J. Ormerod

SUMMARY. To date, scholars who investigate sexual harassment have been disturbingly silent about issues facing women of color. The current study describes results of a qualitative study of sexual and racial harassment conducted with 37 African American women. These data indicate that African American women cannot easily separate issues of race and gender when considering their personal accounts of victimization, which creates a form of racialized sexual harassment. Implications for practice and therapeutic interventions are presented. *[Article copies available for a fee from The Haworth Document Delivery Service: 1-800-HAWORTH. E-mail address: <getinfo@haworthpressinc.com> Website: <http://www.HaworthPress.com> © 2002 by The Haworth Press, Inc. All rights reserved.]*

KEYWORDS. Blacks, sexual harassment, racial harassment

NiCole T. Buchanan, PhD, is Assistant Professor in the Psychology Department at Michigan State University. Alayne J. Ormerod, PhD, is Assistant Professor in the Department of Educational Psychology at the University of Illinois Urbana-Champaign.

Portions of this paper were presented at the 26th Annual Meeting of the Association for Women in Psychology, Los Angeles, CA.

Deep appreciation is expressed to Melanie S. Harned for her generous editing and support and encouragement.

Address correspondence to: NiCole T. Buchanan, Department of Psychology, Michigan State University, East Lansing, MI 48824-1117.

[Haworth co-indexing entry note]: "Racialized Sexual Harassment in the Lives of African American Women." Buchanan, NiCole T., and Alayne J. Ormerod. Co-published simultaneously in *Women & Therapy* (The Haworth Press, Inc.) Vol. 25, No. 3/4, 2002, pp. 107-124; and: *Violence in the Lives of Black Women: Battered, Black, and Blue* (ed: Carolyn M. West) The Haworth Press, Inc., 2002, pp. 107-124. Single or multiple copies of this article are available for a fee from The Haworth Document Delivery Service [1-800-HAWORTH, 9:00 a.m. - 5:00 p.m. (EST). E-mail address: getinfo@haworthpressinc.com].

Sexual harassment is perhaps the most common occupational hazard for working women, with one of every two experiencing unwanted sex-related behavior over the course of their working lives (Morgan, 2001; Sbraga & O'Donohue, 2000). Although it is likely that women have experienced sexual harassment since first entering the work force, serious investigation of this topic has emerged only within the last two decades. In 1979, Catherine MacKinnon argued that sexual harassment violates the Civil Rights Act of 1964 as a form of employment discrimination and has a disparate impact on women. Shortly thereafter, the U. S. Equal Employment Opportunity Commission (EEOC) (1980) established a legal standard that defined sexual harassment for the first time in U. S. history. Under this standard, sexual harassment was categorized as *quid pro quo*, which refers to exchange of sexual favors for special employment treatment, and *hostile environment*, which refers to conduct that creates an intimidating or offensive work atmosphere.

Sexual harassment has also been defined psychologically and behaviorally. As a psychological process, sexual harassment has been conceptualized as a traumatic psychological stressor (Fitzgerald, Swan, & Fischer, 1995). Within this context, the individual must appraise the situation as stressful and initiate a complex coping process, which can vary considerably based on individual factors, contextual factors of the organization, and the nature of the harassment, such as its frequency or severity (Fitzgerald, Swan, & Magley, 1997).

Current behavioral definitions (Fitzgerald, Shullman et al., 1988; Gelfand, Fitzgerald, & Drasgow, 1995) describe sexual harassment as having three distinct but related dimensions. First, *gender harassment* refers to behaviors and comments that serve to insult and degrade women as a group without the goal of gaining sexual cooperation. This can be further divided into two sub-types: *sexist hostility* (misogynistic behaviors that degrade women without explicit sexual content) and *sexual hostility* (explicitly sexual comments, gestures, and jokes). Second, *unwanted sexual attention* includes unwanted touching, stroking, or repeated requests for dates or sexual interactions. Third, *sexual coercion*, which is similar to *quid pro quo* harassment, refers to unwanted sexual attention with direct or implied bribes or threats to one's work or job. These forms of sexual harassment can occur in varying degrees of severity (Langhout et al., 1999).

APPLICATION OF CONCEPTS
TO AFRICAN AMERICAN WOMEN

Despite extensive research on sexual harassment, relatively little has focused on the experience of ethnic minority women. This is surprising given that African American women have a long history of victimization. Perhaps the most egregious examples were the wanton rape and sexual abuse of female slaves by slave owners and their relatives, overseers, and even guests. After slavery was dismantled, and well into the 1960s, African American women were relegated to domestic employment. Black women continued to be at risk for sexual mistreatment because they worked in the homes of White families. Having few options and few financial resources increased their vulnerability and decreased their likelihood of complaining about sexual harassment (Neville & Hamer, 2001).

Despite these challenges, many contemporary Black women have been vocal about abuse in the workplace. For example, an African American woman, who was a victim of both racial and sexual harassment, brought forth the first legal cases used to define case law on sexual harassment (*Meritor Savings Bank FSB v. Vinson*, 1986; *Vinson v. Taylor*, 1985). Furthermore, in 1991, the country witnessed the most public sexual harassment hearing in history, brought forth by professor Anita Hill against [now Supreme Court Judge] Clarence Thomas, both prominent African Americans (McKay, 1992).

The Jezebel and Sapphire images depict Black women as sexually promiscuous, hot-blooded, and hypersexual. These images began during slavery and continue today (Donovan & Williams, 2002 [This volume]). Researchers speculated that Black women are reluctant to label their experiences sexual harassment because, ". . . in their struggle against the image of sexual promiscuity, Black women may not want to draw attention to themselves as targets of sexual attention" (Kalof, Eby, Matheson, & Kroska, 2001, p. 297-298).

Sexual Harassment

Estimates of sexual harassment in the lives of African American women have varied widely. For instance, in one study, Black and White women reported similar rates of gender harassment (Piotrkowski, 1998). Conversely, in another study, White women reported higher rates of sexual harassment when compared to their Black counterparts (53% vs. 34%) (Wyatt & Riederle, 1995). Researchers speculate that Black women in their samples may have underreported their victimization (Wyatt & Riederle, 1994).

However, in most studies, when compared to Caucasian women, women of color reported higher rates of sexual harassment, ranging from 60% to 85% (Cortina, Swan, Fitzgerald, & Waldo, 1998; Mansfield, Koch, Henderson, & Vicary, 1991; Paludi, 1996).

Black women who worked in low status, blue-collar jobs reported the greatest frequency of sexual harassment, which suggests an interaction between race and employment status (Mansfield et al., 1991). Based on the literature, various factors have been linked to increased vulnerability to sexual harassment. They include economic inequalities, stereotypes about sexual availability, being single or divorced, and being youthful, for example, between the ages of 20 and 44. In addition, women are at increased risk for sexual harassment if they are dependent on their jobs, work in low-status or traditionally male jobs, or have a male supervisor (MacKinnon, 1979; Wyatt & Riederle, 1995). Black women's overrepresentation in these categories makes them more vulnerable to workplace abuse (Yoder & Aniakudo, 1995, 1996, 1997).

Racial Harassment

Racial discrimination often has an impact upon an employment decision, job advancement, or some form of work-related opportunity, whereas racial harassment typically involves differential treatment based on race and the maintenance of a hostile or offensive work environment (Harrick & Sullivan, 1995). Racial harassment can have several dimensions, including verbal racial harassment, such as slurs and derogatory comments about the victim's racial or ethnic group, exclusion from work-related or social interactions because of ethnicity (Schneider, Hitlan, & Radhakrishnan, 2000), and physical forms of harassment directed at an ethnic group (Ormerod, Bergman, Palmieri, Drasgow, & Juraska, 2001).

Although the research is limited, racial harassment appears to be a frequent occurrence. In a multiracial sample, between 40% and 76% of respondents experienced one or more incidents of racial harassment within a one-year period (Scarville, Button, Edwards, Lancaster, & Elig, 1999; Schneider et al., 2000). This form of harassment has been associated with deleterious effects for victims. More specifically, it is negatively related to stress, life satisfaction, perceptions of good health, job satisfaction, organizational commitment, and positive organizational climate (Mays, Coleman, & Jackson, 1996; Valentine, Silver, & Twigg, 1999) and positively related to symptoms of posttraumatic stress (Schneider et al., 2000).

Racialized Sexual Harassment

Sexual and racial harassment may be combined in unique ways for African American women. Specifically, the cultural and historical contexts of slavery and sexualized stereotypes of African American women result in sexual harassment that is perceived as racially motivated (Collins, 1998, 2000; Murrell, 1996; Winston, 1991). Moreover, the harassment is likely to take different forms in the lives of Black women than in the lives of White women. For example, although a coworker may refer to a White woman as a whore or a slut, an African American woman may be called a *Black* whore, which creates an experience that combines aspects of both race and gender oppression (Buchanan, 1999). Another example are the infamous tapes from a Texaco board meeting where an African American woman, Bari-Ellen Roberts, was dismissed as a "smart-mouthed little colored girl" (Collins, 1998, p. 12).

There is anecdotal support (Mansfield et al., 1991; Yoder & Aniakudo, 1996) and empirical evidence (Mecca & Rubin, 1999) that "for many African American women, the issue of sexual harassment seems inextricably intertwined with racism" (p. 817). In particular, Black college women described a category of harassment based on racial stereotypes of African American women's sexuality or physical features (e.g., that Black women have large buttocks). Although many respondents were angered by these race-based stereotypes, little research has addressed the emotional outcomes of experiencing racialized sexual harassment. However, victims often perceive multiple forms of harassment to be more severe (Fitzgerald et al., 1997).

According to Murrell (1996), future research should address three primary concerns. First, research should examine whether women of color are differentially exposed to and affected by sexual harassment in the workplace. Second, research must examine whether sexual and racial harassment are inextricably linked for Black victims. Third, research should examine whether the range and severity of outcomes for women of color are different from that of Caucasian women. Additionally, researchers have questioned the cross-cultural meaning of the construct sexual harassment by asking whether the term is an *etic*, that is, a universal construct that does not require cultural adaptations, or an *emic* construct that thus should be examined from the perspective of the specific cultural group being studied (Adams, J. H., 1997; Buchanan, 1999; Mecca & Rubin, 1999).

GOALS OF THE STUDY

Toward these goals, in the current study we will investigate the sexual and racial harassment experiences of African American women. This necessitates an understanding of each construct and how the unique history and experiences of African American women are likely to result in a combined form of harassment. Therefore, in this study we took an *emic*, within-group, qualitative approach. Qualitative methods allow participants to be co-creators in the meaning-making process by voicing their understanding of the harassing experience. Such methods are effective in addressing sensitive topics with women of color (Jarrett, 1993; Madriz, 2000) and in helping to define a phenomenon of interest (Wilkinson, 1999). In addition, we used a focus group interview, which allowed participants to express their points of view. Focus groups are also valuable when studying a phenomenon when little quantitative research is available, such as the relatively new construct proposed here, racialized sexual harassment.

The focus group protocol asked the participants broad questions about the nature of their experience with unwanted sex-related and race-based harassment. We expected that women would describe experiences that combined both forms of harassment (e.g., being called a name combining race and gender, such as *Black whore* versus being called a *whore* without the other qualifier). In addition, we expected that the participants would report being targeted because they were both Black and female. No formal hypotheses were proposed for testing, which is consistent with a grounded theory approach (Strauss & Corbin, 1998). Instead, theory was allowed to emerge from the experiences voiced by participants.

METHODS

Participants

Thirty-seven African American women were recruited via flyers, e-mail listserves for Black women, and referrals from respondents (snowballing) to participate in focus group interviews. The participants were residents in a large or mid-size city in the Midwest. The mean age of the sample was 39 years old, with a range from 23 to 56 years old. They were highly educated, with most holding a bachelor's or master's degree. Only one participant ended her formal education with a high school diploma. The women in the sample were employed in a wide range of professions, including nursing,

mental health, teaching, accounting, librarianship, secretarial, college administration, academic advising, and research assistantships.

Procedure

Six focus group interviews were conducted, each lasting approximately
90 minutes. According to feminist and qualitative researchers, focus group
moderators should closely match the demographics of the participants
(Jarrett, 1993; Krueger, 1994; Madriz, 2000). Accordingly, the first author
and two assistant moderators, all African American women, were present
during the interviews.

Focus groups began with an overview of the general topics to be discussed and an explanation of the moderator's role. The women were also
reminded that participation was voluntary and confidential and that they
should honor the privacy of other group members. The focus group protocol included questions about unwanted race-based and sex-based behaviors experienced personally or described to them by other African
American women. This protocol was used as a loose framework to guide
separate conversations on racial harassment and sexual harassment, while
allowing considerable freedom of discussion among the participants.
Topic introduction was counter-balanced (half began with racial harassment and half with sexual harassment) to ensure adequate coverage of each
across focus groups.

Focus group interviews continued (for a total of six) until reaching a
point of theoretical saturation (Krueger, 1994; Glaser & Strauss, 1967),
that is, when no new information emerged from additional interviews. At
this point, audiotapes of the focus groups were transcribed, reviewed by the
moderator, and corrected for accuracy. In compensation for their time, the
women received lunch, were paid $25, and were entered in a raffle for
$125.

Data Analysis

A grounded theory approach (Glaser & Strauss, 1967) was used to identify themes emerging from the focus group interviews. Initially, the transcripts were subjected to a line-by-line microanalysis in order to discover
salient categories and to uncover relationships between concepts. Based on
the salient categories, a conceptual ordering analysis was used to generate
well-developed themes (Strauss & Corbin, 1998). In particular, information was coded about their experiences with harassment (e.g., sexual ha-

rassment, racial harassment alone, or a combination in the form of racialized sexual harassment).

RESULTS

Although the focus group protocol divided the conversation into race-based and sex-based harassing behaviors, themes of racial harassment or sexual harassment alone were not found. Instead, participants often interwove topics (e.g., describing sex-related behaviors during the designated time for a discussion on race).

Racialized Sexual Harassment

There was considerable evidence of racialized sexual harassment as a distinct construct from either racial harassment or sexual harassment. For example, the women reported that White coworkers and supervisors often felt free to be sexually explicit or request information about the participants' sex lives (e.g., asking about sexual positions participants have tried or telling participants of their own sexual exploits). These discussions occurred without sufficient opportunity to build rapport or a relationship with the participants. Consequently, the women asserted that this behavior reflected an underlying assumption that African American women's sexual boundaries, both the behaviors they will engage in and their comfort in discussing sex, are looser than those of Caucasians.

A second interesting and unexpected finding was that many women reported comments that sexualized their dress and appearance. For example, in preparation for a dinner date with her husband, a participant changed into a red dress. A White colleague told her, "You look like you're getting ready to go stand on the corner," implying that she looked like a prostitute. Several women also reported comments about their shoes. For instance, a coworker told a participant that the color of her shoes made them "too exotic and offensive."

Dimensions of Sexual Harassment

According to previous research, sexual harassment can vary in dimension, such as severity (Langhout et al., 1999). Participants in this sample also identified varying degrees of harassment, categorized here as covert, subtly overt, and overt.

Covert. Although ambiguous in nature, covert events were the most frequently reported and reflected a general bias against African American women. For example, several participants reported conflicts with their White secretaries. More specifically, upon entering their current positions, subordinate White female employees often refused to make coffee, a duty they had performed in the past for a White supervisor. Participants perceived this as a refusal by White employees, both men and women, to engage in behaviors that may be constructed as "serving" a Black woman.

Subtly overt. The second category, subtly overt, included behaviors that were described as sexually harassing, but were not directly racist. Instead, these experiences reflected assumptions and stereotypes about African American women's sexuality, such as their availability for sex. For example, one woman was told by a White male coworker, "I bet you are a slave to sex."

Overt. The final category, labeled as overt, combined obvious racist and sexist intentions. This was the least common experience, but powerful when it occurred. For example, one woman was subjected to repeated unwanted comments from a White male coworker concerning her "sexy black ass," and another was repeatedly asked to pose for pictures because he "loved big, sexy, Black women."

DISCUSSION

In this study, we investigated various forms of harassment in the lives of 37 professional African American women. Qualitative methods and focus group interviews were used. In addition, we employed an emic framework to further develop sexual harassment as a construct that applies to the experience of Black women. These methodologies are a contribution to the literature because they revealed racialized sexual harassment, which is distinct from either racial or sexual harassment alone. This reflects the women's inability or unwillingness to separate their experiences as either racial or sexual. Instead, they perceived them as simultaneously sex- and race-based.

Similar to previous researchers (Fitzgerald et al., 1988), we discovered varying levels of sexual harassment and behaviors that could be categorized as sexual coercion, unwanted sexual attention, and gender harassment. As expected, our participants reported racial variations of these forms of harassment, some of which incorporated direct reference to the legacy of African American enslavement and stereotypes that emerged from that time period (e.g., Black women as insatiable Jezebels) (Buchanan, 1999; Collins, 2000). Although some events were overt, for example, being touched or asked to perform sexual acts, many other behaviors were covert, such as refusing to comply with requests or assignments from a Black woman. These behaviors did not refer to race or gender; however, they were a subtle reminder that Black women should not be in positions of authority. In extreme cases, this behavior can take the form of *contrapower* sexual harassment (e.g., a female professor being harassed by a male student). Black women may be more vulnerable to harassment from male or White subordinates because their achieved status or formal organizational power does not mitigate their lower ascribed status as members of a marginalized group (Rospenda, Richman, & Nawyn, 1998).

Our participants also reported subtly overt harassment, which took the form of inappropriate sexual questions or comments that sexualized the participants' attire. Separately, such events may be easily dismissed. However, taken together, a theme emerges where the color and style of clothing, even if it is neutral, becomes sexualized when worn by African American women. Moreover, although such comments may appear insignificant, they can have implications for how Black women present themselves. For example, in order to protect themselves from the Jezebel stereotype, some African American women feel that they have to be especially conservative and conscientious about their wardrobes (Wilson & Russell, 1996) or avoid initiating professional mentoring relationships with White men (Murrell, 1996). However, it should be noted that White women perpetrated many of these sexualized racist acts. Therefore, some of the safeguards against harassment, such as working in an all-women environment, may not offer protection for African American women.

IMPLICATIONS FOR PRACTICE

Sexual and racial harassments are significant psychological stressors in the lives of many women (Fitzgerald et al., 1997; Mays et al., 1996). However, many mental health professionals are not adequately trained to recognize and treat these forms of victimization (Campbell, Raja, & Grining, 1999). This is unfortunate because many female psychologists will be sexually harassed while providing services (deMayo, 1997), clinical supervisors must assist supervisees after they are sexually harassed by clients (deMayo, 2000), and psychology educators will be faced with sexual harassment in the academy (Rubin, Hampton, & McManus, 1997). In addition, mental health providers may be asked to render an expert opinion regarding the psychological effects of sexual harassment on a litigant (Fitzgerald, Buchanan, Collinsworth, Magley, & Ramos, 1999; Jorgenson & Wahl, 2000).

Although mental health professionals have an integral role in victims' recovery from sexual harassment, there is little information on specific therapeutic interventions (Koedam, 2000; Sherer, 1996; Shrier & Hamilton, 1996), particularly with African American women (Daniel, 1995). However, using the limited literature and our findings, we offer suggestions for how to modify assessment and interventions to address racialized sexual harassment.

Assessment

Sherer (1996) suggested that mental health providers conduct a thorough assessment with survivors of sexual harassment. It should include the following:

Record keeping. Keep in mind that records can be subpoenaed (Benedek, 1996; Jorgenson & Wahl, 2000; Koedam, 2000; Schafran, 1996). Service providers should maintain careful, comprehensive, factually based records that avoid speculation. When appropriate, it may be helpful to include specific quotations from the client. If present, the provider should note the nature, duration, intensity, and chronology of current and past physical or psychological symptoms. In cases of ongoing harassment, the client should be encouraged to maintain her own set of written documentation.

Documenting the harassment. Ask the client to tell her story about the harassment. She should be encouraged to speak freely, including how she felt and reacted to the trauma. Some African American women may respond better when asked to give a testimony (Taylor, 2002) [This volume]). In order to obtain a detailed history, the mental health provider should periodically repeat back or paraphrase the client's information. It is especially important to obtain the story in chronological order, including where and when the harassment occurred, who witnessed the act, and whom the client told, if anyone.

Black women's reactions to sexual harassment may differ based on the ethnicity of the perpetrator (Shelton & Chavous, 1999). Therefore, it is important to inquire about the ethnicity of all the participants. One psychiatrist realized this when she interviewed a middle-aged African American victim of workplace harassment:

I found that I needed her to tell me who was black and who was white, who was accusing whom of sexual misconduct, and who was committing it . . . Had I not first developed the ability to simply ask . . . I might never have succeeded in teasing out the salient issues of the actual sexual harassment. (Sherer, 1996, p. 84-86)

Interviewers should also ask about the ethnic makeup of the workplace. The dynamics of the harassment may be more acute if a Black woman is a *token* or numerical minority in her work environment (Yoder & Aniakudo, 1995, 1996, 1997) or if she is a victim of contrapower harassment perpetrated by a White or male subordinate (Rospenda et al., 1998).

History of victimization. It is especially important for those clients involved in litigation to receive a thorough evaluation of past victimization and its related effects. This will avoid misuse of this history in court (Fitzgerald, Buchanan et al., 1999). Ask about previous experiences, either as a child or an adult, with harassment and victimization. Has the client experienced incest, rape, partner violence, or other forms of harassment in the workplace? In addition, Black women should be asked about racial harassment (e.g., not being allowed to live in certain neighborhoods because of race, being followed by the police, being called racial slurs). Note details, such as numbers of times, ages, and duration of each experience. Discuss the client's coping mechanisms and reaction to these victimizations.

Therapeutic Interventions

Little research has focused specifically on the treatment of sexual harassment survivors (Daniel, 1995; Koedam, 2000; Shrier & Hamilton, 1996). However, therapists can use many of the same interventions that they would use for survivors of other forms of victimization.

Therapeutic stance. It is imperative that therapists avoid causing secondary injury by implying such questions as: What were you saying or doing? What were you wearing? How did you let this happen? Until there is evidence to the contrary, the therapist should assume that the client is not fabricating the event and that her work performance was adequate prior to the harassment. If the client's behavior is exacerbating her problems, these concerns can be addressed after rapport is established. In general, the therapist should create an atmosphere of trust and support (Shrier & Hamilton, 1996).

Addressing reactions to the harassment. Although it is possible for clients to recover and heal, many clients report symptoms that are consistent with posttraumatic stress disorder, and adjustment, mood, or anxiety disorders. Race-based discrimination may exacerbate the stress for African American women. One obvious goal of therapy is to help the client deal effectively with her reactions to the abuse. For some clients, medication may be an effective method for managing symptoms. Others may benefit from learning about the extent and dynamics of sexual harassment, which help to normalize the experience. Family therapy or group therapy can be used to enhance the victim's support system (Mays et al., 1996; Shrier & Hamilton, 1996).

It is common for a survivor to experience a range of feelings, such as confusion, disillusionment, and anger. In addition, she may be grieving numerous losses, including her job, career advancement, and her senses of trust and self-esteem (Shrier & Hamilton, 1996). It is especially important to help the woman develop strategies for coping with these feelings in the work environment. This can be even more challenging for Black women, particularly if they are one of a few ethnic minority women in their work environment. Being a token creates performance pressure, stress, and social isolation (Yoder & Aniakudo, 1997).

Racialized sexual harassment often occurs in the context of other forms of violence. For example, when compared to their nonabused counterparts, Black women with a history of childhood sexual abuse reported higher incidences of sexual harassment (Wyatt & Riederle, 1994). In addition, Black survivors of childhood sexual abuse are at increased risk for physical and sexual violence in their adult intimate relationships (West, Williams, & Siegel, 2000). When appropriate, therapists should help clients make connections between their personal histories of abuse and their current harassment experiences. Ask if the harassment reminds her of any other relationship or experience in her life. This is not to blame the victim; however, understanding these connections can help shed light on the client's coping strategies and reactions to the current victimization (Adams, K. M., 1999). Therapists should also be aware of historical traumas, such as a family history of sexual assaults or lynchings. These stories, which are often passed down through the generations, can exacerbate the current trauma or increase feelings of vulnerability (Daniel, 2000).

Effective therapy with Black survivors of sexual trauma requires counselors to explore the impact of oppressive images. Daniel (1995) contends that "Black women need to be in therapeutic settings in which negative stereotypes and injurious reconstructions are not dominant" (p. 116). For example, the fear of reinforcing the Jezebel stereotype or being labeled as aggressive Sapphires can silence Black women. In addition, Black women may be considered racially disloyal if they reveal sexual harassment committed by Black men.

CONCLUSION

The women in this study gave testimony to the existence of an often ignored form of harassment, labeled here as racialized sexual harassment. This form of harassment was found to have many forms, those that were overtly racist and sexist, such as calling someone a Black whore, and those that were much more subtle or covert, such as making reference to sexualized stereotypes of African American women. Perhaps most striking are the findings that White women were also perpetrators, creating a threatening atmosphere for Black women, even when they were employed in all-women environments. Their stories demonstrate that the harassment experiences of African American women are complex. Moreover, they illustrate the importance of acknowledging and understanding the intertwined experiences of both racial and sexual harassment in the lives of Black women.

REFERENCES

Adams, J. H. (1997). Sexual harassment and Black women: A historical perspective. In W. O'Donohue (Ed.), *Sexual harassment: Theory, research, and treatment* (pp. 213-224). Boston: Allyn and Bacon.

Adams, K. M. (1999). Sexual harassment as cycles of trauma reenactment and sexual compulsivity. *Sexual Addiction & Compulsivity, 6,* 177-191.

Benedek, E. P. (1996). Forensic aspects of sexual harassment: Serving as an expert witness, providing courtroom testimony, and preparing legal reports. In D. K. Shrier (Ed.), *Sexual harassment in the workplace and academia: Psychiatric issues* (pp. 113-132). Washington, DC: American Psychiatric Press.

Buchanan, N. T. (1999, March). *Sexual harassment and the African American woman: A historical analysis of a contemporary phenomena.* Paper presented at the meeting of the Association for Women in Psychology, Providence, RI.

Buchanan, N. T., Langhout, R. D., & Fitzgerald, L. F. (1999). Predictors of African American women's responses to sexual harassment. In L. Fitzgerald (Chair), *Exploring sexual harassment experiences of seldom researched targets.* Symposium conducted at the meeting of the Society for Industrial and Organizational Psychology, New Orleans, LA.

Campbell, R., Raja, S., & Grining, P. L. (1999). Training mental health professionals on violence against women. *Journal of Interpersonal Violence, 14,* 1003-1013.

Civil Rights Act of 1964, Title VII, 42 U.S.C. §2000e *et. Seq.*

Collins, P. H. (1998). *Fighting words: Black women and the search for justice.* Minneapolis, MN: University of Minnesota Press.

Collins, P. H. (2000). *Black feminist thought: Knowledge, consciousness, and the politics of empowerment.* New York: Routledge.

Cortina, L. M., Swan, S., Fitzgerald, L. F., & Waldo, C. (1998). Sexual harassment and assault: Chilling the climate for women in academia. *Psychology of Women Quarterly, 22*, 419-441.

Daniel, J. H. (1995). The discourse on Thomas v. Hill: A resource for perspectives on the Black woman and sexual trauma. *Journal of Feminist Family Therapy, 7*, 103-117.

Daniel, J. H. (2000). The courage to hear: African American women's memories of racial trauma. In L. C. Jackson & B. Greene (Eds.), *Psychotherapy with African American women: Innovations in psychodynamic perspectives and practice* (pp. 126-144). New York: Guilford.

deMayo, R. A. (1997). Patient sexual behavior and sexual harassment: A national survey of female psychologists. *Professional Psychology: Research and Practice, 28*, 58-62.

deMayo, R. A. (2000). Patients' sexual behavior and sexual harassment: A survey of clinical supervisors. *Professional Psychology: Research and Practice, 31*, 706-709.

Donovan, R., & Williams, M. (2002). Living at the intersection: The effects of racism and sexism on Black rape survivors. *Women & Therapy, 25* (3 & 4), 95-105.

Equal Employment Opportunity Commission (EEOC) (1980). Guidelines and discrimination because of sex (Sec. 1604.11). *Federal register, 45*, 746676-4677.

Fitzgerald, L. F., Buchanan, N. T., Collinsworth, L. C., Magley, V. J., & Ramos, A. M. (1999). Junk logic: The abuse defense in sexual harassment litigation. *Psychology, Public Policy, and Law, 5*, 730-759.

Fitzgerald, L. F., Shullman, S. L., Bailey, N., Richards, M., Swecker, J., Gold, Y., Ormerod, A., & Weitzman, L. (1988). The incidence and dimensions of sexual harassment in academia and the workplace. *Journal of Vocational Behavior, 32*, 152-175.

Fitzgerald, L. F., Swan, S., & Fischer, K. (1995). Why didn't she just report him? The psychological and legal implications of women's responses to sexual harassment. *Journal of Social Issues, 51*, 117-138.

Fitzgerald, L. F., Swan, S., & Magley, V. (1997). But was it really sexual harassment: Psychological, behavioral and legal definitions of sexual harassment. In W. O'Donohue (Ed.), *Sexual harassment: Theory, research, and treatment* (pp. 5-28). New York: Allyn & Bacon.

Gelfand, M. J., Fitzgerald, L. F., & Drasgow, F. (1995). The structure of sexual harassment: A confirmatory analysis across cultures and settings. *Journal of Vocational Behavior, 47*, 164-177.

Glaser, B. G., & Strauss, A. L. (1967). *The discovery of grounded theory: Strategies for qualitative research*. Chicago, IL: Aldine.

Harrick, E. J., & Sullivan, G. M. (1995). Racial harassment: Case characteristics and employer responsibilities. *Employee Responsibilities and Rights Journal, 8*, 81-95.

Jarrett, R. L. (1993). Focus group interviewing with low-income minority populations: A research experience. In D. L. Morgan (Ed.), *Successful focus groups: Advancing the state of the art* (pp. 184-201). Newbury Park, CA: Sage.

Jorgenson, L. M., & Wahl, K. M. (2000). Workplace sexual harassment: Incidence, legal analysis, and the role of the psychiatrist. *Harvard Review of Psychiatry, 8*, 94-98.

Kalof, L., Eby, K. K., Matheson, J., & Kroska, R. J. (2001). The influence of race and gender on student self-reports of sexual harassment by college professors. *Gender & Society, 15*, 282-302.

Koedam, W. S. (2000). Sexual harassment and stalking. In F. W. Kaslow (Ed.), *Handbook of couple and family forensics: A sourcebook for mental health and legal professionals* (pp. 120-141). New York: John Wiley & Sons.

Krueger, R. A. (1994). *Focus groups: A practical guide to applied research.* Thousand Oaks, CA: Sage.

Langhout, R. D., Bergman, M. E., Cortina, L. M., Fitzgerald, L. F., Drasgow, F., & Hunter Williams, J. (1999, April). Women's experiences of sexual harassment: A closer look. In T. M. Glomb (Chair), *Expanding conceptualizations of sexual harassment.* Symposium conducted at the meeting of the Society for Industrial and Organizational Psychology, Atlanta, GA.

MacKinnon, C. A. (1979). *Sexual harassment of working women.* New Haven: Yale University Press.

Madriz, E. (2000). Focus groups in feminist research. In N. K. Denzin & Y. S. Lincoln (Eds.), *Handbook of qualitative research* (pp. 835-850). Thousand Oaks, CA: Sage.

Mansfield, P. K., Koch, P. B., Henderson, J., & Vicary, J. R. (1991). The job climate for women in traditionally male blue-collar occupations. *Sex Roles, 25,* 63-79.

Mays, V. M., Coleman, L. M., & Jackson, J. S. (1996). Perceived race-based discrimination, employment status, and job stress in a national sample of Black women: Implications for health outcomes. *Journal of Occupational Health Psychology, 1,* 319-329.

McKay, N. (1992). Remembering Anita Hill and Clarence Thomas: What really happened when one Black woman spoke out. In T. Morrison (Ed.), *Race-ing justice, engendering power: Essays on Anita Hill, Clarence Thomas, and the construction of social reality* (pp. 269-289). New York: Pantheon Books.

Mecca, S. J., & Rubin, L. J. (1999). Definitional research on African American students and sexual harassment. *Psychology of Women Quarterly, 23,* 813-817.

Meritor Savings Bank v. Vinson, 477 U.S. 57, 40 FEP Cases 1822 (1986).

Morgan, P. (2001). Sexual harassment: Violence against women at work. In C. M. Renzetti, J. L. Edleson, & R. K. Bergen (Eds.), *Sourcebook on violence against women* (pp. 209-226). Thousand Oaks, CA: Sage.

Murrell, A. J. (1996). Sexual harassment and women of color: Issues, challenges, and future directions. In M. S. Stockdale (Ed.), *Sexual harassment in the workplace: Perspectives, frontiers, and response strategies* (pp. 51-66). London: Sage.

Neville, H. A., & Hamer, J. (2001). "We make freedom": An exploration of revolutionary Black feminism. *Journal of Black Studies, 31,* 437-461.

Ormerod, A. J., Bergman, M. E., Palmieri, P. A., Drasgow, F., & Juraska, S. (2001, April). Because of your race: The structure of racial ethnic harassment and discrimination in the military. In F. Drasgow (Chair), *Racial ethnic discrimination and harassment: Methodology, measurement, and results.* Symposium conducted at the annual meeting of the Society of Industrial Organizational Psychologists, San Diego, CA.

Paludi, M. (1996). *Sexual harassment on college campuses: Abusing the ivory power.* Albany: State University of New York Press.

Piotrkowski, C. S. (1998). Gender harassment, job satisfaction, and distress among employed White and minority women. *Journal of Occupational Health Psychology, 3,* 33-43.

Rospenda, K. M., Richman, J. A., & Nawyn, S. J. (1998). Doing power: The confluence of gender, race, and class in contrapower sexual harassment. *Gender & Society, 12,* 40-60.

Rubin, L. J., Hampton, B. R., & McManus, P. W. (1997). Sexual harassment of students by professional psychology educators: A national study. *Sex Roles, 37,* 753-771.

Sbraga, T. P., & O'Donohue, W. (2000). Sexual harassment. *Annual Review of Sex Research, 11,* 258-285.

Scarville, J., Button, S. B., Edwards, J. E., Lancaster, A. R., & Elig, T. W. (1999). *Armed Forces Equal Opportunity Survey* (Report No. 97-027). Arlington, VA: Defense Manpower Data Center. (DTIC/NTIS No. AD A366 037).

Schafran, L. H. (1996). Sexual harassment cases in court, or therapy goes to war: Supporting a sexual harassment victim during litigation. In D. K. Shrier (Ed.), *Sexual harassment in the workplace and academia: Psychiatric issues* (pp. 133-152). Washington, DC: American Psychiatric Press.

Schneider, K. T., Hitlan, R. T., & Radhakrishnan, P. (2000). An examination of the nature and correlates of ethnic harassment experiences in multiple contexts. *Journal of Applied Psychology, 85,* 3-12.

Shelton, J. N., & Chavous, T. M. (1999). Black and White college women's perceptions of sexual harassment. *Sex Roles, 40,* 593-615.

Sherer, A. (1996). Psychiatric assessment: A semistructured interview. In D. K. Shrier (Ed.), *Sexual harassment in the workplace and academia: Psychiatric issues* (pp. 79-94). Washington, DC: American Psychiatric Press.

Shrier, D. K., & Hamilton, J. A. (1996). Therapeutic interventions and resources. In D. K. Shrier (Ed.), *Sexual harassment in the workplace and academia: Psychiatric issues* (pp. 95-112). Washington, DC: American Psychiatric Press.

Strauss, A., & Corbin, J. (1998). *Basics of qualitative research: Techniques and procedures for developing grounded theory.* Thousand Oaks, CA: Sage.

Taylor, J. Y. (2002). Talking back: Research as an act of resistance and healing for African American women survivors of intimate male partner violence. *Women & Therapy, 25* (3 & 4), 145-160.

Valentine, S., Silver, L., & Twigg, N. (1999). Locus of control, job satisfaction, and job complexity: The role of perceived racial discrimination. *Psychological Reports, 84,* 1267-1273.

Vinson V. T. *753 F.2d 141, 36 FEP Cases 1423 (D.C. Cir.* (1985).

West, C. M., Williams, L. M., & Siegel, J. A. (2000). Adult sexual revictimization among Black women sexually abused in childhood: A prospective examination of serious consequences of abuse. *Child Maltreatment, 5,* 49-57.

Wilkinson, S. (1999). Focus groups: A feminist method. *Psychology of Women Quarterly, 23,* 221-245.

Wilson, M., & Russell, K. (1996). *Divided sisters: Bridging the gap between Black women and White women.* New York: Anchor Books.

Winston, J. (1991). Mirror, mirror on the wall: Title VII, Section 1981, and the intersection of race, gender, and the Civil Rights Act of 1990. *California Law Review, 4,* 775-825.

Wyatt, G. E., & Riederle, M. (1994). Sexual harassment and prior sexual trauma among African American and White American women. *Violence and Victims, 9,* 233-247.

Wyatt, G. E., & Riederle, M. (1995). The prevalence and context of sexual harassment among African American and White American women. *Journal of Interpersonal Violence, 10,* 309-321.

Yoder, J. D., & Aniakudo, P. (1995). The responses of African American women firefighters to gender harassment at work. *Sex Roles, 32,* 125-137.

Yoder, J. D., & Aniakudo, P. (1996). When pranks become harassment: The case of African American women firefighters. *Sex Roles, 35,* 253-270.

Yoder, J. D., & Aniakudo, P. (1997). "Outsiders within" the firehouse: Subordination and difference in the social interactions of African American women firefighters. *Gender & Society, 11,* 324-341.

"There's a Stranger in This House": African American Lesbians and Domestic Violence

Amorie Robinson

SUMMARY. Although more researchers are investigating violence in lesbian relationships, they continue to neglect the experiences of African American lesbians. The purpose of this article is to describe the experience of a battered African American lesbian and to offer suggestions for

Amorie Robinson, PhD, is a clinical psychologist and community activist. Much of her volunteer time has been spent conducting support groups, including groups for African American lesbians.

The author wishes to express her sincere appreciation to the women who extended their support and expertise throughout this endeavor: Carita Anderson, Tameka Gillum, Kalimah Johnson, Pamela Reid, and the gracious women who were willing to share their personal stories with her in confidence.

Address correspondence to: Amorie Robinson, PhD, Counseling Associates, Inc., 26699 West Twelve Mile Road, Suite 100, Southfield, MI 48034.

[Haworth co-indexing entry note]: "'There's a Stranger in This House': African American Lesbians and Domestic Violence." Robinson, Amorie. Co-published simultaneously in *Women & Therapy* (The Haworth Press, Inc.) Vol. 25, No. 3/4, 2002, pp. 125-132; and: *Violence in the Lives of Black Women: Battered, Black, and Blue* (ed: Carolyn M. West) The Haworth Press, Inc., 2002, pp. 125-132. Single or multiple copies of this article are available for a fee from The Haworth Document Delivery Service [1-800-HAWORTH, 9:00 a.m. - 5:00 p.m. (EST). E-mail address: getinfo@haworthpressinc.com].

intervention, which include techniques for addressing homophobia, providing appropriate referrals, and culturally sensitive treatment. *[Article copies available for a fee from The Haworth Document Delivery Service: 1-800-HAWORTH. E-mail address: <getinfo@haworthpressinc.com> Website: <http://www. HaworthPress.com> © 2002 by The Haworth Press, Inc. All rights reserved.]*

KEYWORDS. Blacks, African Americans, lesbians, battered women

Our safe space is a very small world. And often, that space only exists at our conscious building and vigilant protection. When lesbians of color can move through the world in peace and safety, it means that lesbians and women of color are living in peace and safety. It benefits us all to change the world. (Campbell, 1991, p. 8)

More researchers are turning their attention to battering in lesbian relationships (Burke & Follingstad, 1999; Kaschak, 2001; Leventhal & Lundy, 1999; West, 2002). However, with few exceptions (Butler, 1999; Goetting, 1999; Russo, 2001; White, 1994), investigators have neglected intimate violence in the lives of African American lesbians. As an African American psychotherapist, who has conducted individual psychotherapy and support groups for African American lesbians, I have worked with many domestic violence survivors. The purpose of this article is to describe the experiences of a battered African American lesbian and to offer suggestions for intervention.

CASE STUDY

Akua (a pseudonym) was a 43-year-old, African American lesbian and mother of two daughters, ages 10 and 14, when she entered therapy for depression and anxiety. She had just terminated a three-year relationship with her abusive partner, Kenyetta (a pseudonym).

The Battering Relationship

The couple maintained separate residences. However, they spent much of their time together at Akua's house with her two daughters. Although the children had developed a positive relationship with Kenyetta, Akua felt anxious when her partner interacted with the girls. She was not *out* to her daughters and feared that they would discover her lesbian relationship. Thus, she spent more time at Kenyetta's apartment, where most of the abuse occurred.

Akua began to feel that "things were not right." For example, it was clear that her partner had a drinking problem. Kenyetta became very angry and critical of Akua, as well as her family members and friends. She demanded that Akua limit her contact with relatives and associates. Eventually, Kenyetta's violence escalated from yelling and humiliating remarks to throwing household items, kicking doors, and punching Akua in the face with a closed fist. Kenyetta also threatened to *out* Akua to her daughters and coworkers. Despite Akua's best efforts to comply with her partner's demands, the cycle of violence continued. After each battering episode, Kenyetta apologized, tried to make amends, and promised that the violence would never happen again. Kenyetta's expressions of regret and remorse were so convincing that Akua forgave her abuse. However, tension often followed these endearing moments, which ultimately led to more violence, usually after Kenyetta had been drinking. Akua felt like "there was a stranger in my house."

In response to the battering, Akua began developing depressive symptoms, including social withdrawal, neglect of hygiene, significant weight gain, and crying spells. Although Akua described her partner as physically stronger, she blamed herself for the violence because she fought back in self-defense. Although she felt trapped, isolated, and alone, Akua was reluctant to leave her partner. Her daughters had a special relationship with Kenyetta, which she did not want to disrupt. In addition, Akua had begun to accept her lesbian identity only one year before she met and fell in love with Kenyetta. Consequently, she was invested in maintaining her first lesbian relationship.

At one point, Akua considered seeking assistance. However, disclosing the abuse would also require her to reveal her lesbian identity. In order to protect her privacy, she considered going outside of the African American community to seek a support group or counselor. However, she feared that mental health professionals in the "White suburbs" would not understand her problems, which would add to her discomfort. Calling the police was not an option. She was embarrassed and believed that the police would scrutinize her and dismiss her claim of woman battering.

Case Analysis and Discussion

Akua's experience is not unique. According to researchers, a substantial number of lesbians, between 30%-40%, have been involved in a physically abusive relationship. This violence often occurs in conjunction with emotional and sexual abuse (Burke & Follingstad, 1999; West, 2002). Equally high rates of lesbian battering have been found across ethnic groups (Turrell, 2000).

Kenyetta's behavior is common among batterers, regardless of attractional orientation. For example, Kenyetta had an alcohol problem. Although alcohol consumption may not cause the abuse, it can facilitate and legitimate intimate partner violence. This is true for lesbian relationships as well (Renzetti, 1998). However, the centrality of bars in the social lives of some lesbians, coupled with societal discrimination, can foster alienation and isolation, which, in turn, may contribute to both heavy drinking and partner violence (West, 1998).

Kenyetta's abuse escalated from verbal abuse to physical violence, followed by apologies and remorse. She also insisted that Akua limit her contact with family members and friends, which was an abuse strategy designed to isolate Akua. Batterers, regardless of attractional orientation, often exhibit this cycle of violence (Renzetti, 1998). However, there are several important differences. Lesbian batterers can use homophobic control as a method of psychological abuse. For example, without the permission of the survivor, an abuser may *out* her partner by revealing her attractional orientation to others, including relatives, employers, and property owners. This form of abuse could result in a variety of negative consequences for the survivor, such as being shunned by family members and the loss of a job or housing (Renzetti, 1998). Kenyetta often threatened to *out* her partner. This form of control was effective because Akua had not revealed her lesbian relationship to her daughters or coworkers.

Like many survivors, Akua felt depressed, afraid, and ashamed. She also felt guilty because she used violence in self-defense. She may have internalized stereotypes about lesbian battering. In same-sex relationships, gender cannot be used to distinguish between the aggressor and victim. Consequently, mental health professionals, researchers, and police have often perceived lesbian battering as an "equal fight" or mutual battering. Lesbians sometimes internalize this myth. Regardless of her motivation for using aggression, a victim may feel guilty for using violence against her partner and, as a result, believe that she is also responsible for the abuse (West, 1998).

The lack of resources makes it especially difficult for Akua and other battered African American lesbians to terminate their abusive relationships. Few social service agencies are equipped to meet the needs of battered lesbians (Leventhal & Lundy, 1999). Shelter staff members may not be responsive to the needs of many oppressed groups, including African Americans and lesbians (Donnelly, Cook, & Wilson, 1999). Furthermore, police officers have a history of being unresponsive to battered African American women, particularly when alcohol is involved in the violent incident (Robinson & Chandek, 2000). As a result, African American lesbians often must contend with homophobia, racism, and sexism when they seek assistance.

SUGGESTIONS FOR INTERVENTION

A positive response from service providers can play a major role in breaking the cycle of violence in lesbian relationships. Based on the available research (Kaschak, 2001; Leventhal & Lundy, 1999; Renzetti, 1998), the following suggestions are offered:

Acknowledge the Problem

Identifying the problem is the first step in motivating members of the lesbian community and service providers to recognize and confront same-sex battering. This requires us to conduct more research on the prevalence of lesbian battering and the characteristics of this form of violence. A special effort should be made to include African Americans and other lesbians of color in this research.

Address Homophobia and Heterosexism

Professionals should be aware of subtle forms of homophobia and heterosexism in their interactions with survivors. Seeking treatment often requires a survivor to reveal both her abuse and attractional orientation. Being identified as a lesbian could jeopardize the survivor's personal, financial, or professional status. African American lesbians, who are also marginalized by racism, may be especially fearful of losing their support systems. Helping professionals can alleviate this fear by referring to the abuser in gender-neutral terms, which indicates an awareness that violence can potentially occur in all relationships. As a result, the survivor may be more willing to reveal the gender of her batterer and feel safe to further discuss her situation. In addition, professionals need to address homophobia and discrimination against lesbians in their agencies by developing written and spoken language that is inclusive of same-sex relationships. It is especially important that agencies that serve African American clients, including religious organizations, be responsive and sensitive to the needs of lesbians.

Provide Appropriate Referrals

Inaccessible and insensitive help sources may hamper a survivor's ability to obtain help. For example, lesbian victims may be reluctant to consult friends or family members who are unaware or disapproving of the victim's lesbian relationship. Therefore, when possible, professionals should refer survivors to services that are designed to meet their needs. These agencies should be prepared to address lesbian battering among African Americans, as well as adolescents, bi-attractional women, and lesbians with substance abuse problems.

Provide Appropriate Treatment

Professionals should question the survivor about a broad range of abuse, including physical abuse, sexual abuse, and emotional abuse. For example, ask the survivor if her partner has ever threatened to reveal her attractional orientation without her permission. Asking about relationship dynamics, such as how the couple resolves conflicts around dependency and power imbalances, may also alert professionals to the presence of psychological abuse.

Service providers should also educate themselves about myths and stereotypes surrounding violence. African American women have historically been stereotyped as angry, aggressive, and domineering. Consequently, service providers may perceive them as mutual combatants and, thus, less deserving of protection (Harrison & Esqueda, 1999). In addition, African American lesbians must often contend with the myth of mutual battering. The violence in lesbian relationships is rarely reciprocal. It is important that service providers distinguish between the aggressor and victim. Like their heteroattractional counterparts, a lesbian victim may be quiet, withdrawn, and embarrassed, particularly if she has defended herself or fought back. Although she may blame herself, further questioning reveals that what appears to be mutual abuse is actually the victim's efforts to secure her personal safety, as opposed to hurting her partner. In addition, she may express concern for her partner's well-being and often continues to assume responsibility for the violence long after the relationship has ended. In contrast, batterers often loudly assert their victimization status, while simultaneously displaying controlling and intrusive behavior. Although they may perceive themselves as partially accountable for the relationship violence, they seldom accept full responsibility. Instead, they blame the victim for provoking the violence (Leventhal & Lundy, 1999; Renzetti & Miley, 1996).

To conclude, African American lesbians demonstrate great courage and resilience (Greene, 2000). With the help of culturally sensitive mental health professionals, they can overcome the challenge of partner violence.

REFERENCES

Burke, L. K., & Follingstad, D. R. (1999). Violence in lesbian and gay relationships: Theory, prevalence, and correlational factors. *Clinical Psychology Review, 19*, 487-512.

Butler, L. (1999). African American lesbians experiencing partner violence. In J. C. McClennen & J. Gunther (Eds.), *A professional's guide to understanding gay and lesbian domestic violence: Understanding practice interventions* (pp. 50-57). Lewiston, NY: Edwin Mellen Press.

Campbell, D. (1991, Spring). Lesbians of color: Between a rock and a hard place. *National Coalition Against Domestic Violence*, 7-12.

Donnelly, D. A., Cook, K. J., & Wilson, L. A. (1999). Provision and exclusion: The dual face of services to battered women in three deep south states. *Violence Against Women, 5*, 710-741.

Goetting, A. (1999). *Getting out: Life stories of women who left abusive men*. New York: Columbia University Press.

Greene, B. (2000). African American lesbians and bisexual women in Feminist-Psychodynamic psychotherapies: Surviving and thriving between a rock and a hard place. In L. C. Jackson & B. Greene (Eds.), *Psychotherapy with African American women: Innovations in psychodynamic perspectives and practice* (pp. 82-125). New York: Guilford Press.

Harrison, L. A., & Esqueda, C. W. (1999). Myths and stereotypes of actors involved in domestic violence: Implications for domestic violence culpability attributions. *Aggression and Violent Behavior, 4*, 129-138.

Kaschak, E. (Ed.) (2001). Intimate betrayal: Domestic violence in lesbian relationships [Special issue]. *Women & Therapy, 23* (3).

Leventhal, B., & Lundy, S. E. (Eds.) (1999). *Same-sex domestic violence: Strategies for change*. Thousand Oaks, CA: Sage.

Renzetti, C. M. (1998). Violence and abuse in lesbian relationships: Theoretical and empirical issues. In R. K. Bergen (Ed.), *Issues in intimate violence* (pp. 117-127). Thousand Oaks, CA: Sage.

Robinson, A. L., & Chandek, M. S. (2000). Differential police response to Black battered women. *Women & Criminal Justice, 12*, 29-61.

Russo, A. (2001). *Taking back our lives: A call to action for the feminist movement.* New York: Routledge.

Turrell, S. C. (2000). A descriptive analysis of same-sex relationship violence for a diverse sample. *Journal of Family Violence, 15,* 281-293.

West, C. M. (2002). Lesbian intimate partner violence: Prevalence and dynamics. *Journal of Lesbian Studies, 6,* 119-125.

West, C. M. (1998). Leaving a second closet: Outing partner violence in same-sex couples. In J. L. Jasinski & L. M. Williams (Eds.), *Partner violence: A comprehensive review of 20 years of research* (pp. 163-183). Thousand Oaks, CA: Sage.

White, E. C. (1994). *Chain, chain, change: For Black women in abusive relationships.* Seattle, WA: Seal Press.

Head and Brain Injuries
Experienced by African American
Women Victims of Intimate Partner Violence

Martha E. Banks
Rosalie J. Ackerman

SUMMARY. Regardless of ethnicity, traumatic brain injury (TBI) is one of the most serious, prevalent, and often undiagnosed results of intimate partner violence. Greater severity of violence, coupled with inadequate health care, places battered African American women at increased risk for head injuries. Accordingly, we review the symptoms associated with head injuries in battered women, with a focus on the experiences of Black women. A case study is used to illustrate rehabilitation and treatment options. Assessment was conducted using the Ackerman-Banks Neuropsychological Rehabilitation Battery. Neuropsychological assessment is recommended, as well as culturally relevant and multidisciplinary treatment strategies that can empower clients. *[Article copies available for a fee from The Haworth Document Delivery Service: 1-800-HAWORTH. E-mail address: <getinfo@haworthpressinc.com> Website: <http://www.HaworthPress. com> © 2002 by The Haworth Press, Inc. All rights reserved.]*

Martha E. Banks, PhD, and Rosalie J. Ackerman, PhD, are affiliated with the Research & Development Division of ABackans DCP, Inc.

Portions of this article were presented at 108th Annual Convention of the American Psychological Association in Washington, DC, August, 2000. The authors contributed equally to the development of this article.

Address correspondence to: Martha Banks, ABackans DCP, Inc., Research Division, 1700 West Market St., Dept. RD 301, Akron, OH 44313.

KEYWORDS. Blacks, head injury, traumatic brain injury, battered women, rehabilitation, neuropsychology

According to recent estimates, at least 1.8 million women are beaten by their intimate partners every year in the United States (Mahoney, Williams, & West, 2001). During the course of these assaults, batterers will often target the woman's head, face, or neck in the form of head-banging, head and shoulder-shaking, and hair pulling (Muelleman, Lenaghan, & Pakeser, 1996). These assaults can result in traumatic brain injury (TBI), one of the most serious and prevalent, but often undiagnosed, consequences of intimate partner violence. Severe violence and lack of health care may place Black women at greater risk for such injuries. In this article, we will give an overview of the symptoms associated with head injuries. A case study will be used to illustrate rehabilitation and treatment options.

HEAD INJURIES IN BATTERED WOMEN

As expected, battered women often report abrasions, lacerations, fractures, and dislocations (Kyriacou et al., 1999). They may also suffer less visible injuries, such as neurological damage, with symptoms including headaches and disorganization. As evidence, when compared to their non-victimized counterparts, battered women were more likely to score in the impaired range on the Halstead-Reitan Neuropsychological Battery and the Quick Neurological Screening Test (Deering, Templer, Keller, & Canfield, 2001). In addition, survivors are at increased risk for head injuries, including TBI as well as subtle head injury, which may not be observable through the use of a CT scan or MRI (Mahon & Elger, 1989). According to O'Neal (1992), subtle brain injury can result in a "... general disruption of the speed, efficiency, execution and integration of mental processes" (p. 5) (see also McAllister et al., 1999). Cognitive and emotional symptoms, which are often associated with headaches and dizziness, can appear weeks or even months after the assault.

Unfortunately, little research has investigated the neuropsychological, physical, and psychological consequences of head and brain injuries in battered women. In a multiethnic sample of 26 residents at a battered women's shelter (38% African American), researchers (Monahan & O'Leary, 1999) discovered that 35% had a history of head trauma. Almost one-half of the survivors reported a loss of consciousness at the time of the injury. The majority of these injuries resulted from being hit in the head with a closed fist.

As expected, head injured women reported symptoms that have been consistently associated with subtle to severe head injury, including somatic complaints, cognitive deficits, and emotional symptoms. This is consistent with the findings of other studies (Banks & Ackerman, 1997; Diaz-Olavarrieta, Campbell, Garcia de al Cadena, Paz, & Villa, 1999). (See Table 1.)

TABLE 1. Possible Symptoms of Head Injury Resulting from Partner Violence

Somatic Complaints
Dizziness–Vertigo
Headaches–Migraines
Seizures
Sleep difficulties
Cognitive Difficulty
Concreteness/Difficulty with abstract thinking
Confusion
Difficulty with concentration
Difficulty following directions
Difficulty retaining information (including therapy tasks)
Disorganization
Inability to initiate self-directed behavior
Inability to resume pretrauma levels of job performance
Memory loss
Mental fatigue
Judgment Difficulty
Difficulty with decision-making
Inaccurate assessment of batterer lethality
Emotional Difficulty
Apathy
Agitation
Depressed mood (sometimes with suicidal tendencies)
Irritability
Low frustration tolerance
Behavior Difficulty
Difficulty with anger management
Changes in personality
Medical History
Delay in seeking treatment
Multiple emergency department visits
Untreated hearing, vision, and concentration problems
Untreated loss of consciousness
Appetite and weight changes
Menstrual changes

Adopted from "Post-assault traumatic brain injury Interview & checklist" by Banks & Ackerman, 1997, Akron, OH: ABackans DCP, Inc. "Domestic violence against patients with chronic neurologic disorders" by Diaz-Olavarrieta et al., 1999, *Archives of Neurology, 56*, 681-685; "Head injury and battered women: An initial inquiry" by K. Monahan & K. D. O'Leary, 1999, *Health and Social Work, 24*, 269-278.

Head Injuries in Black Battered Women

Although little research has focused specifically on head injuries in battered Black women, the results are consistent with previous studies (Monahan & O'Leary, 1999; Muelleman et al., 1996). In a hospital that served predominantly Black, low-income patients, victims of domestic violence were 7.5 times more likely to report head, neck, and facial injuries than other trauma patients (Perciaccante, Ochs, & Dodson, 1999). Such high rates of head trauma may explain why battered Black women report diminished functioning and TBI. In a sample of 64 African American women recruited from Bay Area shelters and programs for battered women, the majority of participants (n = 51) were classified as head injured. When compared to their non-head injured counterparts, they reported greater neuropsychological impairment in the area of information processing. In addition, head injured women were more anxious, depressed, and more likely to experience Posttraumatic Stress Disorder (PTSD) (Oden, 2000).

Regardless of ethnicity, victims can receive multiple head injuries, usually without rehabilitation or adequate healing of brain tissue between injuries (Harrison-Felix et al., 1998). Nevertheless, there are several reasons why researchers should focus on injuries among battered Black women. When compared to other ethnic groups, African American women may experience more severe community and intimate partner violence, such as having weapons used against them (Grisso et al., 1999; Jenkins, 2002 [This volume]). The severity of this violence places African American women at a disproportionate risk for head injuries. This problem was so pervasive that one researcher (Oden, 2000) found that making comparisons between head injured and non-injured women was "complicated by the difficulty in finding battered [Black] women without head injuries" (p. 1864). This is consistent with the clinical experience of the authors.

Moreover, battered Black women often receive inadequate medical care (McNutt, van Ryn, Clark, & Fraiser, 2000). For example, darker skin color can mask bruises and other injuries; as a result, health care providers may fail to document those injuries (White, 1994). The lack of good medical care can have tragic results. If undetected, the symptoms associated with head injuries may go untreated. In addition, head injuries predominated as the most common injury documented in emergency rooms before homicide (Wadman & Muelleman, 1999). Service providers who overlook head injuries may miss an opportunity to intervene and protect women from potentially lethal violence.

IMPLICATIONS FOR THERAPY

Head injuries have grave medical, legal, and, of course, psychological implications for battered women. When observed in counseling sessions, head injured women exhibited difficulty with decision-making, judgment, and abstract thinking. It was especially difficult for them to project into the future and process information. Several of the women discussed how their memory, concentration, and ability to reason had been impaired (Monahan & O'Leary, 1999). Head injuries had compromised their abilities to make informed, consistent decisions about shelter, child care, and safety planning. In addition, those women reported depression and difficulty completing job training, which further hampered their efforts to escape their abusive relationships (Monahan & O'Leary, 1999). Given the extent of intimate partner violence and head injuries, mental health providers need to be equipped to treat these clients.

Neuropsychologically informed psychotherapy is the best approach to use with clients who have sustained head or brain injuries. Whereas most therapeutic models place the impetus for change on the client, neuropsychologically informed psychotherapy involves considerable direction from the therapist. This approach involves application of the client's strengths and weaknesses, as assessed through a neuropsychological evaluation. Such clients are often unable to benefit from perceiving the therapist as a role model, due to their inability to interpret other people's emotions and difficulty using environmental stimuli for accurate problem solving. This might be perceived as poor judgment, unless the therapist understands the client's limited ability to integrate information. Therapists working with victims of intimate partner violence must take on the additional role of protector, frequently assessing and reassessing each client's safety.

Client Example

Jane[1] was a 19-year-old African American mother of a 7-month-old girl when she began treatment with the second author. She lived with her boyfriend, a 24-year-old African American restaurant worker. An emergency room physician, who provided follow-up medical treatment, referred Jane for neuropsychological assessment after she had been injured in a slow speed car accident. Her presenting complaints were chronic pain and short-term memory difficulties.

During the initial interview, Jane reported pain in various parts of her body that were inconsistent with the injuries sustained in the car accident.

When asked about the nature of her relationships, she reported being beaten by her boyfriend of two years. She had been bitten on her arms and neck, and struck with a belt strap, which had left welts on her back. Although there was minimal skin discoloration, the bruises and swelling were quite visible. She also reported having an unwanted child. That interview was the first time that she had ever disclosed the sexual assault that led to her pregnancy.

Jane also reported memory problems, such as "losing my keys . . . [I] can't find them." In addition, she had been fired for failing to show up for work on assigned days. A neuropsychological assessment was performed in order to determine the client's neuropsychological strengths and to develop a multidisciplinary treatment plan. The testing included the *Ackerman-Banks Neuropsychological Rehabilitation Battery* (A-BNRB) (Ackerman & Banks, 1994, 2000), the only comprehensive neuropsychological battery normed on clinical populations that included African American women.

According to the test results, Jane's long-term memory was intact; however, she exhibited difficulties in attention, concentration, and short-term memory. During the evaluation, she had crying spells and exhibited low frustration tolerance. She was easily distracted and had difficulty interpreting other people's emotions. Her affect was flat, and she had minimal vocal inflection. During problem-solving tasks, Jane was disorganized, and her solutions reflected poor judgment, in part because she did not pay attention to details. She exhibited symptoms of organic anxiety and depression, manifested by slow concrete thinking and an impulsive response style. Additional neurological symptoms, which were documented before the accident, included slurred speech, weakness of her left hand (poor grip strength), limping (dragging her left leg), and drooping of the left side of her lip.

Jane had a negative CAT scan immediately following the accident. Despite the recommendations for physical and occupational therapy, the emergency room physician did not refer Jane for comprehensive rehabilitation. Based on the gross imaging technique, rather than the more sensitive neuropsychological evaluation (McAllister et al., 1999; Voller et al., 1999), Jane's physician referred her to individual psychotherapy.

Neuropsychologically informed psychotherapy, with a focus on empowerment (Nabors & Pettee, in press), was conducted for 10 months. During that time, Jane was easily distracted by noises outside the office, such as crying babies and people entering the waiting room. Her mind wandered, she was very disorganized, and she continued to misplace her keys. Jane had difficulty making progress in psychotherapy due to re-injury. As noted, her bruises were evident to the therapist. But, financial dependence (having lost her job) and fear of losing custody of her child made Jane reluctant to leave her abusive relationship.

The primary therapeutic goals were to help Jane develop strategies for pain management and to achieve independence from her abusive partner. In order to provide the client with a focused activity to counteract pain, she was trained in deep muscle relaxation, using diaphragmatic breathing and biofeedback. Jane was able to progress slowly, but experienced setbacks with each re-injury. She was highly motivated to work on relaxation as she reported considerable relief from pain. Jane was able to move from the biofeedback to relaxing on her own. She practiced deep breathing to help relax tense muscles and to decrease the pain in her back and left leg. Jane's process took 10 months.

While relaxed, Jane was able to discuss specific issues concerning the abuse and her relationship with the abuser. The psychotherapeutic process involved having the client tell and retell her concerns about the relationship. She recognized the dangers of remaining in the abusive relationship, but she became anxious when considering her options. Jane's muscles would tighten and her pain would increase during the anxious episodes. However, with the retelling process she was able to associate the pain with the negative aspects of the relationship. By realizing that she could control the pain, Jane was able to consider her options.

Fear of being perceived as an unfit mother made Jane reluctant to use the services of a battered women's shelter. In addition, the majority of the staff and clients at the local shelters were European American women, which added to her reluctance. Family members were willing to provide support for Jane and her child; however, they did not live in the area. Because Jane was impulsive and had difficulty with problem solving, she had not considered moving closer to her family.

The level of violence and fear about leaving were decreased when Jane's abusive partner began another relationship. At that point, her ability to benefit from psychotherapy improved considerably. Jane developed a safety plan for herself and her child. She again contacted family members, made them aware of her situation, and decided to move into a relative's home.

Therapy continued, with a focus on moving and seeking employment. Due to her memory difficulties, a supportive work environment was pursued through the local rehabilitation service. The employer had a commitment to helping battered women reenter the work force. Because the employer was aware of her cognitive difficulties and memory lapses, multiple cues were built into Jane's work, which improved her functioning.

Formal psychotherapy was terminated after employment had been arranged and plans had been made for Jane and her child to move in with relatives. Follow-up involved weekly telephone contacts for one month, biweekly for the next two months, and then occasionally for two years. Within one month of terminating psychotherapy, Jane had successfully moved and started a new job. She continued to use relaxation techniques during the first year post-treatment.

Case Analysis and Discussion

Jane's overall constellation of symptoms was not consistent with the injuries from the car accident.[2] Her symptoms were similar to those exhibited by people diagnosed with PTSD, generalized anxiety disorders, and attention disorders. The difference between the symptoms of those psychologically-based disorders and neurologically-based disorders is the awareness of physical injury involving the head, and therefore the brain, and the lack of response to traditional psychotherapy.

It is common for African American women to be overlooked as candidates for cognitive and motor sensory rehabilitation (Asbury, Walker, Belgrave, Maholmes, & Green, 1994; Banks, Ackerman, & Corbett, 1995; Uswatte & Elliott, 1997). Ideally, Jane would have been treated by a multidisciplinary staff: a neurologist to further assess her left-sided weakness; a physiatrist to oversee physical rehabilitation; a neuropsychologically informed rehabilitation psychologist to address cognitive difficulties; an occupational therapist for improving job skills; a psychotherapist to deal with anxiety and depression; a physical therapist to address left-sided weakness and gait problems; a speech therapist to help with short-term memory and slurred speech; a social worker to deal with living options; and a vocational counselor for job placement (Ackerman & Banks, in press; Malec & Basford, 1996). In addition, if medication were needed, referral to a psychiatrist, who was sensitive to neurological problems, would have been appropriate.

Because Jane's mind wandered and she continued to misplace her keys, therapists could perceive such a client as uncooperative and noncompliant. However, this behavior can reflect memory problems, the inability to learn new approaches to problems, and/or re-injury due to continued physical abuse. Therapists must be aware of these symptoms. In addition, Jane might be misdiagnosed as having borderline intellectual skills, rather than dementia resulting from repeated beatings. With this misdiagnosis, parenting issues could be brought to the attention of social workers, which could result in loss of custody, a fear that Jane had expressed. Her fear certainly was justified. Increasing numbers of Black battered women are losing their children when social service agencies suspect that their children have been exposed to violence (Johnson, 1998). Additionally, Jane was reluctant to use the services of a battered women's shelter. Shelter staff members are not always responsive to the needs of oppressed groups, including African American women, lesbians, and mentally ill clients (Donnelly, Cook, & Wilson, 1999).

Jane's experiences are consistent with previous research that indicates that head injured battered women have greater difficulty making informed, consistent decisions about shelter, child care, and safety planning (Monahan & O'Leary, 1999). It should be noted that Jane was in therapy for 10 months before completion and follow-up care. In contrast, clients without re-injury generally completed similar therapy in four months. More time was required before Jane could begin making informed, consistent decisions, and enacting the necessary steps to accomplish her plans.

CONCLUSION

Intimate partners will batter substantial numbers of African American women. In this article, we have described the impact of head injuries sustained by these women and provided recommendations for treatment. We suggest conducting neuropsychological assessments with survivors of intimate partner violence (Voller, Auff, Schnider, & Aichner, 2001). Neuropsychological assessment should lead to culturally relevant and sensitive multidisciplinary treatment strategies that help empower clients.

NOTES

1. A pseudonym is used to protect the identity of the client.
2. When similar physical asymmetry is observed in older people, they are usually assessed for strokes. It is appropriate to assess younger people, especially African American women, with such asymmetry for neurological disorders, including strokes.

REFERENCES

Ackerman, R. J., & Banks, M. E. (in press). Assessment, treatment, and rehabilitation for interpersonal violence victims: Women sustaining head injuries. *Women & Therapy*.
Ackerman, R. J., & Banks, M. E. (1994, 2000). *Ackerman-Banks Neuropsychological Rehabilitation Battery.* © Akron, OH: ABackans DCP, Inc.

Asbury, C. A., Walker, S., Belgrave, F. Z., Maholmes, V., & Green, L. (1994). Psychosocial cultural and accessibility factors associated with participation of African Americans in rehabilitation. *Rehabilitation Psychology, 39,* 113-121.

Banks, M. E., & Ackerman, R. J. (1997). *Post-assault traumatic brain injury interview & checklist.* Akron, OH: ABackans DCP, Inc.

Banks, M. E., Ackerman, R. J., & Corbett, C. A. (1995). Feminist neuropsychology: Issues for physically challenged women. In J. Chrisler & A. Hemstreet (Eds.), *Variations on a theme: Diversity and the psychology of women* (pp. 29-49). Albany: State University of New York Press.

Deering, C., Templer, D. I., Keller, J., & Canfield, M. (2001). Neuropsychological assessment of battered women: A pilot study. *Perceptual and Motor Skills, 92,* 682-686.

Diaz-Olavarrieta, C., Campbell, J., Garcia de la Cadena, C., Paz, F., & Villa, A. R. (1999). Domestic violence against patients with chronic neurologic disorders. *Archives of Neurology, 56,* 681-685.

Donnelly, D. A., Cook, K. J., & Wilson, L. A. (1999). Provision and exclusion: The dual face of services to battered women in three deep south states. *Violence Against Women, 5,* 710-741.

Grisso, J. A., Schwarz, D. F., Hirschinger, N., Sammel, M., Brensinger, C., Santanna, J., Lowe, R. A., Anderson, E., Shaw, L. M., Bethel, C. A., & Teeple, L. (1999, December 16). Violent injuries among women in an urban area. *New England Journal of Medicine, 25,* 1899-1905.

Harrison-Felix, C., Zafonte, R., Mann, N., Dijkers, M., Englander, J., & Kreutzer, J. (1998). Brain injury as a result of violence: Preliminary findings from the Traumatic Brain Injury Model Systems. *Archives of Physical Medicine and Rehabilitation, 79,* 730-737.

Jenkins, E. J. (2002). Black women and community violence: Trauma, grief, and coping. *Women & Therapy, 25* (3 & 4), 29-44.

Johnson, L. D. (1998). Caught in the crossfire: Examining legislative and judicial response to the forgotten victims of domestic violence. *Law and Psychology Review, 22,* 271-286.

Kyriacou, D. N., Angulin, D., Taliaferro, E., Stone, S., Tubb, T., Linden, J. A., Muelleman, R., Barton, E., & Kraus, J. F. (1999). Risk factors for injury to women from domestic violence against women. *New England Journal of Medicine, 16, 341,* 1892-1898.

Mahon, D., & Elger, C. (1989). Analysis of posttraumatic syndrome following a middle head injury. *Journal of Neuroscience Nursing, 21,* 382-384.

Mahoney, P., Williams, L. M., & West, C. M. (2001). Violence against women by intimate relationship partners. In C. M. Renzetti, J. L. Edleson, & R. K. Bergen (Eds.), *Sourcebook on violence against women* (pp. 143-178). Thousand Oaks, CA: Sage.

Malec, J. F., & Basford, J. S. (1996). Postacute brain injury rehabilitation. *Archives of Physical Medicine & Rehabilitation, 77,* 149-207.

McAllister, T. W., Saykin, A. J., Flashman, L. A., Sparling, M. B., Johnson, S. C., Guerin, S. J., Mamourian, A. C., Weaver, J. B., & Yanofsky, N. (1999). Brain activation during working memory 1 month after mild traumatic brain injury: A functional MRI study. *Neurology, 53,* 1300-1308.

McNutt, L., van Ryn, M., Clark, C., & Fraiser, I. (2000). Partner violence and medical encounters: African American women's perspectives. *American Journal of Preventive Medicine, 19,* 264-269.

Monahan, K., & O'Leary, K. D. (1999). Head injury and battered women: An initial inquiry. *Health & Social Work, 24,* 269-278.

Muelleman, R. A., Lenaghan, P. A., & Pakeser, R. A. (1996). Battered women: Injury locations and types. *Annals of Emergency Medicine, 28,* 486-492.

Nabors, N. A., & Pettee, M. F. (in press). Womanist therapy with African American women with disabilities. *Women & Therapy.*

Oden, T. M. (2000). Insult denied: Traumatic brain injury in battered African American Women. *Dissertation Abstracts International, 61*(04), DAI-B (UMI no. 9968071).

O'Neal, J. (1992). Toward a more precise definition of subtle brain injury. *Headlines, 3,* 5.

Perciaccante, V. J., Ochs, H. A., & Dodson, T. B. (1999). Head, neck, and facial injuries as markers of domestic violence. *Journal of Oral Maxillofac Surgery, 57,* 760-762.

Uswatte, G., & Elliott, T. R. (1997). Ethnic and minority issues in rehabilitation psychology. *Rehabilitation Psychology, 42,* 61-71.

Voller, B., Auff, E., Schnider, P., & Aichner, F. (2001). To do or not to do? Magnetic resonance imaging in mild traumatic brain injury. *Brian Injury, 15,* 107-115.

Voller, B., Benke, T., Benedetto, K., Schnider, P., Auff, E., & Aichner, F. (1999). Neuropsychological, MRI and EEG findings after very mild traumatic brain injury. *Brain Injury, 13,* 821-827.

Wadman, M. C., & Muelleman, R. L. (1999). Domestic violence homicides: ED use before victimization. *American Journal of Emergency Medicine, 17,* 689-691.

White, E. C. (1994). *Chain, chain, change: For Black women in abusive relationships.* Seattle, WA: Seal Press.

BREAKING SILENCE: ACTIVISM AND HEALING

Talking Back: Research as an Act of Resistance and Healing for African American Women Survivors of Intimate Male Partner Violence

Janette Y. Taylor

Janette Y. Taylor is Assistant Professor in the College of Nursing, University of Iowa. She received both her PhD in Nursing Science and the graduate certificate in Women's Studies from the University of Washington-Seattle. Dr. Taylor is certified as a Women's Health Care Nurse Practitioner. Her research interests are in women's health. Her current research focuses on resilience and recovering among African American women survivors of intimate male partner abuse, as well as on incarcerated abused women.

This research was supported by Women's Health Nursing Research Training Grant NINR T3NR07039, NRSA from NINR 5F31NR0718702, Nurses Educational Fund, Inc., Sigma Theta Tau, Psi Chapter-at-Large and Hester McLaws Award, University of Washington School of Nursing, Seattle, WA. Special thanks to the women who shared their testimonies.

Address correspondence to: Janette Y. Taylor, College of Nursing, The University of Iowa, Iowa City, IA 52242 (E-mail: janette-taylor@uiowa.edu).

[Haworth co-indexing entry note]: "Talking Back: Research as an Act of Resistance and Healing for African American Women Survivors of Intimate Male Partner Violence." Taylor, Janette Y. Co-published simultaneously in *Women & Therapy* (The Haworth Press, Inc.) Vol. 25, No. 3/4, 2002, pp. 145-160; and: *Violence in the Lives of Black Women: Battered, Black, and Blue* (ed: Carolyn M. West) The Haworth Press, Inc., 2002, pp. 145-160. Single or multiple copies of this article are available for a fee from The Haworth Document Delivery Service [1-800-HAWORTH, 9:00 a.m. - 5:00 p.m. (EST). E-mail address: getinfo@haworthpressinc.com].

145

SUMMARY. The purpose of this article is to use a Black feminist/
womanist framework to: (a) explore the historical factors that discourage
Black women's participation in the research process; (b) demonstrate how
research can be a potential avenue of resistance and healing for African
American women survivors of intimate male partner violence; and
(c) suggest ways for practitioners and researchers to encourage the participation of this population. Benefits from the research process emerged
as three themes: (a) healing the self, (b) helping others, and (c) envisioning new life directions. *[Article copies available for a fee from The Haworth
Document Delivery Service: 1-800-HAWORTH. E-mail address: <getinfo@
haworthpressinc.com> Website: <http://www.HaworthPress.com> © 2002 by
The Haworth Press, Inc. All rights reserved.]*

KEYWORDS. Blacks, battered women, interviews, ethics

Moving from silence into speech is for the oppressed, the colo-
nized, the exploited, and those who stand and struggle side by side
a gesture of defiance that heals, that makes new life and new
growth possible. It is that act of speech, of "talking back," that is
no mere gesture of empty words, that is the expression of our
movement from object to subject–the liberated voice. (hooks,
1989, p. 9)

Scholars and practitioners, including therapists, nurses, and shelter
workers, are often collaborative partners on research projects pertaining
to violence in the lives of women. Although all these professionals are
committed to reducing the victimization of women, working together
toward this goal can be challenging (Riger, 1999). Based on a national
survey, practitioners were especially concerned about the ethical treatment of survivors. Specifically, they feared that researchers lacked understanding of, and empathy for, the plight of the survivors. Concerns
about re-victimization made some practitioners in this study reluctant to
facilitate victim involvement in the research process (National Violence
Against Women Prevention Research Center, 2001).

In response, scholars have documented the therapeutic value of research performed through interviews, focus groups, descriptive research with the completion of questionnaires, and interviews on
sensitive topics. Participants may receive a variety of benefits from
their involvement in the research process, including catharsis, self-ac-

knowledgement, a sense of purpose, self-awareness, empowerment, and healing. In addition, research can offer a voice to disenfranchised participants (Banks-Wallace, 1998; Hutchinson, Wilson, & Wilson, 1994; Kavanaugh & Ayres, 1998).

Although diverse populations can potentially benefit from the research process, African American women have been especially reluctant to participate. Moreover, little is known about the potential benefits of this process for Black women. Having this information may encourage a collaborative relationship between practitioners and researchers, which can increase Black women's participation in research endeavors. Accordingly, the purpose of this paper is to use a Black feminist/womanist framework to: (a) explore the historical factors that discourage Black women's participation; (b) demonstrate how research can be a potential avenue of resistance and healing for African American women survivors of intimate male partner violence; and (c) offer strategies to increase African American women's participation in the research process.

HISTORICAL OVERVIEW

African Americans continue to be mistrusting and suspicious of public health prevention programs and government sponsored health research (Earl & Penney, 2001; Shavers-Hornaday, Lynch, Burmeister, & Torner, 1997). For example, Freedman (1998) interviewed Black women about their health-illness beliefs and values. One participant articulated lingering concerns about oppressive medical research practices when she commented, "As black people, we become the guinea pig for white people" (p. 945). In addition to feeling like disposable objects, rather than valued collaborators in the process, many participants feel exploited. These feelings are justifiable because some researchers have abandoned projects or communities after grant funding ended (Fontes, 1998).

In order to understand why African American women are keenly aware of the coercive and one-sided nature of scientific and medical research, and thus avoid participation, we must first review their long history as subjects of pseudo-scientific research. In the early nineteenth century, European natural scientists attempted to distinguish and rank various racial differences. George Cuvier, a prominent naturalist, determined that Saartjie (Sarah) Bartman, an African woman from the Kung tribe of Bushmen, was a model specimen to illustrate his claims of racial inferiority. She was called the "Hottentot Venus" and displayed for public amusement. Strangers ridiculed her prominent Africanoid features and physically molested her buttocks and genitalia. After Sarah Bartman's death, her mummified body, skull, skeleton, and disembodied vagina were preserved in a specimen jar and displayed at various museums (Byrd & Clayton, 2000; Sharpley-Whiting, 1999).

During slavery in the antebellum South, Black women continued to be forced participants in scientific experiments. Many of these procedures attempted to manipulate Black women's reproductive capacity. For example, some owners engaged in slave breeding, which was an experimental selective process that forced enslaved women and men to reproduce for the purpose of creating efficient workers (Roberts, 1997). Physicians were also more agreeable towards the use of novel procedures on enslaved women; consequently, the medical establishment also exploited Black women. J. Marion Sims, a noted surgeon and *Father of Modern Gynecology*, performed surgery on 30 enslaved women. Over the course of four years, some of these women endured multiple operations before he successfully perfected a method to repair vesicovaginal fistulas, which are openings and tears in the vaginal wall that allow a continuous slow leakage of urine from the bladder into the vagina. Likewise, early surgical techniques involving Cesarean section-birth used Black women as objects of experimentation (Axelsen, 1985; Byrd & Clayton, 2000). Although enslaved Black women contributed to scientific advancement in a variety of ways, there were vast differences between the benefits received by the scientist and the subject. As Savitt (1978) noted, "Usually the end result was notoriety for the physician and anonymity or oblivion for the patient" (p. 293).

Perhaps the most memorable and widely publicized experiment is the Tuskegee study, which lasted from 1932 to 1972. During this 40-year period, the United States Public Health Service withheld treatment from 400 impoverished African American men diagnosed with syphilis. According to physicians, the purpose of the experiment was to learn more about the progression of the disease which, in its later stages, is characterized by blindness, paralysis, and damage to the cardiovascular and central nervous system. This study was particularly unethical because the medical community knew the complications associated with the disease *before* the study was conducted (Jones, 1993).

Little research has focused on the African American women and children, the invisible victims of this experiment. Based on limited knowledge, researchers confirmed that family members were sick as well. At least 50 unnamed women and children contracted syphilis from the untreated men. Their needs were ignored until 1975 when the government approved treatment for 27 wives who tested positive for syphilis and 17 children and 2 grandchildren with congenital syphilis (Gamble, 1997). Ironically, Eunice Rivers, a Black nurse who cared for the dying men, became the focus of ethical dilemmas raised by the experiment. Long after her death, researchers continue to ask why she, the least powerful person in the medical community, did not actively work to stop the exploitation of her patients (Hammonds, 1994). In addition, the Tuskegee study continues to be a powerful metaphor within the Black community because it represents participants' vulnerability and the medical community's disregard for African Americans. Even today, knowledge of this study is associated with greater mistrust of medical researchers and reluctance to participate in medical research (Earl & Penney, 2001; Shavers, Lynch, & Burmeister, 2001).

Medical and scientific research continues to flourish in an atmosphere that promotes racism and the use of underprivileged and disadvantaged groups as specimens and subjects (Byrd & Clayton, 2000). For example, during the 1970s forced sterilization of African American women via unnecessary hysterectomies was common practice. Although the practice was performed across the country, these procedures were so common in the South that they were referred to as *Mississippi appendectomies*. More recently, long-acting contraceptives, such as Norplant and Depo-Provera, have been used to control the reproduction of poor women of color, particularly those who are drug addicted (Roberts, 1997).

TALKING BACK: SILENCE, RESISTANCE, AND HEALING

Community members and leaders often fear that research findings will be misinterpreted or used to reinforce negative images of African Americans. In response to these concerns, a "political gag order" has been imposed, which discourages survivors from discussing their victimization with community outsiders. Discussing her experience as a rape survivor, Pierce-Baker (1998) writes:

> Black women have survived by keeping quiet not solely out of shame, but out of a need to preserve the race and its image. In our attempts to preserve racial pride, we black women have often sacrificed our own souls. (p. 84)

However, remaining silent neither secures safety nor promotes health and well-being. Instead, silence is a betrayal of the self that steals vitality and life (Lorde, 1984). Ultimately, this silence impedes research efforts (Crenshaw, 1994; West, C. M., 2002).

Although it has not been safe for Black women to speak, they have a long history of breaking silence around their victimization. According to Black feminist scholars, marginalized individuals have learned to express their resistance in a narrative form of opposition. Commonly referred to as *talking back* or *back talk*, this form of speech occurs when individuals engage in ". . . speaking as equal to an authority figure. It meant daring to disagree and sometimes it just meant having an opinion" (hooks, 1989, p. 5).

Historically, Black women have been denied access to academic institutions and the media. As a result, they had developed other methods for disseminating their oppositional speech (Collins, 2000). Talking back often occurs in the form of testimony, defined as ". . . to bear witness, to bring forth, to claim and proclaim oneself as an intrinsic part of the world. The act of testifying or giving testimony has deep roots in African American history, reaching back to slavery (and before)" (p. 2). The expressive act of testimony is a way to connect with one's Creator, humanity, history, and community. It is through testimony that African American women renew themselves by sharing portions of their lives that were often kept silenced and hidden (Cody, 2001; Gates, 1991; West, T. C., 1999). This knowledge, for example, how to keep oneself safe from sexual abuse, is then passed from generation to generation along with memories of other racial traumas (Daniel, 2000).

Although bearing witness or testifying can be healing, it can also be dangerous for Black women to engage in public oppositional talk. Consequently, Black women had to develop more subtle and safe ways to convey their reality. On the surface, their narratives often conform to dominant cultural language, but deeper analysis reveals a discourse of stories that emphasizes their resistance and resilience (Etter-Lewis, 1993; King, 1998). These stories are analogous to Black women's hair texture:

> Like permed or color treated hair, the texture of their narratives is often different above and below the surface. Above the surface, there is acceptable public appearance (e.g., straight hair/"standard language"), but close to the root/core is a more natural and appealing form (e.g., nappy hair/the language of resistance that sometimes is disguised or hidden). (Etter-Lewis, 1993, p. 155)

The word *nappy* refers to the natural texture of many African American women's hair. Nappy hair, in its natural state, is very curly, voluminous, strong, and far more resilient than chemically treated hair. Natural hair is often chemically treated (e.g., relaxed or permed) to straighten it so that it adheres to Euro-American standards of beauty (Bonner, 1990; Ferrell, 1993). The goal of using chemicals is to suppress the natural state of the hair and to socialize it to conform to an acceptable standard. African American hair, much like the women, is oppressed as well as pressed to conform (e.g., by a hot iron or daily living). However, when the new growth of hair appears, it is untreated, with a fuller texture and strength. It is referred to as "nappy at the root" and can be thought of as a site of resistance. Natural hair represents "tenacity, resilience and creativity of people of African descent" (Nelson, 1998, p. A-31). Similar to their hair structure, the narratives of African American women must be listened to and analyzed in ways that connect with their deeper symbolic meaning.

In order to understand African American women's participation in clinical studies, therapists and scholars must go beyond the surface and explore how Black survivors perceive the research process. The following questions need to be addressed: Considering their history of scientific exploitation, why do African American victim-survivors of domestic violence participate in the research process? What benefits do they receive from their involvement? How can practitioners and researchers work together to encourage Black women's participation, while protecting them from exploitation? Information presented in this paper is based on a larger study, which focused on the resilience-recovery experience of 21 African American survivors of intimate male partner violence (Taylor, 2002 [This volume]).

METHOD

Sample

A purposive sample of 21 African American women was recruited. The women lived in Snohomish, Pierce, and King counties in Washington state. In order to be included in the study, the woman had to be a self-identified African American survivor of intimate male partner abuse by an African American male partner or male partner of color. The women were between the ages of 24 and 70, with a mean age of 39. The length of recovery ranged from 6 months to 21 years, with a mean of 6 years. With the exception of 3 women, all of the participants had a high school diploma or GED. A majority of the women (81%) were employed outside the home. The participants' gross annual income ranged from $4,000 to $52,000, with a median income of $20,500. Two-thirds of the women were the primary caretakers of their children. Although the women were extremely busy working and taking care of their families, they were willing to set aside time to participate in the research process. Interviews took place in their residences, workplace, or a public location, such as a library, shopping mall, YWCA, or restaurant. Safety, comfort, privacy, and convenience were factors that influenced the women's selections of meeting places.

Data Collection and Analyses

Interview narratives were gathered through an in-depth semi-structured guided interview format (Mishler, 1986; Spradley, 1979). Each woman had an opportunity to be interviewed over two sessions. The purpose of the first interview was to gather information about resiliency and recovery. The second interview provided an opportunity for the women to verify and validate my interpretation of their stories and emerging themes. At the end of the interview, each woman was asked, "How do you feel right now about telling your story?" All the interviews were audiotaped and transcribed verbatim onto computer diskettes. Field notes, taken after interviews or during field observations, were also transcribed onto computer diskettes. The data were retrieved, coded, and systematically organized according to patterns and themes. Data analysis was modeled after Spradley's (1979) ethnographic research methodology. The ethnographer uses qualitative content analysis to inductively derive themes or patterns from the data. Themes were carefully extracted through the process of logical analysis of content from all data sources.

This study was a womanist ethnographic investigation. A significant feature of this methodology is the consideration of how concepts, such as race, class, and gender, produce material consequences in the lives of African American women. One goal of womanist ethnographic research is to discover the cultural knowledge African American women use to organize their behavior and to interpret their experiences. The overall approach to a womanist-centered data analysis is to examine the interview narratives, which are personal testimonies, and frame them within a larger social context (Banks-Wallace, 2000; Neville & Hamer, 2001; Taylor, 1998).

RESULTS

The women were introspective and reflective as they provided additional information about themselves. They disclosed the therapeutic value of the interview and research process and how they benefited from participation. The benefits emerged as three themes: (a) healing the self; (b) helping others; and (c) envisioning new life directions.

Healing the Self

In the initial interview, women reviewed their lives and focused on their previous and current abilities to effectively navigate barriers and to cultivate opportunities. This occasion to explore their lives felt like a healing space within the context of the interview process. One survivor commented:

> I think that since I have spoken with [you] about being a survivor of domestic violence, that has helped me to grow as a person . . . since I spoke with you a couple of months back, it has really started me on a real healing path . . . I think this interview alone has helped. (age 38, recovering 8 years)

Women expressed a range of emotions about themselves and the courses of their lives. Several women were engaged in a continued struggle to overcome feelings of shame and sadness. However, they felt a sense of relief (or release) when sharing their stories. For many participants, the therapeutic part of the interview process was the freedom to talk without fear of judgment. This helped them to move past their shame. The women valued the presence of an empathic listener, as well as an opportunity to provide information through the interviews.

> When talking about it, you get it out. It makes you feel better . . . Because sometimes things happen to you—you feel ashamed to explain it to [another person], but after you get it out, you're glad you got it out. And I feel that way now. I'm glad that I told you these things. (age 70, recovering 17 years and 11 months)

For several participants, talking about experiences of abuse and violence was similar to offering a testimonial. Several of the participants used the word *testimony* to define their interview experience. For example, in the initial interview, one participant explained why she wanted to be in this study and how she conceptualized talking about her past experiences: "In church they say you overcome by testimonies. So when I go and share [my story of abuse and drug use], it doesn't have power over me any more" (age 38, recovering 1 year). During the second interview, she commented further on the meaning of testimony: "What it means is how you are living today and how you've overcome. Every time you share [your story], it breaks it down [and] makes it more real. You are hearing yourself. People listen when you have lived it." Testimony is a vehicle by which women share their stories and perform self-healing, affirmation, and empowerment. As noted, when "You are hearing yourself," it is self-affirming and heightens awareness of the woman's personal power and the ability to shape her world via self-activity. Likewise, the testifier provides a living example that can facilitate the healing of others.

Helping Others

Many of the African American women who volunteered to participate in this research study made introductory statements similar to the following: "If my story will help, yes, I'd like to talk with the interviewer or researcher." These women wanted to contribute to the understanding of African American women's experiences with intimate male partner violence. This was an opportunity to talk to and reach a wider audience. In addition, the interview served as a pivotal event that supported some women's readiness to engage in activities which advocate for other victim-survivors of intimate male violence: "It [the interview] has helped me to be able to tell other women [and to] work in a community-based clinic" (age 47, recovering 12 years and 1 month).

The women who participated in the study viewed themselves as part of the broader African American society and, as such, were responsible for each other. This sense of connectedness fostered feelings of social responsibility that supported their efforts to speak out, talk back, and participate in telling their stories via research interviews. They wanted to expose, inform, and spark other women's consciousness about violence in the lives of Black women. The participants appeared comfortable with self-disclosure, especially because it provided information that was potentially helpful to other women. This desire to help others has been echoed in interviews with other battered Black women (Goetting, 1999).

Envisioning New Life Directions

In addition to its therapeutic value, the interview process was an opportunity for the women to experience further self-discovery and to
clarify personal areas for future growth:

> I noticed that I shared a little bit more [information] even now than
> I have [shared in the past]. And I don't talk; I don't deal a lot with
> the rape. I think I'm going [to] ponder that a little bit more now. It
> might determine what kind of group I go to, 'cause maybe I don't
> need a domestic violence support group. I might just need a single
> parent group or maybe a group for women survivors of sexual
> abuse. (age 32, recovering 6 months)

For other participants, the interview process was a consciousness
raising experience. This interaction was a safe space for new personal
insights to emerge and a chance for some women to consider further
challenges in their lives. These insights were an unexpected, but pleasant, outcome of talking to the researcher. In general, the women fin-
ished the interview process feeling self-affirmed. Several participants also
expressed an appreciation for the methodology that moved the research experience away from the popular impression of traditional research methods
(e.g., sterile, distant, oppressive). One woman commented, "This has
been a very good experience because I feel you did it in a very professional way, very talented and very creative . . ."

IMPLICATIONS FOR PRACTICE

Although the research outcomes presented here are limited by the
small sample size and geographic homogeneity of the participants, the interviews yielded significant insights. Despite a long history of scientific
oppression, Black women are willing research participants, particularly
when the study is conducted in a culturally sensitive manner. Moreover,
the process can be empowering, therapeutic, and a method for healing
themselves, helping others, and envisioning new life directions.

When considering the limited knowledge regarding violence in the
lives of Black women, it is imperative that we include these women in
the research process and use appropriate methodologies to interpret the
results. The following suggestions are based on previous research
(Brzuzy, Ault, & Segal, 1997; Fontes, 1998; Massat & Lundy, 1997),

findings from this study, recommendations of the participants, and my own experience during the process.

Enhancing Individual-Community Willingness to Participate

Historical traumas, such as the Tuskegee experiment, are deeply engrained in the collective memories of African Americans. In order to recruit participants successfully, practitioners and researchers need to acknowledge this history. They also need to develop ways to reduce suspicion and to restore trust in researchers and the scientific process (Earl & Penney, 2001; Shavers et al., 2001). This requires a sustained and ongoing presence in the community at various neighborhood fairs, churches, and other ethnic events. When appropriate, the professional can include family members and friends in such activities. The extended involvement demonstrates a greater level of commitment and provides an additional context in which to view the researcher (Freedman, 1998). For one year prior to collecting data, I attended several survivor support groups and co-facilitated another group.

Results of a study can be briefly described and presented in newsletters, which can be mailed to households in diverse communities. Likewise, results can be placed in local newspapers and presented as public service announcements on ethnic radio stations. These actions reflect the researchers' willingness to share their knowledge with the larger community (Fontes, 1998). The women in this study were offered copies of the transcribed interviews and copies of the dissertation, and were invited to the dissertation defense, which is a public presentation of the results. Several women eagerly accepted all invitations.

Using Language to Access Knowledge Claims

We can use language that draws on Black women's cultural experiences. A womanist epistemology values concrete experience and the use of dialogue in assessing knowledge claims (Collins, 2000). Therefore, the use of testimonials and bearing witness is congruent with African American women's ways of knowing. Testimony or bearing witness shifts the focus and power from the researcher to the individual and allows her to speak to the collective and in a collective mode. The use of such language symbolically represents a deeper interest in the subject matter and may enhance the quality of the narrative data collected (Tarpley, 1995). Based on feedback from sessions with the women, I changed my recruitment flyers. The bold and centered first line at the top of the flyers was changed from "Tell Your Story" to "A Call to Witness."

Involve Participants in the Research Process

When a project is being conceptualized, investigators should invite community members and leaders to discuss how partner violence can best be defined and measured in their community. Focus groups are an effective way to gather this information (Buchanan & Ormerod, 2002 [This volume]; Morgan, 1997). Integrated research teams should also include Black feminists, who can help interpret the research findings. Researchers explain the importance of this strategy by writing, "Because the principal investigator and other authors of this article are upper-middle class White female feminists, we chose to collaborate with Black feminist women to aid in understanding and interpreting the Black women's experiences with abuse" (Moss, Pitula, Campbell, & Halstead, 1997, p. 434). African American researchers and activists should participate in the data collection as well. For example, they can accompany the researcher to community events, make introductions, and explain the research process and benefits to potential participants (Freedman, 1998).

When working with survivors, researchers and practitioners should develop a safety protocol. For example, they should develop procedures for contacting participants, conducting interviews, and maintaining confidentiality (Langford, 2000). It is also important to be respectful of survivors and their communities. A community leader can act as a conduit between the investigator and participants, which can help build trust. This may minimize participants' concerns about disclosing personal information or airing "dirty laundry" to community outsiders.

Having interviewers or group leaders who match pertinent demographic variables of the participants can make the project more attractive. The recruitment flyer for this study underwent an additional change to read, "African American nurse researcher seeks African American women survivors of domestic violence to participate in a study." Once the flyers were altered, more women were eager to participate. One survivor explained that the first flyer led her to believe that the study was being conducted by a White researcher "who wants to come to our community and get into our business!" However, it should not be assumed that all Black researchers would establish immediate rapport with Black participants. Although race and gender may be unifying issues, social class and skin color differences can still pose barriers (Johnson-Bailey, 1999).

CONCLUSION

For many African American women survivors in this study, participating in this research project was a symbolic way of talking back to the men who abused them and to social structures that attempt to maintain them in positions of silence and subjugation. Participation in narrative research about violence is a less visible form of political activism, yet an equally important form of resistance, particularly in light of historical and contemporary scientific exploitation. As practitioners and researchers, we must continue to ask ourselves: How do we help marginalized women bear witness to the violence in their lives? How can we create spaces for them to speak and heal, while contributing to the desperately needed knowledge about their lives and health? As we seek answers to such questions, we must consider how and why marginalized people's research participation is truly a movement "from silence into speech . . . that is the expression of our movement from object to subject–the liberated voice" (hooks, 1989, p. 9). Such involvement is an act of healing that benefits individuals, communities, and the research process.

REFERENCES

Axelsen, D. E. (1985). Women as victims of medical experimentation: J Marion Sims' surgery on slave women, 1845-1850. *Sage: A Scholarly Journal of Black Women, 2*, 10-13.

Banks-Wallace, J. (1998). Emancipatory potential of storytelling in a group. *Image: Journal of Nursing Scholarship, 30*, 17-21.

Banks-Wallace, J. (2000). Womanist ways of knowing: Theoretical considerations for research with African American women. *Advances in Nursing Science, 22*, 33-45.

Bonner, L. B. (1990). *Good hair: For colored girls who've considered weaves when the chemicals become to ruff.* New York: Crown Trade Paperbacks.

Brzuzy, S., Ault, A., & Segal, E. A. (1997). Conducting qualitative interviews with women survivors of trauma. *Affilia, 12*, 76-83.

Buchanan, N. T., & Ormerod, A. J. (2002). Racialized sexual harassment in the lives of African American women. *Women & Therapy, 25* (3 & 4), 107-124.

Byrd, W. M., & Clayton, L. A. (2000). *An American health dilemma: A medical history of African Americans and the problem of race.* New York: Routledge.

Cody, W. K. (2001). Bearing witness-not bearing witness as synergistic individual-community becoming. *Nursing Science Quarterly: Theory, Research, and Practice, 14*, 94-100.

Collins, P. H. (2000). *Black feminist thought: Knowledge, consciousness, and the politics of empowerment.* New York: Routledge.

Crenshaw, K. W. (1994). Mapping the margins: Intersectionality, identity politics, and violence against women of color. In M. A. Fineman & R. Mykitiuk (Ed.), *The public nature of private violence: The discovery of domestic violence* (pp. 93-118). New York: Routledge.

Daniel, J. H. (2000). The courage to hear: African American women's memories of racial trauma. In L. C. Jackson & B. Greene (Eds.), *Psychotherapy with African American women: Innovations in psychodynamic perspectives and practice* (pp. 126-144). New York: Guilford Press.

Earl, C. E., & Penney, P. J. (2001). The significance of trust in the research consent process with African Americans. *Western Journal of Nursing Research, 23,* 753-762.

Etter-Lewis, G. (1993). *My soul is my own: Oral narratives of African American women in the professions.* New York: Routledge.

Ferrell, P. (1993). *Where beauty touches me: Natural hair care and beauty book.* Washington, DC: Cornrows & Co.

Fontes, L. A. (1998). Ethics in family violence research: Cross-cultural issues. *Family Relations, 47,* 53-61.

Freedman, T. G. (1998). "Why don't they come to Pike street and ask us?" Black American women's health concerns. *Social Science & Medicine, 47,* 941-947.

Gamble, V. N. (1997). The Tuskegee syphilis study and women's health. *Journal of American Women's Medical Association, 52,* 196-197.

Gates, H. L. (Ed.). (1991). *Bearing witness: Selections from African American autobiography in the twentieth century.* New York: Pantheon Books.

Goetting, A. (1999). *Getting out: Life stories of women who left abusive men.* New York: Columbia University Press.

Hammonds, E. M. (1994). Your silence will not protect you: Nurse Eunice Rivers and the Tuskegee syphilis study. In E. C. White (Ed.), *The Black women's health book: Speaking for ourselves* (pp. 323-331). Seattle, WA: Seal.

hooks, b. (1989). *Talking back: Thinking feminist, thinking Black.* Boston: South End Press.

Hutchinson, S. A., Wilson, M. E., & Wilson, H. S. (1994). Benefits of participating in research interviews. *Image: The Journal of Nursing Scholarship, 26,* 161-164.

Johnson-Bailey, J. (1999). The ties that bind and the shackles that separate: Race, gender, class, and color in a research process. *Qualitative Studies in Education, 12,* 659-670.

Jones, J. H. (1993). *Bad blood: The Tuskegee syphilis experiment.* New York: Free Press.

Kavanaugh, K., & Ayres, L. (1998). "Not as bad as it could have been": Assessing and mitigating harm during research on sensitive topics. *Research in Nursing & Health, 21,* 91-97.

King, D. W. (1998). *Deep talk: Reading African American literary names.* Charlottesville, VA: University Press of Virginia.

Langford, D. R. (2000). Pearls, pith, and provocation: Developing a safety protocol in qualitative research involving battered women. *Qualitative Health Research, 10,* 133-142.

Lorde, A. (1984). *Sister outsider.* Trumansburg, NY: The Crossing Press.

Massat, C. R., & Lundy, M. (1997). Empowering research participants. *Affilia, 12*, 33-56.

Mishler, E. G. (1986). *Research interviewing: Context and narrative.* Cambridge, MA: Harvard University Press.

Morgan, D. L. (1997). *Focus groups as qualitative research.* Newbury Park, CA: Sage.

Moss, V., Pitula, C., Campbell, J., & Halstead, L. (1997). The experience of terminating an abusive relationship from an Anglo and African American perspective: A qualitative descriptive study. *Issues in Mental Health Nursing, 18*, 433-454.

National Violence Against Women Prevention Research Center (2001). *Fostering collaborations to prevent violence against women: Integrating findings from practitioner and researcher focus groups.* Charleston, SC: Author.

Nelson, J. (1998, November 28). Stumbling upon a race secret. *The New York Times*, pp. A-31.

Neville, H. A., & Hamer, J. (2001). "We make freedom": An exploration of revolutionary Black feminism. *Journal of Black Studies, 31*, 437-461.

Pierce-Baker, C. (1998). *Surviving the silence: Black women's stories of rape.* New York: W. W. Norton.

Riger, S. (1999). Working together: Challenges in collaborative research on violence against women [Special issue]. *Violence Against Women, 5*.

Roberts, D. (1997). *Killing the Black body: Race, reproduction, and the meaning of liberty.* New York: Pantheon.

Savitt, T. L. (1978). *Medicine and slavery: The diseases and health care of Blacks in antebellum Virginia.* Chicago: University of Illinois Press.

Sharpley-Whiting, T. D. (1999). *Black Venus: Sexualized savages, primal fears, and primitive narratives in French.* Durham, NC: Duke University Press.

Shavers, V. L., Lynch, C. F., & Burmeister, L. F. (2001, Jan 1). Factors that influence African-Americans' willingness to participate in medical research studies. *Cancer* (Suppl. 91), 233-236.

Shavers-Hornaday, V. L., Lynch, C. F., Burmeister, L. F., & Torner, J. C. (1997). Why are African Americans under-represented in medical research studies? Impediments to participation. *Ethnicity and Health, 2*, 31-45.

Spradley, J. P. (1979). *The ethnographic interview.* New York: Holt, Rinehart, & Winston.

Tarpley, N. (1995). On giving testimony, or the process of becoming. In N. Tarpley (Ed.), *Testimony: Young African Americans on self-discovery and Black identity* (pp. 1-10). Boston: Beacon Press.

Taylor, J. Y. (1998). Womanism: A methodologic framework for African American women. *Advances in Nursing Science, 21*, 53-64.

Taylor, J. Y. (2002). "The straw that broke the camel's back": African American women's strategies for disengaging from abusive relationships. *Women & Therapy, 25* (3 & 4), 79-94.

West, C. M. (2002). Black battered women: New directions for research and Black feminist theory. In L. H. Collins, M. Dunlap, & J. Chrisler (Eds.), *Charting a new course: Psychology for a feminist future* (pp. 216-237). Westport, CT: Prager.

West, T. C. (1999). *Wounds of the spirit: Black women, violence, and resistance ethics.* New York: New York University Press.

Fragmented Silhouettes

Salamishah Tillet

SUMMARY. The intersection of racism and sexism within the African American community has privileged the bodies of Black men over the bodies of Black women. Oftentimes, violent crimes against Black women become issues of African American racial division rather than of solidarity. I propose that we change our racial schema, in which issues of police brutality and racial profiling overshadow the continual trauma of Black women's bodies by Black men. I suggest these issues no longer be seen as distinctly separate or divisive, but that we create a world in which Black men and Black women have absolute authority of their bodies. *[Article copies available for a fee from The Haworth Document Delivery Service: 1-800-HAWORTH. E-mail address: <getinfo@haworthpressinc.com> Website: <http://www.HaworthPress.com> © 2002 by The Haworth Press, Inc. All rights reserved.]*

KEYWORDS. Blacks, rape, activism, violence

This is an essay about secrets. Quietly kept secrets of violence, injury, and assault. Not secrets of police brutality and racial profiling. Of

Salamishah Tillet is a PhD candidate in the History of American Civilization program at Harvard where she studies African American and Caribbean literature and history. Her doctoral work focuses on contemporary cultural representations of slavery in the United States. She is also a co-founder of a non-profit organization that sponsors the multimedia performance *A long walk home: A story of a rape survivor*, which uses art to document the journeys of African American women from rape victims to survivors.

Address correspondence to: Salamishah Tillet, Committee on Higher Degrees in the History of American Civilization, 12 Quincy Street, Cambridge, MA 02138.

[Haworth co-indexing entry note]: "Fragmented Silhouettes." Tillet, Salamishah. Co-published simultaneously in *Women & Therapy* (The Haworth Press, Inc.) Vol. 25, No. 3/4, 2002, pp. 161-177; and: *Violence in the Lives of Black Women: Battered, Black, and Blue* (ed: Carolyn M. West) The Haworth Press, Inc., 2002, pp. 161-177. Single or multiple copies of this article are available for a fee from The Haworth Document Delivery Service [1-800-HAWORTH, 9:00 a.m. - 5:00 p.m. (EST). E-mail address: getinfo@haworthpressinc.com].

Amadou Diallo. Or Thomas Jones. Or Abner Louima. Or that Black men have their bodies routinely searched and seized by the hands of police officers. Or that Black men, regardless of class or status, still feel vulnerable to random racial harassment. No, this essay is about the secrets of Black women. Of rape. And of sexual assault. Of how our daily abuses are continually sidelined and how we are forced to remain silent, because of American patriarchal racism on the one hand and African American sexism on the other. Secrets of how we, as African Americans, do not mourn the rape of Black women with the same intensity and the same immediacy as we do the slaying, lynching, and beating of Black men. Secrets of how many White Americans have been taught to devalue the bodies of Black people and have learned never to acknowledge the specific horrors committed against Black women. Secrets of how Black women remain quiet, because to speak out is regarded as an act of betrayal.

Do not be overwhelmed by our secrets.
Hear our words, our muffled cries.

And know that hidden in the deep recesses of our American past and present is the fact that African American women know that their bodies can be searched and seized almost everyday by almost everyone.

Black Body lies on Cold Wet Ground/Prodded into/Hands Pinned Down/Screams Fisted Shut/Black Body attempts to Move/To Flee/

OH, WHERE, OH WHERE HAS MY BODY GONE: FROM LYNCHING TO POLICE BRUTALITY

This past summer, I attended the *Without Sanctuary*[1] lynching exhibit at the New York Historical Society. The walls were filled with photographs and postcards of either anti-lynching crusaders or people who had been lynched. For the first time in my life, I was able to peer into the faces of the White mobs that surrounded the lynched bodies. And for the first time, I was able to visualize what had been in my collective memory all along–Black men hanging from trees. Dragged. Charred. Murdered. Underneath each photograph was a brief description, a caption almost, reading "Unidentified corpse of African American male. A large gathering of lynchers. Circa 1900, location unknown."

As a late 20th century onlooker, I quietly watched each photograph, trying to understand this historical horror. As I stared at these photographs, I slowly began to merge history with the present. Many of these men were assaulted simply for being Black. I saw that there were similarities between contemporary police brutality and these lynchings. The trajectory, the line from then to now, had been drawn for me: Black men have always been and continue to be victims of organized, racist violence. African American men, such as Jesse Washington, John Lee, and William Brown, were lynched because they were suspected of having committed crimes against White women. Recently, Nicholas Heyward, Jr., Amadou Diallo, and Patrick Dorisman were all young Black men who were accidentally killed by police officers. They were caught in the crossfire of justice as police officers searched for a suspect who matched their racial profile. All of these deaths are now part of our historical memory of racialized trauma.

> *Thwarted with more violence/Paralyzed/Eyes Glare at Black Body/Hands pressing Black Body Down/Heavy Blows on the face/The Ribs/The Legs/Legs Opened Wider/Stick inside of Legs/*

And then I saw her. At first, she did not really stand out. She was subsumed in the gendered-racial horror in which Black men are the only ones remembered as victims of lynching. I probably did not notice her because I had never really thought about the lynching of Black women. But she followed me in the room. Hung on a bridge with her son. The caption read: "The barefoot corpse of Laura Nelson. May 25, 1911, Okemah, Oklahoma." Laura Nelson and her son, L. W. Nelson, were accused of killing Deputy George Loney. Although the murder was in self-defense, Laura and her son were dragged and lynched at a newly constructed bridge. There was no investigation of their deaths.

While the death of her son, L. W. Nelson, is not specifically recalled in our lynching memory, his body is. The memory of his lynched body is part of a masculinized memory of lynching while Laura's lynched body is not. Lynching is often remembered as a masculine experience and, in many ways, is central to how the history of African American men, and the larger African American experience, is understood. African American women like Laura Nelson, Mary Turner and Cordella Stevenson are invisible (Brown, 1995). The lynching of these women, who were accused of robbing or assaulting their White male employers, has been absent in our recollection of lynching. They do not shape the way we discuss violence aimed at Black bodies, or receive media attention, or are placed in our historical textbooks. They are mere backdrops in our race conversations. They are fragmented silhouettes in our memories.

> *Black Body cries Out Loud/Within/Thinks of body somewhere else/*
> *But weight suddenly shifts/Pushing Black body deeper/*
> *Deeper into Nothingness/*

While the majority of lynched victims were African American men, African American women were also victims of racially motivated and sexually violent acts. The virtual invisibility of African American women in our lynching memories is largely due to the way history has been shaped and not by the actual numbers of Black women lynched. Within our minds, the history of violence within the African American community is often equated with the status of Black males. Violence done against Black men has become essential to African American antiracist political discourse. From anti-slavery language to anti-lynching campaigns to anti-police brutality marches to anti-racial profiling blockades, Black oppression has often come to mean Black male oppression. According to Brown (1995), these images continue

> an ideology of Blackness, group identity, that equates the status, condition, and progress of the race–the good of the race–with men. ... It is an ideology that looks to improve the lot of men while not just omitting women from the picture but often accepting the violence against them. (p. 114)

> *Black Body Blanks out/Loses consciousness/Tries to get up*

Because the violence against Black men is privileged in our political outrage and moral contempt, we rarely think about the bodies of Black women. Although Black women chronically experience violence, from lynching to rape to police brutality to domestic violence, we erase their stories from the annals of history and from the surface of our minds. We push these narratives away and say we will deal with them after we are emancipated, have gained Civil Rights, established Black power, and ended racial profiling.

> *Cannot get up/Because Juice is flowing from Her legs/Not because she wants it there/Because she never had the right to her body in the first place/*

EVERYDAY VIOLENCE:
A GLIMPSE INTO THE LIVES OF BLACK WOMEN

In August 1997, I went to the Philadelphia sex crime unit to give a statement about being raped in my first year of college. I had finally mustered enough courage and strength to publicly acknowledge that I had been raped. Although I was raped in October 1992, I had never before this moment felt comfortable pressing charges. My perpetrator had been a friend, another African American, on our predominately White college campus. At first, I pretended that nothing ever happened, that I was not raped. It was only when I came face-to-face with the brutality of the rape again that I could no longer run from this trauma. I knew my case would be a long shot because I was just within the five-year statute of limitations and because I knew that most rape cases end with a not guilty verdict. Nonetheless, I wanted to assert my right to press charges.

When I visited the Philadelphia District Attorney's office, I was so incredibly afraid to tell my story to the White, male, complete stranger who sat before me behind his desk. After I completed my story, he told me that this case was unprosecutable. He did tell me that he believed my story because it was filled with too many holes, too many inconsistencies, for me to just make up. He reasoned, however, that in 1992 the *No-means-No* rape clause did not yet exist. In his judgment, according to the law in 1992, I was not legally raped.

I waited until after graduation to give my statement to the police. I realized now why I never attempted to press charges when I was in college. I felt then, as I do now, that my campus was an unsafe place to disclose my rape history. On the one hand, the university itself provided very few judicial and public forums for these silences to be broken. On the other hand, within our African American campus community, the fight against racism and race-based violence constantly superceded sexism and gender-based crimes. For example, during my junior year, African American men assaulted two of my very close Black women friends. In the first scenario, my friend went to the university police. The campus judicial system did a good job of protecting the rights of her assailant. He was never formally charged with the crime of physical assault, and she spent the better part of our senior year in fear of his fists. She received no protection from the campus judicial system. In the second situation, my friend pressed charges with the Philadelphia police. Here the victim had physical evidence, pictures taken by the police of bruises to her face and chest. The judge, however, did not believe the charge of attempted sexual assault. Although he could not dismiss the pictures, he did not believe that my friend was beaten up because she was resisting rape.

> *Black body now hides Herself behind already Cracked Mirror/*
> *As she watches his Body walk away.*

As these women courageously stepped forward with their stories of domestic violence and attempted sexual assault, they were socially scorned within our African American community on campus. Some people automatically dismissed their stories as made-up, and they were considered bitter, angry women. Very few people came to their aid. Although most people took a stance of communal indifference, there were those who spat words of disbelief in their faces because they saw these women as rabble-rousers. Troublemakers. Man haters. Many of the more politically active Black men on campus said they were taking no sides and often never listened to, talked to, or believed these women. Many of the more politically active Black women on campus took a stance of silence and continued to critique the blatant racism on our campus without critiquing the sexism.

There were no real spaces in which we could talk. In which those women could publicly be outraged, feel safe, and speak out. Although their assailants still attended the same school, no one offered to walk these women home late at night. No one, except for a small community of women gatherers who formed rings of protection around their sistah-spirits, wanted to believe that these women cried and walked alone, bruised inside and out. And yet, I write their stories into a narrative of violence done against Black bodies because their testimonies are at risk of being remembered only by these two women. Their stories of pain, defeat, and eventual survival are my story. We are casualties in global war against women that is lost every minute. Battered bodies. Tightly guarded souls. Sullen eyes, which no longer can see the world as theirs.

The bodies of these women, like my body, were not considered under siege, but accessible and able to be abused without consequences to the abuser. Their stories were not believed because the Black men in question were seen as unlikely perpetrators of such acts. In these moments, the judicial racism towards Black men does not only hurt Black men. It unfairly puts Black women who have been raped or abused in positions in which they feel like they are further criminalizing Black men rather than saving their own racial-sexual selves (McKay, 1992).[2]

The myth of the Black male rapist is directly connected to the lynching exhibit I attended. Beneath many of the photographs was the explanation that these men were lynched after being accused of raping a White girl or woman. Although the most pervasive justification for lynching Black men was the myth of their hypersexuality, there is little evidence to support this belief. Anti-lynching crusader Ida B. Wells astutely realized that many of the liaisons between these "raped" White women and Black men "rapists" were often consensual and romantic (Royster, 1997).[3] Ida B. Wells, like abolitionist Frederick Douglass, also noted that the Black male rapist stereotype became most popular after slavery and was created to terrorize newly freed Black communities.[4] Many African Americans realized that the men in their community were being accused of raping White women so that White authorities and mobs could justify their use of violence. The cries of rape by White women against Black men were often fraudulent and fatal (Davis, 1981). Many African Americans rejected the myth because they knew it was merely a product of Southern racism.

This pattern continues today. From lynching to police brutality and racial profiling, the image of the hypersexual and pathologically violent Black man has been used to legitimize the beatings and murders of Black men by law enforcement officers. African American male leaders have often spoken out about these atrocities. They have also rejected the popularized image of the Black rapist and criminal. Furthermore, they have created formal, public resistance to the search and seizure of Black men's bodies. The notion of the Black male rapist has been discarded by some and seen as merely racist propaganda.

But somehow in our collective cleansing, we have held on, ever so tightly, to its female counterpart: the myth of the Black whore (Collins, 2000; Davis, 1981). The Black whore is the image that emerges in our minds when we hear a Black woman accuse a man, either Black or White, of rape, sexual harassment, or physical assault. It underlies the assumption that she has lied, exaggerated what really happened, or misunderstood his intentions. Although the image of the hypersexual, libido-driven Black woman was used to justify the sexual coercion and rape of Black women during and after slavery, it continues to be used to excuse the violence done against African American women within both Black and White America today. This myth affects how much we believe Black women's stories of sexual harassment, rape, and domestic violence. Historically, Black women were not considered to be truthful. It was believed that "a woman who was likely to have sex could not be trusted to tell the truth. Because Black women were not expected to be

chaste, they were likewise considered less likely to tell the truth"
(Crenshaw, 1992, p. 412).

This logic was used against Anita Hill in the congressional hearings
surrounding the nomination of Supreme Court Justice, Clarence
Thomas. When he was first introduced as the seeming replacement for
Thurgood Marshall, his position against affirmative action and his lack
of experience sent chills of disgust within many circles. And yet, his rat-
ings increased in the Black community when he used the lynching metaphor to counter Anita Hill's sexual harassment allegations (Brown,
1995).[5] His eventual confirmation by the predominately White male
Senate and the lack of vocal critical leadership in the African American
community meant that Anita Hill's testimony was lost in this muddy
process. His presence as a Supreme Court judge can only mean that she
was not believed because she was considered both dishonest and inca-
pable of being harassed.

This is also the logic used against Desiree Washington, a Black
beauty pageant contestant, who accused Mike Tyson of raping her in a
hotel room. Instead of crying shame against the horrific crimes against
Black women's bodies, we questioned her character, judgment, and integrity. When Mike Tyson, a boxer with a history of violence against
women, was released from prison, many national Black leaders attended his prison release parade in Harlem.[6] While many of these leaders would later protest the racism and police brutality in the Amadou
Diallo and Abner Louima cases, they saw Desiree Washington's story
as false and vengeful. Many did not believe that she had been raped because they believed the myth that Black women are always asking for
sex and then later lie about being raped.

In each of these scenarios, including my own personal case, once
these women were assumed to be liars, their cries and accusations of
sexual and physical assault carried very little weight in the court of law
or public opinion. Our perpetrators were protected from facing social or
legal consequences. Instead of being seen as victims of gender-hate
crimes, we, Black women, became people who could never be victimized. Our bodies are no longer our own. We are now objects that everyone else has the right to touch in the office and in the street.

> *When we say "NO!," where are the parades, the rallies, the media
> attention, the highway blockades, the church services, the legisla-
> tion, the political lobbying, the sit-ins, the gun-toting, the hip-hop
> lyrics, the movies, the boycotting of violence against Black
> women?*

Hear us cry:

- Black girls are frequent victims of child sexual abuse and incest;
- The combination of race, class, and gender oppression makes Black women vulnerable to rape in their own communities;
- The police are less likely to intervene to help Black battered women, even when their children witness the violence;
- Many battered Black women receive inadequate medical care;
- Battering makes it more difficult for Black women to make the welfare-to-work transition.

Why don't these facts ever roll off our leaders' tongues? (Brush, 2001; McNutt, van Ryn, Clark, & Fraiser, 2000; Robinson & Chandek, 2000; West, Williams, & Siegel, 2000).

Unfortunately, violence against Black women's bodies has become everyday violence. It has become normalized and silenced. It has become too common, too ordinary to be considered a major political issue or to receive major media coverage. I now know more Black women who have been physically or sexually assaulted than I know who have not been victimized. And I am sure this is true for many of us. Ask our grandmothers, mothers, daughters, and sistah-friends. I know women who have been sexually or physically abused by their fathers, grandfathers, police officers, babysitters, friends, boyfriends, teachers, and employers. I know far too many women who have been ostracized, ignored, or verbally attacked once they break their silence.

Black women's bodies are swallowed whole in a society that practices race- and gender-based crimes against the human body. Because our attackers tend to look like us, those in sociopolitical power tend to look away because these issues are seen as divisive for African American progress. Although our bodies have seen so much firsthand violence, Black women who cry out in the middle of the night that we were beaten, harassed, assaulted, and raped are sidelined and silenced. Instead of hearing our voices, we are all too often asked, "What were you doing there in the first place?"

ALTERNATIVE WORLDS: RAPE LEGISLATION, RESISTANCE, AND A NATIONAL CRISIS

We have no real answers to, "What were you doing there in the first place?" because the question comes from a place of absurdity and oppression. It comes from a culture that pretends that rape happens quietly, and infrequently, and without real consequence. It comes from a culture in which patriarchy, racism, and homophobia have found their niche, their meeting place, and their bedrock. For a brief moment, I ask you to travel to another place with me. Suspend all that you know as real. Forget the very painful history I have already painstakingly laid out for you. Pretend that we are in an alternate universe, another spatial plane in which the racial-sexual hierarchy remains the same but the faces of rape victims have changed. Pretend that we live in a country in which middle-class, non-imprisoned, White men are disproportionately more likely to be raped than any other group. Let's take a quantum leap together to see how rape would be politicized if this were the reality.

Elected public officials would vie for the proper stance on the rape issue. More conservative politicians would claim that rapists should be imprisoned for no fewer than 20 years and be ineligible for parole until the maximum sentence was served. New legislation which promised stronger policing of rape related crimes and more anti-rape education programs would pass in Congress. On the other hand, more liberal politicians would discuss the government's responsibility to give more money to counseling programs for rape victims. Police officers, judges, and public defenders would be more sensitive to rape victims because they would see the rape of White men as a national crisis, which needed to be contained. White male rape victims would feel comfortable pressing charges, testifying, and speaking out against their perpetrators because there would be institutional support. We would be in the midst of a political catastrophe because White men's bodies were being searched and seized at will. We would be flooded with media attention of White male rape testimonies and narratives.

Somehow, this world is too difficult to imagine because middle-class, heterosexual White men are the least likely victims of race- and gender-based hate crimes. It seems absurd to make claims of what the world would look like if they were more likely to be raped than any other group because we have no racial-gender framework from which to imagine this. But I ask that you see this absurdity as a symbol for the tragedy of the violence against Black bodies. We cannot imagine this world because there is a precedent for searching and seizing Black bodies.

Now, imagine for a second what the world would look like if African American men were disproportionately more likely to be raped than any other group. They would not necessarily receive better medical treatment, more police sensitivity, or judicial compassion than African

American women, but there would be a conscious historical memory of, and resistance against, their trauma in which hanged bodies and raped bodies would be equally mourned. The National Association for the Advancement of Colored People (N.A.A.C.P.) and the Congressional Black Caucus would have anti-rape rhetoric as part of their national race initiatives. African American leaders would consistently try to have bills passed to end rape against Black men. Anti-rape marches would be led by and include both African American men and women. The word *rape* would be part of our vocabulary of political resistance, and we would empathize with the brutal experiences of everyday Black men who had their bodies sexually and physically violated. African American male leaders would call upon White and Black America to work together to end this madness.

If these strategies were ineffective, we would try to combat this outrage on all fronts, by any means necessary–in the classroom, in the church, and in our homes. We would have a generation of hip-hop artists lyrically narrate their experience as rape victims. We would have Sunday morning sermons and organized Black church speak-outs creating community-based resistance. And we would have young Black boys, soon to be young Black men, incessantly warned about the violence to which they were vulnerable. Many African Americans would know that one in three men would be raped in their lifetime. And we would see rape and domestic violence as further endangering the African American man.

Of course, I realize that these are severe quantum leaps that I am asking you to take. Granted, I do not take into account the race and gender of the perpetrators of this violence. I do not reveal that young White and Black boys, not yet men, are victims of sexual assault and rape-based crimes. In these examples, I do not suggest how rape is directly tied to power. And that power in the United States is directly tied to White supremacy, heterosexism, and capitalism. And that rape is used to dispossess and curtail the power of women. It keeps us in our separate and unequal place. I do not state whether the perpetrators are White or Black or male or female, so perhaps there is a looseness and incredibility to my argument. Because of the severity of homophobia and sexism, we do not live in a world in which men, Black and non-Black, live with the daily fear of rape. Because in our world most heterosexual men have been exempt from sexual violence committed by men, they have not had to fully imagine what it means to occupy the precarious position of women. They have benefited from the homophobia of men by which their bodies are not the primary victims of rape. They have been able to close their eyes and not remember the nightmares of their bodies being ripped open by those they know.

These are two imaginary worlds that I have created in which the response to rape is directly connected to the systemic power of the victim. In the first case, I suggest that anti-rape legislation and anti-rape language would be structurally in place if the rape victims were White men, the beneficiaries of patriarchy and racism. In the second scenario, Black bodies would still be at risk, but the discourse among many African Americans would change. A sort of hysteria and political immediacy would occur, and our coded cultural silences would be broken. I offer these two alternate worlds, not as models, but as kaleidoscopes in which we temporarily can see another prism of rape. These are examples of how we would respond to the issue of rape differently if the victim were of another race or gender. However, given the current reality of violence done against women, and specifically African American women, why is the issue of rape not treated as an epidemic?

SISTAH SPIRITS LIVING IN AN ANTI-RAPE WORLD

Black body is sexual/And innocent/And curious/

This is no longer an essay about secrets. It breaks those silences. It articulates the burdens that many Black women face when they experience flashbacks, body memories, or see their perpetrators. It is an article that paints the landscape of historical trauma and present realities. I want to alter our racial schema and collective memories. I want to insert into our collective memories women who have been forgotten and systematically abandoned. I then want to offer viable alternatives to our dispossession.[7]

Black Body trusts her Own judgment/Is Free/Laughs/
And Stares in the Mirror to see her Beauty/

I write of a world in which there is continued coalition building among White women and women of color. In which violence against women is the primary cause. In which coalition building among Whites and Blacks and freedom building are seen as life giving and essential. In which African American men and women work together, in dialogue to end the violence done to Black women's bodies. In which women can tell these stories without feeling the incredible weight of shame and danger.

Within African American political activism, our notions of Blackness can be expanded to include both Black men and women. African American political resistance will only support the victimization of Black men if we continue to masculinize Black oppression. By this, I mean that violence against Black bodies is coded as *police brutality,* or *lynching,* or *racial profiling,* or Black men committing crimes against other Black men. From the abolitionist movements, to Garvey nationalism, to the Civil Rights Movement, to the Nation of Islam, to the Black Power Movement, to the Million Man and Woman Marches, African American women have been asked to serve these movements quietly and faithfully, while our specific grievances of violence have been unheard. We can only achieve full equality in political movements when we acknowledge the pervasive sexism within these very same movements. There is room on our political platforms to call for an end to racial-gender violence done against all African Americans.

We can create anti-violence and anti-rape rallies, marches, and blockades in which we publicly resist the rape of African American women by Black and non-Black men. Although there have been some African American men who have historically, and presently, acknowledged and fought against the horror of Black women's rape, many of our African American male leaders and political activists continue to deny the severity of this violence. We must collectively fight for the end of rape within the African American community. Within both public and private spaces, we can discuss rape with the same vigor and the same indignation with which we discuss police brutality, racial profiling, and lynching.

It is within these intellectual and political circles that African American women are able to tell their stories without immediate disbelief. In this place, we will hear about the everyday lives of African American rape survivors. We can also hear a deafening silence. However, these silences do not mean that these women have healed or have become whole, but rather that they cannot speak out. Their victimization is coupled with guilt, inadequacy, self-blame, and self-mutilation. These women walk around with generations of pain inside their bodies, which they then pass on to their daughters and their sons. All the while never letting on that this too happened to them once. Or twice. Or over and over again. These women cry alone, not always having the language or a community with whom they can speak.

Black Body walks in the street Late at Night/Comfortable/
Dressed in cloth of Her own choosing/

Fortunately, some courageous Black women have listened to these stories and found them worth capturing, worth recording. They see themselves in these women's silent testimonies because they are their own stories, too. They have dedicated their lives to stopping the violence against Black women's bodies. Sistah-spirits who use their stories, their pain, and their survival to tell the world that Black women are raped everyday by someone, somewhere. Sistah-spirits who incorporate the testimonies of Black men who fight in the war against rape. In her beautifully written book, *Surviving the Silence: Black Women's Stories of Rape*, Charlotte Pierce-Baker (1998) is the first writer to quilt Black women's narratives together to create a polyphonic cry against rape. Page after page, she allows us to enter those sacred spaces that Black women have never shared with anyone. She helps us collectively to heal because she tells us that the wounds are there to be mended.

Filmmaker Aishah Shahidah Simmons (2002 [This volume]) continues to articulate the stories of Black women rape and incest survivors in her feature length documentary, *NO!* The film focuses on the specific nuances of intraracial rape between Black men and Black women. Simmons has dedicated the past five years of her life to making this herstoric film that challenges our silence and inserts into our cultural memory the history of rape against Black women. She reshapes our racialized-gendered landscape with the violent reality of rape of Black girls and women and the amazing courage of these survivors to speak out in the face of their pending invisibility.

Following the lessons of Pierce-Baker (1998) and Simmons (2002 [This volume]), photographer Scheherazade Tillet has created a multimedia photography exhibition and slide show presentation, *A Long Walk Home: A Story of a Rape Survivor*. It uses pictures and dramatic choreography to capture my own personal journey from rape victim to rape survivor. Through her project, many people have felt comfortable releasing the shame and guilt of their victimization. With her camera, she has captured what the world looks like for women after they have been raped and how, with support and courage, they are able to finally heal.

Although race, gender, and rape have brought these three women together, each woman has found the other through art and the courage to articulate these realities. They have begun to create a world in which it is a bit safer for Black women to tell their stories, and a world closer to the one in which I choose to live. A world in which Black women are not vulnerable to rape. In which Black women are not disproportionately raped more than any other group because we live at the crossroads of race and gender and class. One in which we teach young African American girls how to physically defend themselves at a very young age. In which we never learn that female bodies can be bought and sold at will. One in which we can unlearn that Black girls, soon to be Black women, are the most sexually available and the least credible rape victims, and unlearn that boys, soon to be men, have the social and economic right to search and seize female bodies.

Black Body enters club/Hotel Room/Classroom/
Church meeting/Bedroom/Office/Factory Floor/

We need to create political spaces in which Black men not only feel morally outraged by this issue, but also are politically outspoken and active.[8] We can use preexisting anti-violence organizations to form language and counter-discourses that are anti-racist in agenda, action, and political aspiration. In our new world, we will replace the violence of the past. In our new world, Black women will occupy multiple spaces of their own choosing, with their own definitions of equality, liberation, and sexuality.

And walks out Unscathed.

NOTES

1. The *Without sanctuary: Lynching photography in America* exhibit is a collection of photographs and postcards taken as souvenirs at lynchings. The collector James Allen investigated this extraordinary legacy for 25 years. These photographs were on display at the New York Historical Society. They were also published as a book (Allen, 2000).

2. McKay (1992) describes the multiplicity of oppression in America as "racial-sexual oppression that is neither wholly racial nor wholly sexual, but as inseparable as the racial-sexual self" (p. 279).

3. Royster (1997) details how Ida B. Wells concluded that White women's rapes were not the cause of lynching at all. Blacks were lynched for allegations of murder, burglary, arson, poisoning water and livestock, insulting Whites, being insolent, and other perceived offenses. Sometimes, the victim was never charged with a crime.

4. Fredrick Douglass points out that Black men were not indiscriminately labeled as rapists during slavery. Furthermore, if Black men possessed this animalistic urge to rape, this alleged rape instinct would certainly have been activated when White women

were left unprotected by White men who were fighting in the Confederate Army. In fact, no Black man was publicly accused of raping a White woman during the Civil War. For Douglass this was proof that, "Negro accusers have been compelled to invent new [rape] charge[s] to suit the times" (Davis, 1981, p. 184).

5. Clarence Thomas made the following comments about the proceedings:

> From my standpoint, as a Black American, as far as I'm concerned, it's a high-tech lynching for uppity blacks who in any way deign to think for themselves, to do for themselves, to have different ideas . . . You will be lynched, destroyed, caricatured by a committee of the U.S. Senate, rather than hung from a tree. (Brown, 1995, p. 101)

6. See Nelson (1997) for a Black feminist analysis of the May 1995 Harlem parade for boxer and convicted rapist Mike Tyson.

7. See Daniel (2000) for therapeutic strategies for addressing traumatic racial memories.

8. Black feminist scholars discovered that Black men who were anti-rapist activists rejected rape myths and endorsed more egalitarian attitudes toward women than nonactivists (White, Potgieter, Strube, Fisher, & Umana, 1997).

REFERENCES

Allen, J. A. (2000). *Without sanctuary: Lynching photography in America.* Santa Fe, NM: Twin Palms.

Brown, E. B. (1995). Imagining lynching: African American women, communities of struggle and collective memory. In G. Smitherman (Ed.), *African American women speak out on Anita Hill-Clarence Thomas* (pp. 100-124). Detroit, MI: Wayne State University Press.

Brush, L. D. (2001). Poverty, battering, race, and welfare reform: Black-White differences in women's welfare-to-work transitions. *Journal of Poverty, 5,* 67-89.

Collins, P. H. (2000). *Black feminist thought: Knowledge, consciousness, and the politics of empowerment.* New York: Routledge.

Crenshaw, K. (1992). Whose story is it, anyway? Feminist and antiracist appropriations of Anita Hill. In T. Morrison (Ed.), *Race-ing justice, en-gendering power: Essays on Anita Hill, Clarence Thomas, and the construction of social reality* (pp. 402-436). New York: Pantheon Books.

Daniel, J. H. (2000). The courage to hear: African American women's memories of racial trauma. In L. C. Jackson & B. Greene (Eds.), *Psychotherapy with African American women: Innovations in psychodynamic perspectives and practice* (pp. 126-144). New York: Guilford Press.

Davis, A. (1981). *Women, race, and class.* New York: Random House.

McKay, N. Y. (1992). Remembering Anita Hill and Clarence Thomas: What really happened when one woman spoke out. In T. Morrison (Ed.), *Race-ing justice, en-gendering power: Essays on Anita Hill, Clarence Thomas, and the construction of social reality* (pp. 269-289). New York: Pantheon Books.

McNutt, L., van Ryn, M., Clark, C., & Fraiser, I. (2000). Partner violence and medical encounters: African American women's perspectives. *American Journal of Preventive Medicine, 19,* 264-269.

Nelson, J. (1997). *Straight, no chaser: How I became a grown-up Black woman.* New York: G. P. Putnam's Sons.

Pierce-Baker, C. (1998). *Surviving the silence: Black women's stories of rape.* New York: W. W. Norton.

Robinson, A. L., & Chandek, M. S. (2000). Differential police response to Black battered women. *Women & Therapy, 12,* 29-61.

Royster, J. J. (Ed.). (1997). *Southern horrors and other writings: The anti-lynching campaign of Ida B. Wells, 1892-1900.* Boston, MA: Bedford Books.

Simmons, A. S. (2000). Using celluloid to break the silence about sexual violence in the Black community. *Women & Therapy, 25* (3 & 4), 179-185.

West, C. M., Williams, L. M., & Siegel, J. A. (2000). Adult sexual revictimization among Black women sexually abused in childhood: A prospective examination of serious consequences of abuse. *Child Maltreatment, 5,* 49-57.

White, A. M., Potgieter, C. A., Strube, M. J., Fisher, S., & Umana, E. (1997). An African-centered Black feminist approach to understanding attitudes that counter social dominance. *Journal of Black Psychology, 23,* 398-420.

Using Celluloid to Break the Silence About Sexual Violence in the Black Community

Aishah Shahidah Simmons

SUMMARY. I am the producer, writer, and director of *NO!*, a feature length documentary that addresses intra-racial sexual assault in the Black community. Through this film, I hope to break the silence and give visual voice to a chorus of Black women rape survivors and Black women and men activists, historians, poets, attorneys, psychologists, and musicians. Their messages are conveyed through testimonies, scholarship, dance, music, and poetry. *[Article copies available for a fee from The Haworth Document Delivery Service: 1-800-HAWORTH. E-mail address: <getinfo@haworthpressinc.com> Website: <http://www.HaworthPress.com> © 2002 by The Haworth Press, Inc. All rights reserved.]*

Aishah Shahidah Simmons is an award-winning Black feminist, lesbian, independent filmmaker and activist at AfroLez® Productions based in Philadelphia, PA. Her internationally known short films include: *Silence . . . Broken*, *In My Father's House*, and *NO!* (A Work-in-Progress), which explore the issues of race, gender, homophobia, rape, and misogyny. She has screened her work and given international lectures on the intersections of oppressions in African American women's lives. Her awards include the 1994 Philadelphia Gay Pride Award, the 1995 Atlantic City Black Film Festival Filmmaker Award, the 1998 Audre Lorde Legacy Award, and the 2000 Bread and Roses Community Fund's Waters Award for Intergenerational Activism.

Address correspondence to: Aishah Shahidah Simmons, AfroLez Productions, P.O. Box 58085, Philadelphia, PA 19102-8085 (E-mail: AfroLez@aol.com).

[Haworth co-indexing entry note]: "Using Celluloid to Break the Silence About Sexual Violence in the Black Community." Simmons, Aishah Shahidah. Co-published simultaneously in *Women & Therapy* (The Haworth Press, Inc.) Vol. 25, No. 3/4, 2002, pp. 179-185; and: *Violence in the Lives of Black Women: Battered, Black, and Blue* (ed: Carolyn M. West) The Haworth Press, Inc., 2002, pp. 179-185. Single or multiple copies of this article are available for a fee from The Haworth Document Delivery Service [1-800-HAWORTH, 9:00 a.m. - 5:00 p.m. (EST). E-mail address: getinfo@haworthpressinc.com].

KEYWORDS. Blacks, rape, activism, media

> We can learn to work and speak when we are afraid in the same
> way we have learned to work and speak when we are tired. For we
> have been socialized to respect fear more than our own needs for
> language and definition and while we wait in silence for that final
> luxury of fearlessness, the weight of that silence will choke us.
> (Lorde, 1984, p. 44)

SISTER OUTSIDER

In the spring of 1990, at the ripe age of 21, I read *Sister Outsider* by
Audre Lorde (1984). This book transformed my life. I literally de-
voured every word as if my life depended on it. This book was my fresh
well of Black, lesbian, feminist, mother, warrior-poet, spring water in
the middle of a vast racist, homophobic, sexist, and classist sweltering
hot desert. Audre Lorde's words initiated the cleansing of my internalized homophobia wounds, my incest wounds, my rape wounds which
resulted in my unwanted pregnancy wounds at age 19, and my safe legal
abortion six weeks later at age 20. Even though I have never had the
honor or privilege of meeting Audre Lorde, her written words touched
my spirit, captured my soul, and saved my life.

To own these aspects of my identity is an act of self-revelation and
my way of not allowing the pain and, in some instances, the horror to
fester inside of me, eating away at my organs like a deadly virus. I know
that I am not alone. Unfortunately, too many women suffer alone because they are afraid to break their silences and to tell their truth for fear
of societal and cultural retaliation. Instead of keeping the secrets and
hiding the wounds, I want to use my writings and videos to expose them
to the world. Through this process, my wounds are healing and are
slowly, but very surely, turning into warrior marks. These warrior
marks are expressed in my long-lasting commitment to use my art to
fight against racism, sexism, rape, and other forms of misogyny, homophobia, and classism in the United States and internationally.

I believe in the power of spoken and written words, as well as in the
power of screen images. I am a Black feminist, lesbian, cultural worker,
and activist because I want to break silence that Black women have kept
about incest, rape, sexual abuse, and domestic violence. I began thinking about making what has now become the film entitled *NO!* during the

Mike Tyson rape trial in 1992, as I watched and listened to many of the so-called Black male leaders–the very same ones who in 1989 defended Tawana Brawley when she alleged that she had been raped and sodomized by four White men–accuse Desiree Washington of betraying the Black community.

I am the producer, writer, and director of *NO!*, a forthcoming feature-length documentary that will expose and address the Black community's collective silence about the rape, sexual assault, physical, and verbal abuse of Black girls and women by Black boys and men. *NO!* will create a sacred space in which Black women and men, who are outraged about intra-racial abuse, can challenge the Black community to look inward and confront this issue. *NO!* will initiate healing of the political, psychic, and cultural scars of sexual assault. In the film, *NO!*, narrative vignettes, archival footage, testimonies, interviews, music, dance, and poetry will be used to simultaneously address the violent manifestations of racial, gender, and sexual oppression.

This is a tremendous undertaking, one that I dare not do alone. Since 1994, I have worked with Tamara L. Xavier, a Haitian-American feminist, dancer, choreographer, and co-producer of *NO!* We have raised money through grant proposals to traditional media arts funding sources, grassroots fundraising efforts, and speaking engagements at various academic institutions and conferences across the United States, England, and Canada. After four years of "beating-the-pavement and shaking-the-money-trees," we have received more institutional and individual rejections than acceptances. I am an "out" lesbian; we are African and Haitian American feminists; and we are not veteran filmmakers. These facts, I believe, have served as justification for the lack of support for this very important documentary. The fact is intra-racial rape and sexual assault in the Black community are taboo topics for many people. And there is very little concern, if any, about this issue in the mainstream community at large. My beliefs are reinforced by questions and statements such as: Why are you only focusing on Black women and the Black community? Don't most women really mean "yes" when they say "no"? Given that you are a lesbian, what's your ax to grind by making *NO!*?

In spring 1995, I realized that time was critical with the declining health of Essex Hemphill, the award-winning, gay Black poet whose work was featured in Marlon Riggs' masterpieces *Tongues Untied* and *Black Is . . . Black Ain't*, Isaac Julien's classic *Looking for Langston*, and Shari Frilot's groundbreaking *Black Nations Queer Nations*. Tamara and I solicited and received support from a group of Philadelphia-based Black women and men filmmakers. In May and June of 1995, they donated their time and labor to film Essex Hemphill performing his poem "To Some Supposed Brothers." He died five months later in November 1995. We were also able to film three candid testimonies with Black women survivors: Rosetta Williams, Queen, and my mother, Gwendolyn Zoharah Simmons.

In 1996, we requested $35,000 for *NO!*'s research and development budget from a publicly funded foundation. In response, they wrote the following sexist and misogynistic reasons for not granting the request:

> Strong point of view and the concept is good, however, the example of Mike Tyson's case and the indifference from the [Black] community might be due, in part, to the moral point of view that one does not go to a man's room in the early morning; that opinion cannot be ignored . . .

I could not believe that, given the racism and sexism in Black women's *herstory* in the United States, this foundation, which is funded by our tax dollars, would use the question of Black women's morality as a legitimate reason for not funding this documentary. I was so outraged by the response that I e-mailed and snail mailed it across the United States and England. In 1997, the Astraea National Lesbian Action Foundation was the first foundation to give a pre-production grant to *NO!*

BUT SOME OF US ARE BRAVE . . .

Joan Brannon, a Black feminist filmmaker who is the associate producer, co-writer, and director of photography of *NO!*, and I realized that in order to expose and address intra-racial sexual assault in the 20th and 21st centuries, we needed to examine Black women's herstory in the United States. Our decision was based on the fact that many people, regardless of their backgrounds, often had negative reactions to the documentary because they did not understand this legacy. In many instances, American society defines Black as male and woman as White. This is most evident in expressions such as *Blacks and women*, which implies that these two categories are mutually exclusive. Consequently, Black women are rendered invisible (Hull, Scott, & Smith, 1982). Based on numerous screenings of *NO!: A Work-in-Progress* at universities, community centers, film festivals, and conferences across the United States, Europe, and South Africa, I believe that many people view Black men as the primary victims of this racist and classist society. Although it is true that Black men are victims of racism, expressed in the form of police brutality, racial profiling, higher rates of incarceration and unemployment, and lack of access to decent education, Black women experience both the harsh realities of racism and sexism in their daily lives. As a result of racism, patriarchy, and sexism, Black men can be simultaneously victims and perpetrators of violence (Tillet, 2002 [This volume]).

Given this reality, we decided to expose and address intra-racial sexual violence, while also feminizing Black history. In the film, we move from the enslavement of African people in the United States to contemporary interviews with survivors, Black women and men activists, historians, poets, attorneys, psychologists, and musicians.[1] Dance is used as a metaphor of the healing process as Black women move through the trauma of sexual violence and find wholeness and wellness of body, mind, and spirit.

Too often, people who make documentaries are not a part of the community, which may lead to distorted views. I believe that women behind the *NO!* camera should be representative of the women featured in front of the camera. Since the beginning of this film in 1994, the creative production and advisory team has included lesbians, low-income women, and younger and older women. Many of these women are of African descent. All of these women have agreed to work at reduced rates. On July 10, 1999, thanks to grants, cash, and in-kind donations received from individuals and women-based community funds and foundations, the production of *NO!* began in Philadelphia.[2] I, with the technical and creative assistance of a predominately Black woman production crew, completed production in August 2000.

THE STRUGGLE CONTINUES

There have been many times when I wanted to throw my hands up in the air and say, "To hell with this; I can't do this any longer!" Then I would pause, take a deep breath, and remind myself that every institutional and individual racist, homophobic, and sexist rejection reinforces the need for the film *NO!* This type of resistance refuels my passionate rage to make this film. I pour libations, call on the Creator, and my blood and spirit ancestors, to continue to guide the *NO!* team on this journey. On June 15, 2001, Sharon M. Mullally, a White feminist filmmaker and editor of *NO!*, and I created a 1 hour and 21 minute *NO!* documentary rough cut, from 42 hours of footage.

Sometimes the truth hurts when it is spoken aloud, but it also can be healing. I am interested in healing not only the wounds of sexual assault, but also the wounds that result in uterine fibroid tumors, high blood pressure, cancer, AIDS, chronic depression, fatigue, heart disease, and substance abuse. These are all health problems, I believe, that disproportionately impact Black women because our bodies are at the intersection of race, gender, class, and homophobic oppression. So, while *NO!* has everything to do with rape and sexual assault, it also has everything to do with the wholeness and wellness of Black women's lives. Once completed, *NO!* will be a part of Black women's sacred space and a testament to Black women's strength, resilience, and courage.

NOTES

1. The following interviews and performances are featured in the documentary rough cut: Samiya A. Bashir, poet, *Treason*; Elaine Brown, former Chairperson of the Black Panther Party; Pat Clark, Director, Criminal Justice Program, American Friends Service Committee; Johnnetta B. Cole, President Emeritus, Spelman College; Adrienne Davis, legal scholar at University of North Carolina; John T. Dickerson, Bluegrass Rape Crisis Center; Ulester Douglas and Sulaiman Nuriddin, Men Stopping Violence; Farah Jasmine Griffin, scholar and author, Columbia University; Beverly Guy-Sheftall, historian and author at Spelman College; (the late) Essex Hemphill, poet, *To some supposed brothers*; Audree Irons, Administrative Associate, Spelman College; Honoree Jeffers, poet, *that's proof she wanted it*; Rev. Reanae McNeal, Imani Revelations; Charlotte Pierce-Baker, author of *Surviving the silence: Black women's stories of rape*; Queen, a poet; Loretta Ross, former director, Washington, DC Rape Crisis Center; Gwendolyn Zoharah Simmons, Islamic scholar and former SNCC organizer; Michael Simmons, human rights activist; Barbara Smith, scholar, author, and activist; Salamishah Tillet, writer and graduate student; Scheherazade Tillet, photographer; Traci West, author of *Wounds of the spirit: Black women, violence and resistance ethics*; Aaronette M. White, social psychologist and activist; Janelle White, Leanne Knot Violence Against Women Project; Rosetta Williams, visual artist and poet; Black Feminist Dance Statement; Blues Migration Dance; *A State of Rage,* a narrative choreopoem; vignettes exposing inter- and intra-racial rape and sexual assault during enslavement and Reconstruction.

2. Women Make Movies (WMM), is the 501 [c][3] non-profit fiscal sponsor for *NO!*. WMM is a multicultural, multiracial, non-profit media arts organization, which facilitates the production, promotion, distribution, and exhibition of independent films and videotapes by and about women. WMM was established in 1972 to address the underrepresentation and misrepresentation of women in the media industry. The organization provides services to both users and makers of film and video programs, with a special emphasis on supporting work by women of color. WMM facilitates the development of feminist media through an internationally recognized distribution service and production assistance program.

Ms. Simmons also has been a recipient of several grants including three grants from the Valentine Foundation, two grants from Astraea National Lesbian Action Foundation and the WOMENS Way Discretionary Fund, and the Bread and Roses Community Fund.

REFERENCES

Hull, G. T., Scott, P. B., & Smith, B. (Eds). (1982). *All the women are White, all the Blacks are men, but some of us are brave: Black women's studies.* New York: The Feminist Press.

Lorde, A. (1984). *Sister outsider.* Trumansberg, NY: Crossing Press.

Simmons, A. S. (Producer/Writer/Director) & Xavier, T. (Co-Producer). (2002, expected) *NO!* [Motion Picture]. United States: Women Make Movies. (Available from AfroLez® Productions, P. O. Box 58085, Philadelphia, PA 19102-8085.

Tillet, S. (2002). Fragmented silhouettes. *Women & Therapy, 25* (3 & 4), 161-177.

Striving for a More Excellent Way

Rosalyn R. Nichols

SUMMARY. On March 2, 1998, my childhood friend, Rosmari Pleasure, was gunned down by a male acquaintance in the driveway of her
Memphis home. A More Excellent Way, Inc. (AWay) was created in response to this tragedy and is committed to bringing an end to these violent acts that plague our community. In addition to the annual *Sisters4Life*
5K race, AWay, Inc. sponsors: an annual conference, entitled *A Conversation of Love: Preventing Relationship Violence*; preventive educational initiatives such as *Circles of Courage*; and the *Very Special People (VSP)
Scholarship* to assist former victims of domestic violence. *[Article copies
available for a fee from The Haworth Document Delivery Service: 1-800-
HAWORTH. E-mail address: <getinfo@haworthpressinc.com> Website: <http://
www.HaworthPress.com> © 2002 by The Haworth Press, Inc. All rights reserved.]*

KEYWORDS. Blacks, battered women, activism, pastoral counseling

Reverend Rosalyn R. Nichols is Founder and Director of A More Excellent Way,
Inc. A native of Memphis, she graduated from Memphis Theological Seminary summa
cum laude with a Master of Divinity degree. In 1997, Rev. Nichols served as a visiting
professor at the Baptist Theological Seminary in Zimbabwe, Africa. She went on to
serve as Associate Pastor at Metropolitan Baptist Church. Rev. Nichols has preached
and conducted workshops across the nation. Although the focus of her ministry is relationship violence, her greater mission is to reach out and help others reevaluate, reexamine, and redefine their relationships.

Address correspondence to: Rev. Rosalyn R. Nichols, 766 S. Highland, Memphis, TN
38111 (YMCA Central Office) (www.amoreexcellentwayinc.org; E-mail: sisters4life@
angelfire.com).

[Haworth co-indexing entry note]: "Striving for a More Excellent Way." Nichols, Rosalyn R. Co-published simultaneously in *Women & Therapy* (The Haworth Press, Inc.) Vol. 25, No. 3/4, 2002, pp. 187-192; and:
Violence in the Lives of Black Women: Battered, Black, and Blue (ed: Carolyn M. West) The Haworth Press, Inc.,
2002, pp. 187-192. Single or multiple copies of this article are available for a fee from The Haworth Document Delivery Service [1-800-HAWORTH, 9:00 a.m. - 5:00 p.m. (EST). E-mail address: getinfo@haworthpressinc.com].

As an ordained minister, I am called to challenge the sexism of our faith that destroys intimacy. I am convinced that until we learn as men and women what it means to have healthy, loving, spiritually and physically intimate personal relationships, we will never truly be able to solve the problems of the world. A More Excellent Way, Inc. (AWay, Inc.), is the vehicle I use to do this work. It is my tribute to my childhood friend who was killed because a man thought more of the control he demanded than the love she freely gave. I do this for my girlfriend's daughter who was trusting and whose trust was violated by a gunshot. I do this for my friend whose mother- and father-in-law decided to keep it a secret that her new husband had brutalized the other women in his life. I do this for the little boy who watched his mother being beaten and fears that he might strike out in anger. I do it for my aunt who ran in the night and my cousin who ran with her. I do this work for myself in the hope that it will quiet my nightmares.

MY FRIEND ROSE

Rosmari Elaine Celeste Pleasure, the peculiar little girl with the contagious giggle and funny smile, was my friend. We had grown up together. People called us sisters when we were in school. They often got us confused with one another. Sometimes, it was because our names were so much alike, Rosalyn and Rosmari–two little high yella girls with tight eyes and funny, warm smiles.

The year during recess at Memphis State University Campus School, we picked four-leaf clovers together. I remember that we would lie there for what seemed like hours, underneath the trees in the sunshine. We would lie on our stomachs looking for clovers. We talked about teachers, boys, music, and our families. We were in search of the clover that was different from the rest. Its tiny leaves were unlike the others. It was unique. Others may call that special clover peculiar, odd, or a little strange. After all, it was unlike the regular, three heart-shaped leaves. This one was different, but it made no effort to stand out from the rest. It was not arrogant or boastful. It did not build itself up. Nor did it grow in a way that it rubbed out the others. No, in fact, it just quietly and gently stood in the midst of all the rest. But every now and then, one of us would find the peculiar, little heart-shaped clover, and because it made us feel special, we would keep it for ourselves. I still have those clovers.

I first learned how to change the world with Rose. Without permission or pomp and circumstance, Rose and I, along with our friends and classmates, integrated the gymnastics program at Memphis State Campus

School. Every day after school, we would sit in at practice. We would be dressed, but the coach would not call our name. We didn't know it was racism, or any kind of *-ism* for that matter. All we knew was that there were no Black children on the gymnastics team. We just kept showing up, day in and day out, until one day the coach called us forward and let us try out. After that, there were Black children all over the program. We were good, too. I had waged a sit-in with Rose and didn't even know it.

By the time we graduated from high school, we didn't talk nearly as much. Our lives were taking different paths. I had the distractions of a high school sweetheart. She had distractions as well. We kept in touch through our mothers. I remember the last words her mother said to me one Sunday on the church parking lot. Rose was at church that Sunday with a young man. Her mother, all bright, golden, and dignified, was not fond of this young man. She asked me to speak to Rose about her friend. I didn't. I thought it was Rose's business, not mine. After all, parents are always overly concerned. I had problems of my own. Rose and I smiled indirectly about the matter and said goodbye.

We were no longer as close as we once had been. In fact, there was a pleasant distance between us. After her mother's rape and murder, Rose became distant, keeping others and me at arm's length. I wasn't angry. Nor did I feel she was being rude. After all, her loss was great, and she had the right to work through it as best she knew how. Perhaps, to see me brought back memories of her mother, and that called back her pain and loss. Still, Rose was my friend.

"YOU KNOW ROSE"

The last time I saw Rose, it was at a friend's house. I turned in the sea of people, and there stood Rose, just like that unique little clover we picked as children. We spoke politely and parted ways. My childhood friend, Rosemari Pleasure, a 34-year-old woman with a love for life, was violently plucked from us on March 2, 1998. She was gunned down in the driveway of her Memphis home, shot in the back of her head, and pistol-whipped by a former boyfriend.

I was at a loss for words when Reverend Pleasure, Rose's father, called me. What do you say at a time such as this? Reverend Pleasure and I exchanged polite words. He called to ask me to be here in the morning. It was the act of a parent working feverishly to maintain order in the midst of the ungodly. He said, "I need you, baby, because you know Rose." I hung up the phone, and, for the first time in three days since hell had touched the hem of my garment, I finally cried because it was true.

I spoke these words at my friend's funeral in March 1998:

> To Reverend Pleasure, Robert William David, Mrs. Jo Pleasure and the entire Pleasure family:
>
> I do not have words to express, nor am I arrogant enough to even imagine that I know your pain and grief. I do wish, however, to say I grieve with you and for you. My heart, and the hearts of all who are here and who long to be here, breaks open in the sadness that words never fully express. This is pain that only tears and silence contain. As I stand here, I know heaven and earth have broken open in grief with you. It is my prayer that the One who is greater than all of us, whose heart contains all of our hearts, who can bear our pain, our anger, and our despair, will somehow break through the sorrow that engulfs us to hold you in the center of love. I pray that when you find there is no-where to turn, the Divine Spirit, who does not explain but who is al-ways there, will guide you when your heart feels faint, when the numbness fades, and people turn away. May the Spirit of the Divine be there to catch you. May the spirit of the Divine make her presence known to you when rational and intellect can no longer support you.

As I looked down at Rose in the funeral home, I saw my own reflection. I realized that my choices in relationships had not been perfect, but for God's grace I could have been Rose. It was too much for me. As I drove home, I reflected. This was the third funeral that I had attended. Rose was the third young woman killed at the hands of a former boyfriend. She never saw her 35th birthday, and my two other friends never saw 30. I could not just simply walk away and say, "Ah, what a shame" until the next death. I had to do something.

A MORE EXCELLENT WAY

In the *Christian New Testament,* the Apostle Paul wrote these words to the faith community at Corinth, "But strive for the greater gift and behold I will show you still a more excellent way" (I. Cor. 12.31). Following this message, the Apostle Paul began a beautiful passage by saying, "If I speak with the tongues of men and of angels . . . if I have prophetic powers and understand all mysteries, if I have all faith, if I give all of my possessions away and have not love I am nothing." Paul reminds us that love is patient. Love is kind. Love is not envious, boastful, arrogant, or rude. Love does not insist on its own way, is not irritable or resentful.

I believe that Love is the more excellent way. This led me to establish A More Excellent Way, Inc., a non-profit ministry that has 10 board members, 9 faith advisory board members, and a large volunteer pool. Our vision statement reads:

> A More Excellent Way, Inc. is a nonprofit urban Christian ministry which promotes and encourages individuals to enter into, engage in and maintain spiritually and personally, loving, healthy relationships with others in the home, school, workplace, neighborhood and places of worship toward the elimination of violence.

We seek to accomplish these goals through the following projects:

Sisters4Life–The Rosmari Pleasure Memorial 5K Walk/Run

This event was first held on November 14, 1998 as a race to end violence in the African American community. The intent was to call attention to the loss of productive and talented African American citizens as a result of relationship violence. The first memorial run, which was sanctioned by the Memphis Runners and Track Club, indicated a need to do more: a need to broaden the mission to "race for life: saving lives, families and communities–one sister at a time"; a need to partner with others toward the prevention of relationship violence; a need to collaborate with others for improved delivery of educational activities toward the prevention of relationship violence; a need to supplement the current responses to survivors of relationship violence; and a need to seek ways to connect with perpetrators at the moment of crisis.

A Conversation of Love: Preventing Relationship Violence

This event is held each year to address the issues of violence in relationships and to form new partnerships to end relationship violence. Each forum will raise pertinent questions, seek appropriate answers, strategize for the prevention of relationship violence, and offer resources and plans to build communities of love. The inaugural *Conversation* engages faith leaders who represent the highest form of community leadership. Subsequent *Conversations* will engage community stakeholders, social service agencies, survivors, perpetrators, and other groups who are able to effect change toward saving lives, families, and communities.

Circles of Courage

The *Circle of Courage* in a church, synagogue, or other community of faith is a group of women and men who are committed to developing skills and using their courage to intervene with perpetrators of relationship violence. In order to participate, the volunteer has to commit to training from the agency's staff members.

Very Special People (VSP) Scholarship

This scholarship program is designed to help former victims pursue an education. The scholarship is named in honor of three young women, Deeta Rose Venson, Wylea Estee Smith, and Rosmari Pleasure, all women who lost their lives to relationship violence.

I am grateful for the opportunity to share this story and the work we do with A More Excellent Way, Inc. I hope this information can be helpful in seeing how some of us find ourselves called to the work of preventing relationship violence. I am not the voice of the survivor, or the family member *per se*, but the voice of the community that refuses to be a co-conspirator to the silence that kills us.

"I Find Myself at Therapy's Doorstep": Summary and Suggested Readings on Violence in the Lives of Black Women

Carolyn M. West

SUMMARY. This volume used a Black feminist framework to investigate childhood sexual abuse, intimate partner violence, sexual assault, sexual harassment, and community violence in the lives of African American women. This article will summarize the authors' findings, review their suggestions for intervention, and provide a list of readings and resources. *[Article copies available for a fee from The Haworth Document Delivery Service: 1-800-HAWORTH.*

Carolyn M. West is Assistant Professor of Psychology in the Interdisciplinary Arts and Sciences Program at the University of Washington, Tacoma, where she teaches a course on Family Violence. She received her doctorate in Clinical Psychology from the University of Missouri, St. Louis (1994), and has completed a clinical and teaching postdoctoral fellowship at Illinois State University (1995) and a National Institute of Mental Health research postdoctoral research fellowship at the University of New Hampshire's Family Research Laboratory (1995-1997). In 2000, the University of Minnesota's Institute on Domestic Violence in the African American Community presented Dr. West with the Outstanding Researcher Award. Her current research focuses on partner violence in ethnic minority families and oppressive images of Black women.

Deep appreciation is expressed to Drs. Ellyn Kaschak, Beverly Greene, Suzanna Rose, and Laurie Roades for their support and encouragement, to Bronwyn Pughe for her generous editing, to Karin Dalesky for her research assistance, and to Dr. Beverly Goodwin for the thoughts that inspired this article.

Address correspondence to: Carolyn M. West, PhD, Interdisciplinary Arts & Sciences, Box 358436, 1900 Commerce Street, Tacoma, WA 98402-3100 (E-mail: carwest@u.washington.edu; or www.drcarolynwest.com).

[Haworth co-indexing entry note]: " 'I Find Myself at Therapy's Doorstep': Summary and Suggested Readings on Violence in the Lives of Black Women." West, Carolyn M. Co-published simultaneously in *Women & Therapy* (The Haworth Press, Inc.) Vol. 25, No. 3/4, 2002, pp. 193-201; and: *Violence in the Lives of Black Women: Battered, Black, and Blue* (ed: Carolyn M. West) The Haworth Press, Inc., 2002, pp. 193-201. Single or multiple copies of this article are available for a fee from The Haworth Document Delivery Service [1-800-HAWORTH, 9:00 a.m. - 5:00 p.m. (EST). E-mail address: getinfo@haworthpressinc.com].

E-mail address: <getinfo@haworthpressinc.com> Website: <http://www. HaworthPress.com> © 2002 by The Haworth Press, Inc. All rights reserved.]

KEYWORDS. Blacks, battered women, rape, sexual abuse, sexual harassment, intervention

> Who, then, can I turn to when I hurt real bad? . . . I find myself at therapy's doorstep. Will the counselor usher me to insanity? Because if she does not openly deal with the fact that there is a very low premium on every aspect of my existence, if she does not acknowledge the politics of Black womanhood, now that would surely drive me nuts. (Johnson, E., 1983, p. 320)

This volume used a Black feminist perspective to investigate violence in the lives of Black women. More specifically, the authors in this volume discussed a broad range of violence, including childhood sexual abuse, dating violence, partner abuse in intimate relationships, sexual assault, sexual harassment, and community violence. A special effort was made to focus on marginalized populations, such as Black lesbians and battered Black women who had sustained head injuries. The final section of this volume was devoted to activism and healing. The purpose of this article is to summarize the authors' findings within a Black feminist framework, to review their suggestions for intervention, and to provide a list of suggested readings and resources.

BLACK FEMINIST THEORY

Scholars have used Black feminist theory to investigate domestic violence (West, 1999), rape (Neville & Hamer, 2001), and childhood sexual abuse (Wilson, 1994). The purpose of this volume has been to add to this growing body of literature. Consistent with previous researchers, the authors used a Black feminist framework that considers how living at the intersection of multiple oppressions shapes Black women's experience with violence, uses a broad definition of violence, acknowledges diversity among Black women, explores the influence of historical events and oppressive images on victimization, and values Black women's activism and resistance.

Intersectionality. In order to understand the complexity of violence in the lives of Black women, Black feminists contend that we must acknowledge the overlap and intersections of multiple forms of oppression (Collins, 1998). This means that "a middle-class, African-American heterosexual Christian woman is not just African-American, not just middle-class, not just Christian, and not just female. Instead, her life is located at the intersection of these dimensions" (Phillips, 1998, p. 682). In this volume, the authors demonstrated how living at the inter-· section of oppression can create different forms of violence, such as "racialized sexual harassment" (Buchanan & Ormerod), and make it difficult for Black women to disclose their sexual assaults (Donovan & Williams).

Broad range of violence. Because Black women live at the intersection of oppressions, they are vulnerable to a broad range of violence in all areas of their lives, including their intimate relationships, their communities, and their workplaces. It is important to investigate victimization across the life span, from childhood, through adolescence, and into adulthood. Consequently, this volume included articles on childhood sexual abuse, intimate partner violence (dating and married), sexual assault, sexual harassment, and community violence. Future researchers should investigate violence in the lives of elderly Black women (Griffin, 1999).

Diversity among Black women. Therapists and scholars should acknowledge the diversity among African American women. For example, the authors in this volume investigated violence in the lives of low-income Black women (Banyard, Williams, Siegel, & West), Black college women (Few & Bell-Scott), and professional Black women (Buchanan & Ormerod). Some groups of Black women are especially vulnerable to victimization. Consequently, the authors addressed violence in the lives of Black lesbians (Robinson) and Black women who had sustained head injuries (Banks & Ackerman). Future researchers should focus on Black women across the Diaspora (Johnson, P. C., 1998) and across economic groups (Russo, Denious, Keita, & Koss, 1997). There should be a special effort to include Black women who are especially marginalized, such as Black women who are HIV positive (Jackson-Gilfort, Mitrani, & Szapocznik, 2000) and Black women who are trapped in the criminal justice system (Richie, 1996) or welfare system (Raphael, 2000).

Black women's history. Consistent with Black feminist theory, the authors explained how Black women's history of sexual violence, in the form of rape and forced breeding, has influenced Black women's experience with sexual harassment (Buchanan & Ormerod) and rape (Donovan & Williams). Tillet focused on the history of lynching, a form of violence that has remained in the collective memories of African-Americans and has shaped our discourse about intra-racial sexual assault. The authors also traced the history of oppressive images, such as the subordinate Mammy and sexually promiscuous Jezebel. These images continue to influence Black survivors' self-perceptions and the responses they receive from service providers. Legal scholars are beginning to use Black feminist theory to challenge perceptions of Black survivors in the court system (Ammons, 1995; Kupenda, 1998; Moore, 1995). When appropriate, therapists should make similar efforts to explore traumatic racial memories and the origins or consequences of oppressive images (Daniel, 2000).

Resilience and activism. Despite the challenges faced by African American survivors, the authors in this volume documented their resilience (Banyard and colleagues) and their strategies for terminating abusive dating (Few & Bell-Scott) and marital relationships (Taylor). The authors also demonstrated how participation in the research process (Taylor), the arts (Simmons), and spirituality (Nichols) could be used as forms of activism.

SUGGESTIONS FOR INTERVENTION

Although many Black survivors are resilient, based on literature reviews (Jenkins; West), it is clear that some survivors experience psychological distress in the form of depression, anxiety, stress, and somatic complaints. Despite their symptoms, several authors discovered that some Black survivors were reluctant to participate in therapy (Donovan & Williams; Few & Bell-Scott). This volume was designed to provide culturally sensitive techniques, which we hope will enable practitioners to appropriately respond to the needs of Black women. The following suggestions for intervention were consistently discussed throughout this volume:

1. *Educate professionals.* Many service providers, including therapists, nurses, and police officers, will be called to serve the needs of Black survivors. All professionals should become more knowledgeable about violence in the lives of Black women (see Appendix for references).

2. *Conduct a comprehensive assessment.* Service providers should develop the skills to take abuse histories (Young, Read, Barker-Collo, & Harrison, 2001). Given the "web of trauma" experienced by many Black women, providers should ask about a broad range of violence in their lives, including violence in their homes, communities, and workplaces. Service providers should also note historical violence, which was committed against African Americans as a group or against the survivor's family members, and violence based on race, social class, or sexual orientation (Scurfield & Mackey, 2001).

3. *Draw on the survivor's strengths.* The service provider should assume a competence orientation that acknowledges successful strategies used by survivors.

4. *Encourage activism.* Researchers, mental health providers, community activists, and survivors should develop collaborative relationships. Activism can take many forms. For example, community members can help develop media campaigns or violence prevention programs, and professionals could assist by volunteering their services. It is particularly helpful if activism takes place in a Black feminist environment in which participants are working to eliminate race, class, and gender oppression (White, 2001; White, Strube, & Fisher, 1998).

5. *Improve social support networks.* With education about the risk factors and symptoms associated with victimization, friends, relatives, and community members can help survivors rebuild their lives. If these individuals are not available or are not an appropriate option, therapists should consider referring the survivor to a culturally sensitive support group.

6. *Acknowledge oppressive images.* Both survivors and therapists may internalize oppressive images of Black women (e.g., Mammy, Jezebel). These images can influence the survivor's self-perception or the therapist's response to the survivor. These images should be acknowledged and addressed.

7. *Understand the importance of literature, art, and music.* Using resources that reflect the experiences and challenges faced by Black women may promote healing for some survivors. If appropriate, the survivor could be encouraged to keep a journal or use literature or music that she perceives to be soothing and empowering.

8. *Understand the importance of spirituality.* Faith, religion, or spirituality can be used as a form of Black feminist activism or a source of comfort for some Black survivors. Service providers should not minimize spirituality in the lives of survivors.

Many Black survivors will find themselves at "therapy's doorstep." Before coming to therapy, Black survivors may ask the same question that was asked by Black feminist Eleanor Johnson (1983): "Will the counselor usher me to insanity?" How will mental health professionals respond to this question? With culturally sensitive training and a commitment to social change, therapists can help usher clients toward healing.

REFERENCES

Ammons, L. L. (1995). Mules, Madonnas, babies, bathwater, racial imagery and stereotypes: The African American woman and the battered woman syndrome. *Wisconsin Law Review*, 1003-1080.

Collins, P. H. (1998). The ties that bind: Race, gender, and US violence. *Ethnic and Racial Studies, 21*, 917-938.

Daniel, J. H. (2000). The courage to hear: African American women's memories of racial trauma. In L. C. Jackson & B. Greene (Eds.), *Psychotherapy with African American women: Innovations in psychodynamic perspectives and practice* (pp. 126-144). New York: Guilford Press.

Griffin, L. W. (1999). Elder maltreatment in the African American community: You just don't hit your momma!!! In T. Tatara (Ed.), *Understanding elder abuse in minority populations* (pp. 27-48). Philadelphia, PA: Brunner/Mazel.

Jackson-Gilfort, A., Mitrani, V. B., & Szapocznik, J. (2000). Conjoint couple's therapy in preventing violence in low income, African American couples: A case report. *Journal of Family Psychotherapy, 11*, 37-60.

Johnson, E. (1983). Reflections on Black feminist therapy. In B. Smith (Ed.), *Home girls: A Black feminist anthology* (pp. 320-324). New York: Kitchen Table Women of Color Press.

Johnson, P. C. (1998). Danger in the Diaspora: Law, culture, and violence against women of African descent in the United States and South Africa. *Journal of Gender, Race, & Justice*, 472-527.

Kupenda, A. M. (1998). Law, life, and literature: A critical reflection of life and literature to illuminate how laws of domestic violence, race, and class bind Black women based on Alice Walker's book *The third life of Grange Copeland. Howard Law Journal, 42*, 1-26.

Moore, S. (1995). Battered woman syndrome: Selling the shadow to support the substance. *Howard Law Journal, 38*, 297-352.

Neville, H. A., & Hamer, J. (2001). "We make freedom": An exploration of revolutionary Black feminism. *Journal of Black Studies, 21*, 437-461.

Phillips, D. S. (1998). Culture and systems of oppression in abused women's lives. *Journal of Obstetric, Gynecologic, and Neonatal Nursing, 27*, 678-683.

Raphael, J. (2000). *Saving Bernice: Battered women, welfare, and poverty.* Boston, MA: Northeastern University Press.

Richie, B. E. (1996). *Compelled to crime: The gender entrapment of battered Black women.* New York: Routledge.

Russo, N. F., Denious, J. E., Keita, G. P., & Koss, M. P. (1997). Intimate violence and Black women's health. *Women's Health: Research on Gender, Behavior, and Policy, 3,* 315-348.

Scurfield, R. M., & Mackey, D. W. (2001). Racism, trauma and positive aspects of exposure to race-related experiences: Assessment and treatment implications. *Journal of Ethnic & Cultural Diversity in Social Work, 10,* 23-47.

West, T. C. (1999). *Wounds of the spirit: Black women, violence, and resistance ethics.* New York: New York University Press.

White, A. M. (2001). I am because we are: Combined race and gender political consciousness among African American women and men anti-rape activists. *Women's Studies International Forum, 24,* 11-24.

Wilson, M. (1994). *Crossing the boundary: Black women survive incest.* Seattle, WA: Seal Press.

White, A. M., Strube, M. J., & Fisher, S. (1998). A Black feminist model of rape myth acceptance: Implications for research and antirape advocacy in Black communities. *Psychology of Women Quarterly, 22,* 157-175.

Young, M., Read, J., Barker-Collo, S., & Harrison, R. (2001). Evaluating and overcoming barriers to taking abuse histories. *Professional Psychology: Research and Practice, 32,* 407-414.

APPENDIX

SUGGESTED READINGS

Bent-Goodley, T. B. (2001). Eradicating domestic violence in the African American community: A literature review and action agenda. *Trauma, Violence, and Abuse, 2,* 316-330.

Bograd, M. (1999). Strengthening domestic violence theories: Intersections of race, class, sexual orientation, and gender. *Journal of Marital and Family Therapy, 25,* 275-289.

Boyd, J. A. (1998). *Can I get a witness?: For sisters, when the blues is more than a song.* New York: Dutton Book.

Eugene, T. M., & Poling, J. N. (1998). *Balm for Gilead: Pastoral care for African American families experiencing abuse.* Nashville, TN: Abingdon Press.

Gillum, T. L. (2002). Exploring the link between stereotypic images and intimate partner violence in the African American community. *Violence Against Women, 8,* 64-86.

Heron, R. L., Twomey, H. B., Jacobs, D. P., & Kaslow, N. J. (1997). Culturally competent interventions for abused and suicidal African American women. *Psychotherapy, 34,* 410-424.

Jackson-Gilfort, A., Mitrani, V. B., & Szapocznik, J. (2000). Conjoint couple's therapy in preventing violence in low income, African American couples: A case report. *Journal of Family Psychotherapy, 11*, 37-60.

Jackson, L. C., & Greene, B. (2000). *Psychotherapy with African American women: Innovations in psychodynamic perspectives and practice.* New York: Guilford Press.

McClure, F. H. (1996). Sexual abuse: Case illustration of Sheila: A 15-year-old African American. In F. H. McClure & Teyber, E. (1996), *Child and adolescent therapy: A multicultural-relational approach* (pp. 91-123). Fort Worth, TX: Harcourt Brace.

Mitchell, A., & Herring, K. (1998). *What the blues is all about: Black women overcoming stress and depression.* New York: Perigee Books.

Morrison, T. (Ed.) (1992). *Race-ing justice, en-gendering power: Essays on Anita Hill, Clarence Thomas, and the construction of social reality.* New York: Pantheon Books.

Nader, K., Dubrow, N., & Stamm, B. H. (Ed.) (1999). *Honoring differences: Cultural issues in the treatment of trauma and loss.* Philadelphia, PA: Brunner/Mazel.

Pierce-Baker, C. (1998). *Surviving the silence: Black women's stories of rape.* New York: W. W. Norton & Company.

Puente, A. E., & Perez-Garcia, M. (2000). Neuropsychological assessment of ethnic minorities: Clinical issues. In C. Israel (Ed.), *Handbook of multicultural mental health: Assessment and treatment of diverse populations* (pp. 420-433). San Diego, CA: Academic Press.

Raphael, J. (2000). *Saving Bernice: Battered women, welfare, and poverty.* Boston, MA: Northeastern University Press.

Richie, B. E. (1996). *Compelled to crime: The gender entrapment of battered Black women.* New York: Routledge.

Robinson, T. L. (2000). Making the hurt go away: Psychological and spiritual healing for African American women survivors of childhood incest. *Journal of Multicultural Counseling and Development, 28*, 160-176.

Scurfield, R. M., & Mackey, D. W. (2001). Racism, trauma and positive aspects of exposure to race-related experiences: Assessment and treatment implications. *Journal of Ethnic & Cultural Diversity in Social Work, 10*, 23-47.

Smith, D. (1993). African American women teachers speak about child abuse. In J. James & R. Farmer (Eds.), *Spirit, space, and survival: African American women in (White) academe* (pp. 158-178). New York: Routledge.

Smitherman, G. (Ed.) (1995). *African American women speak out on Anita Hill-Clarence Thomas.* Detroit, MI: Wayne State University Press.

Taylor, J. Y. (2000). Sisters of the yam: African American women's healing and self-recovery from intimate male partner violence. *Issues in Mental Health Nursing, 21*, 515-531.

Washington, P. A. (2001). Disclosure patterns of Black female sexual assault survivors. *Violence Against Women, 7*, 1254-1283.

West, T. C. (1999). *Wounds of the spirit: Black women, violence, and resistance ethics.* New York: New York University Press.

White, E. C. (1994). *Chain, chain, change: For Black women in abusive relationships.* Seattle, WA: Seal Press.

Williams, O. J., & Griffin, L. W. (2000). Domestic violence in the African American community [Special issue]. *Violence Against Women, 6*(5).

Wilson, M. (1994). *Crossing the boundary: Black women survive incest.* Seattle, WA: Seal Press.

WEB RESOURCES

http://drcarolynwest.com This Website provides an extensive reference list on violence in the lives of African Americans.

http://www.dvinstitute.org Institute on Domestic Violence in the African American Community (University of Minnesota, School of Social Work). The Institute's mission is to provide an interdisciplinary vehicle and forum by which scholars, practitioners, and observers of family violence through research findings, the examination of service delivery and intervention mechanisms, and the identification of appropriate and effective responses, can prevent/reduce family violence in the African American community.

http://www.incite-national.org Incite! Women of Color Against Violence. Incite is a national activist organization of radical feminists of color advancing a movement to end violence against women of color and their communities though direct action, critical dialogue, and grassroots organizing.

Diversity and Complexity in Feminist Therapy, edited by Laura Brown, PhD, ABPP, and Maria P. P. Root, PhD (Vol. 9, No. 1/2, 1990). *"A most convincing discussion and illustration of the importance of adopting a multicultural perspective for theory building in feminist therapy. . . . This book is a must for therapists and should be included on psychology of women syllabi."* (Association for Women in Psychology Newsletter)

Fat Oppression and Psychotherapy, edited by Laura S. Brown, PhD, and Esther D. Rothblum, PhD (Vol. 8, No. 3, 1990). *"Challenges many traditional beliefs about being fat . . . A refreshing new perspective for approaching and thinking about issues related to weight."* (Association for Women in Psychology Newsletter)

Lesbianism: Affirming Nontraditional Roles, edited by Esther D. Rothblum, PhD, and Ellen Cole, PhD (Vol. 8, No. 1/2, 1989). *"Touches on many of the most significant issues brought before therapists today."* (Newsletter of the Association of Gay & Lesbian Psychiatrists)

Women and Sex Therapy: Closing the Circle of Sexual Knowledge, edited by Ellen Cole, PhD, and Esther D. Rothblum, PhD (Vol. 7, No. 2/3, 1989). *"Adds immeasureably to the feminist therapy literature that dispels male paradigms of pathology with regard to women."* (Journal of Sex Education & Therapy)

The Politics of Race and Gender in Therapy, edited by Lenora Fulani, PhD (Vol. 6, No. 4, 1988). *Women of color examine newer therapies that encourage them to develop their historical identity.*

Treating Women's Fear of Failure, edited by Esther D. Rothblum, PhD, and Ellen Cole, PhD (Vol. 6, No. 3, 1988). *"Should be recommended reading for all mental health professionals, social workers, educators, and vocational counselors who work with women."* (The Journal of Clinical Psychiatry)

Women, Power, and Therapy: Issues for Women, edited by Marjorie Braude, MD (Vol. 6, No. 1/2, 1987). *"Raise[s] therapists' consciousness about the importance of considering gender-based power in therapy. . . welcome contribution."* (Australian Journal of Psychology)

Dynamics of Feminist Therapy, edited by Doris Howard (Vol. 5, No. 2/3, 1987). *"A comprehensive treatment of an important and vexing subject."* (Australian Journal of Sex, Marriage and Family)

A Woman's Recovery from the Trauma of War: Twelve Responses from Feminist Therapists and Activists, edited by Esther D. Rothblum, PhD, and Ellen Cole, PhD (Vol. 5, No. 1, 1986). *"A milestone. In it, twelve women pay very close attention to a woman who has been deeply wounded by war."* (The World)

Women and Mental Health: New Directions for Change, edited by Carol T. Mowbray, PhD, Susan Lanir, MA, and Marilyn Hulce, MSW, ACSW (Vol. 3, No. 3/4, 1985). *"The overview of sex differences in disorders is clear and sensitive, as is the review of sexual exploitation of clients by therapists. . . . Mandatory reading for all therapists who work with women."* (British Journal of Medical Psychology and The British Psychological Society)

Women Changing Therapy: New Assessments, Values, and Strategies in Feminist Therapy, edited by Joan Hamerman Robbins and Rachel Josefowitz Siegel, MSW (Vol. 2, No. 2/3, 1983). *"An excellent collection to use in teaching therapists that reflection and resolution in treatment do not simply lead to adaptation, but to an active inner process of judging."* (News for Women in Psychiatry)

Current Feminist Issues in Psychotherapy, edited by The New England Association for Women in Psychology (Vol. 1, No. 3, 1983). *Addresses depression, displaced homemakers, sibling incest, and body image from a feminist perspective.*

Index

A Long Walk Home: A Story of a Rape Survivor, 174
A More Excellent Way, Inc. (AWay), 187-192
Abdul-Kabir, S., 18
A-BNRB. *See* Ackerman-Banks Neuropsychological Battery (A-BNRB)
Abortionist movements, 173
Abuse
 premarital, 9
 psychological, defined, 60
 sexual, childhood, 7-8
 substance, violence in Black women and, 16
Abusive relationships, disengaging from, Black women's strategies for, 79-94
 defining moments in, 84-88,85t,91
 moving away in, 85t,88-90,91-92
 moving on in, 90-91,93
 study of, 82-84
  clinical implications of, 91-92
  data analysis in, 83-84
  data collection in, 83
  design of, 82
  participants in, 82-83
  results of, 84
Ackerman, R.J., 3,133
Ackerman-Banks Neuropsychological Battery (A-BNRB), 138
Activism, in Black feminist theory, 196
Acute stress disorder, 34
Acute stress reaction, 33
African American women. *See* Black women

Aggression, community violence and, 36
Alcohol use, violence in Black women and, 16
Alexander, I., 64,65
Anti-rape world, Sistah spirits in, 172-175
Apostle Paul, 190
Appendectomy(ies), Mississippi, 149
Astrae National Lesbian Action Foundation, 182
Atlanta Medical Examiners Office, 34
Attention, sexual, defined, 108
AWay. *See* A More Excellent Way, Inc. (AWay)

Banks, M.E., 3,133
Banyard, V.L., 2,8,45,49,50,52,53
Bartman, S., 147,148
Battered, Black, and Blue, 4,5-27
Battered women, head injuries in, 134-136,135t
Battering relationship, case study of, 126-127
Bell-Scott, P., 3,10,12,59
Black community, sexual violence in, in breaking silence about, 179-185
Black couples, dating violence among, 60-61. *See also* Psychologically abusive dating relationships, Black women's coping strategies in
Black feminist theory, 194-196
 Black women's history in, 195-196
 broad range of violence in, 195

diversity among Black women in, 195
intersectionality in, 195
resilience and activism in, 196
Black Is...Black Ain't, 181
Black lesbians, domestic violence and,
    125-132
    acknowledging problem in, 129
    addressing homophobia and
        heterosexism in, 129-130
    case study of, 126-129
    providing appropriate referrals in,
        130
    providing appropriate treatment in,
        130-131
    suggestions for intervention in,
        129-131
Black Nations Queer Nations, 181
Black Power Movement, 173
Black rape survivors, effects of racism
        and sexism on, 95-105
    addressing oppressive images in,
        101-102
    encouraging social support and
        activism in, 102
    historical overview of, 96-97
    oppressive images of, 97-100
    supportive therapeutic stance in,
        100-101
    therapeutic interventions for, 100-102
Black whore, 112
Black women
    in abusive relationships,
        disengaging from, 79-94. *See
        also* Abusive relationships,
        disengaging from, Black
        women's strategies for
    childhood sexual abuse in, 45-58.
        See also Childhood sexual
        abuse (CSA), in Black
        women
    and community violence, 29-44.
        See also Community
        violence, Black women and
    everyday violence in lives of,
        165-169

and leaving process, 80-81
    racialized sexual harassment in,
        107-124. *See also* Sexual
        harassment, racialized, in
        Black women
    as victims of intimate partner
        violence
    enhancing individual-community
        willingness to participate in,
        156
    head and brain injuries in,
        133-143. *See also* Head
        injuries, in Black women
        victims of intimate partner
        violence; Traumatic brain
        injury (TBI)
    historical overview of, 147-149
    implications for practice,
        155-157
    involving participants in
        research process in, 157
    research as act of resistance and
        healing for, 145-160
    study of
        data collection and analyses
            in, 152
        method of, 151-152
        participants in, 151-152
        results of, 153-155
    using language to access
        knowledge claims in, 156-157
    violence in lives of
        intervention for, 196-198
        overview of, 5-27
        summary and suggested readings
            on, 193-201
Blacks and Women, 182
Book(s), self-help, as coping strategy
        for Black women in
        psychologically abusive
        dating relationships, 71
Brannon, J., 182
Brawley, T., 181
Breaking free, 62
Brown, E.B., 164

Brown, W., 163
Brutality, police, 162-164,173
Buchanan, N.T., 2-3,14-15,107
Bukszpan, D., 52

Campbell, J.C., 17
Carmona, J.V., 46
Childhood sexual abuse (CSA), in
        Black women, 7-8,45-58
    consequences of, 49-51
    intervention for, 54-55
    The Women's Study, 47-49
Christian New Testament, 190
Circle of Courage, 192
Civil Rights Act of 1964, 108
Civil Rights Movement, 173
Clark, M., 60
Coercion, sexual, defined, 108
Collins, P.H., 98
Community Mental Health Council, 32
Community violence, Black women
        and, 29-44
    aggression due to, 36
    community level in, 40-41
    coping in, 38-39
    exposure to violence, 30-32
    individual level in, 40
    intervention for, 39-41
    loss and grief due to, 35
    loss of significant others effects on, 32
    parenting and, 37-38
    physical health affected by, 36-37
    psychological distress due to, 33-35
Congressional Black Caucus, 171
Conversation, 191-192
Coping, community violence and, 38-39
Coping strategies, of Black women, in
        psychologically abusive
        dating relationships, 59-77.
        See also Psychologically
        abusive dating relationships,
        Black women's coping
        strategies in
Courtship violence, 9

Cox, I., 20
CSA. *See* Childhood sexual abuse
    (CSA)
Cuvier, G., 147

Daniel, J.H., 119
Dating relationships, abusive,
        psychologically, Black
        women's coping strategies in,
        59-77. *See also*
        Psychologically abusive
        dating relationships, Black
        women's coping strategies in
Dating violence
    among Black couples, 60-61. *See
        also* Psychologically abusive
        dating relationships, Black
        women's coping strategies in
    in Black women, 8-10
David, R.W., 190
Davis, A.Y., 6
Defining moments, in disengaging
        from abusive relationships,
        84-88,85t,91
Depression, violence in Black women
        and, 17
Diallo, A., 163
Dinero, T.E., 53
Disengaging, 62
Domestic violence, 10-12
    Black lesbians and, 125-132. *See
        also* Black lesbians, domestic
        violence and
Donovan, R., 3,13,95
Dorisman, P., 163
Douglass, F., 167

EEOC. *See* Equal Employment
    Opportunity Commission
    (EEOC)
Equal Employment Opportunity
    Commission (EEOC), 13, 108
Ethnography

traditional, 82
  womanist, 82
Etic, defined, 111
Everyday violence, 165-169
Excellent resilience, 53

Fantuzzo, J.W., 18
Father of Modern Gynecology, 148
Few, A.L., 3,10,12,59
Flitcraft, A., 18
Foley, L.A., 97
Fragmented silhouettes, 161-177
Freaks, 98
Freedman, T.G., 147
Frilot, S., 181

Garvey nationalism, 173
Gender entrapment, 50-51
Gender harassment, defined, 108
Grief, loss and, community violence
  and, 35

Halstead-Reitan Neuropsychological
  Battery, 134
Harassment, gender, defined, 108
Havey, M.R., 54
Head injuries
  in battered women, 134-136,135t
  in Black women victims of intimate
    partner violence, 133-143
    case example of, 137-141
    therapy for, 137-141
Healing, research as act of, for Black
  women survivors of intimate
  male partner violence,
  149-151
Health problems, physical, violence in
  Black women and, 18-19
Hemphill, E., 181,182
Heterosexism, addressing of, 129-130
Heyward, N., Jr., 163

Hien, D., 52
Hill, A., 109,168
Hill, H.M., 31,37,38-39
Hine, D.C., 99
Holiday, B., 6
Homophobia, addressing of, 129-130
Hoochies, 98
Hoodrats, 98
Hostility
  sexist, defined, 108
  sexual, defined, 108
"Hottentot Venus," 148
Hyman, B., 53
HyperRESEARCH, 83

"I Find Myself at Therapy's
  Doorstep," 193-201
Intimate partner violence, Black
  women as victims of, 10-12
  head and brain injuries in, 133-143.
    See also Head injuries, in
    Black women victims of
    intimate partner violence;
    Traumatic brain injury (TBI)
  research as act of resistance and
    healing for, 145-160. *See also*
    Black women, as victims of
    intimate partner violence

Jenkins, E.J., 29
Jezebel image, 97-98
Johnson, E., 198
Journal(s), as coping strategy for Black
  women in psychologically
  abusive dating relationships,
  70-71
Julien, I., 181

Kenny, M.C., 46
Koss, M.P., 53

Landenburger, K.M., 61
Leaving process, 61-62
    Black women and, 80-81
Lee, J., 163
Legislation, rape, 169-172
Lesbian(s), Black, domestic violence and,
    125-132. *See also* Black
    lesbians, domestic violence and
Loeb, T.B., 46
Looking for Langston, 181
Lorde, A., 180
Los Angeles Head Start Mothers, 32
Loss, and grief, community violence
    and, 35
Lynching, 162-164,173

MacKinnon, C., 108
Marshall, T., 168
Mary Mahoney Professional Nurses'
    Organization, 83
Matriarch image, 99-100
McEachern, A.G., 46
Memphis Runners and Track Club, 191
Memphis State University Campus
    School, 188-189
Million Man and Woman Marches,
    173
Mississippi appendectomies, 149
Mohr, W.K., 18
Moss, V.A., 80
Moving away, in disengaging from
    abusive relationships, 85t,
    88-90,91-92
Moving on, in disengaging from
    abusive relationships,
    90-91,93
Mullally, S.M., 183
Murrell, A.J., 111

N.A.A.C.P. *See* National Association
    for the Advancement of
    Colored People (N.A.A.C.P.)

Nappy, defined, 151
Nation of Islam, 173
National Alcohol Survey, 16
National Association for the
    Advancement of Colored
    People (N.A.A.C.P.), 171
National Center for Injury Prevention
    and Control, 8-9
National Crime Victimization Survey,
    12
National Family Violence Survey, 11
Nationalism, Garvey, 173
Nelson, L., 163
New York Historical Society, 162
Nichols, R., Rev., 3,20
Nichols, R.R., 187
NO!, 182,183,184
NO!: A Work-in-Progress, 182
Not going back, 62

OCR. *See* Office of Civil Rights
    (OCR)
Office of Civil Rights (OCR), 13
O'Leary, K.D., 60
Ormerod, A.J., 3,14-15,107
Other-mothers, 92

Parenting, community violence and,
    37-38
Physical health, community violence
    and, 36-37
Physical health problems, violence in
    Black women and, 18-19
Pierce-Baker, C., 102,149,174
Pleasure, R.E.C., 187,188-190
PMWI. *See* Psychological
    Maltreatment of Women
    Inventory (PMWI)
Police brutality, 162-164,173
Posttraumatic stress disorder (PTSD),
    33-34,136
Premarital abuse, 9

Principles of salience, 64
Psychological abuse, defined, 60
Psychological distress, community
      violence and, 33-35
Psychological Maltreatment of Women
      Inventory (PMWI), 64
Psychologically abusive dating
      relationships, Black women's
      coping strategies in, 59-77
   intervention techniques for, 74-75
   journals in, 70-71
   leaving process in, 61-62
   self-help books in, 71
   social support network in, 72-73
   spirituality in, 71-72
   study of
      data analysis in, 64-65
      data collection in, 64
      discussion of, 73-75
      goals of, 63
      leaving as process in, 65,67-70,
         67t
      method in, 63-65
      participants in, 63
      results of, 65,66t
PTSD. *See* Posttraumatic stress
      disorder (PTSD)

Queen, 182
Quick Neurological Screening Test,
      134

Racial discrimination, in Black
      women, 110
Racial profiling, 173
Racism, effects on Black rape
      survivors, 95-105. *See also*
      Black rape survivors, effects
      of racism and sexism on
Rape legislation, 169-172
Rape survivors, Black, effects of
      racism and sexism on,

95-105. *See also* Black rape
      survivors, effects of racism
      and sexism on
Recovery, 62
Reissman, C., 64
Relationship violence, prevention of,
      191-192
Resilience
   in Black feminist theory, 196
   defined, 53
   excellent, 53
   in The Women's Study, 53-54
Resistance, research as act of, for
      Black women survivors of
      intimate male partner
      violence, 149-151
Re-victimization
   in adulthood, in The Women's
      Study, 51-53
   defined, 51
Richie, B.E., 50
Riggs, I., 181,182
Rivers, E., 149
Roberts, B-E, 111
Robinson, A., 3,11,125
Rose, S., 9
Rouse, L., 60

Salience, principles of, 64
Savitt, T.L., 148
Secret(s), 161-177
Self-help books, as coping strategy for
      Black women in
      psychologically abusive
      dating relationships, 71
Sexism, effects on Black rape
      survivors, 95-105. *See also*
      Black rape survivors, effects
      of racism and sexism on
Sexist hostility, defined, 108
Sexual abuse, childhood, 7-8
   in Black women, 45-58. *See also*
      Childhood sexual abuse
      (CSA), in Black women

Sexual assault, in Black women, 12-13
Sexual attention, unwanted, defined,
        108
Sexual coercion, defined, 108
Sexual harassment
    in Black women, 13-15
    racialized, in Black women,
        107-124
        application of concepts to,
            109-111
        implications for practice,
            116-119
        study of
            data analysis in, 113-114
            discussion of, 115-116
            goals of, 112
            methods of, 112-114
            participants in, 112-113
            procedure of, 113
            results of, 114-115
Sexual hostility, defined, 108
Sexual violence, in Black community,
        breaking silence about,
        179-185
Sexually transmitted diseases (STDs),
        violence in Black women
        and, 18
Sherer, A., 117
Siegel, J.A., 2,8,36,45,49,50,51,52,53
Significant others, loss of, effect on
        Black women, 32
Silence, research as act of, for Black
        women survivors of intimate
        male partner violence,
        149-151
Simmons, A.S., 3,20,174,179
Simmons, G.Z., 182
Sims, J.M., 148
Sistah spirits, in anti-rape world,
        172-175
Sister Outsider, 180-182
Sisters4Life–The Rosmari Pleasure
        Memorial 5K Walk-Run, 191
Smith, B., 6
Smith, W.E., 192

Social support network, as coping
        strategy for Black women in
        psychologically abusive
        dating relationships, 72-73
Soeken, K.L., 17
Solis, B., 46
Spirituality, as coping strategy for
        Black women in
        psychologically abusive
        dating relationships, 71-72
Spradley, J.P., 82,152
Stark, E., 18
STDs. *See* Sexually transmitted
        diseases (STDs)
Stevenson, C., 163
Strong Black Woman, 99
Substance abuse, violence in Black
        women and, 16
Suicide attempts, violence in Black
        women and, 17-18
*Surviving the Silence: Black Women's
        Stories of Rape,* 174

Taylor, J.Y., 3,12,19,79,145
TBI. *See* Traumatic brain injury (TBI)
Termination process
    assessment of relationship in, 65,
        67-69,67t
    declaration of self-empowerment
        in, 67t,70
    reestablishing social networks and
        activities in, 67t,69
    separation from partner in, 67t,69
    stages in, 65,67-70,67t
The Women's Study, of childhood
        sexual abuse in Black men,
        47-49
    participants in, 47-48
    procedures of, 48-49
    resilience in, 53-54
    re-victimization in, 51-53
    review of research on, 49-54
Thomas, C., 109,168
Thompson, C.L., 99

Tillet, S., 3,161,174
"To Some Supposed Brothers," 182
Tolman, R., 64
Tongues Untied, 181
Traditional ethnography, 82
Trauma History Screen, 54-55
Traumatic brain injury (TBI), in Black
        women victims of intimate
        partner violence, 133-143
    case example of, 137-141
    therapy for, 137-141
Tully, M.A., 55
Turner, M., 163
Turning point, 62
Tyson, M., 168,181

United States Public Health Service,
        148
Unwanted sexual attention, defined,
        108

Vanzant, I., 71
Venson, D.R., 192
Very Special People (VSP)
        Scholarship, 192
Violence
    community, Black women and,
        29-44. *See also* Community
        violence, Black women and
        courtship, 9
    dating
        among Black couples, 60-61.
        See also Psychologically
        abusive dating relationships,
        Black women's coping
        strategies in
        in Black women, 8-10
    domestic, 10-12
        Black lesbians and, 125-132. *See
        also* Black lesbians, domestic
        violence and
        everyday, 165-169

exposure to
        among Black women, 30-32
        impact of, 32-38
    intimate partner
        in Black women, 10-12
        Black women as victims of,
            research as act of resistance
            and healing for, 145-160. *See
            also* Black women, as victims
            of intimate partner violence
    in lives of Black women
        childhood sexual abuse, 7-8
        dating violence, 8-10
        depression related to, 17
        healing for, steps toward, 19-20
        intimate partner violence, 10-12
        overview of, 5-27
        physical health problems related
            to, 18-19
        psychological sequelae of, 15-19
        sexual assault, 12-13
        sexual harassment, 13-15
        STDs related to, 18
        substance abuse related to, 16
        suicide attempts related to,
            17-18
        summary and suggested readings
            on, 193-201
        types of, 7-15
    relationship, prevention of, 191-192
    sexual, in Black community,
            breaking silence about,
            179-185. *See also* Sexual
            violence, in Black
            community, breaking silence
            about
VSP Scholarship. *See* Very Special
        People (VSP) Scholarship

Washington, D., 168,181
Washington, J., 163
Washington State Association of Black
        Professionals in Health Care,
        83

Welfare queens, 98
Wells, I.B., 167
West, C.M., 2,4,5,8,9,52-53,193
West, J.A., 45
White, A.M., 19
Whore(s), Black, 112
Wife battering, 10-12
Williams, L.M., 2,8,45,49,50,51,52,53
Williams, M., 3,13,95

Williams, R., 182
Without Sanctuary, 162
Wolfer, T.A., 31-32,39
Womanist ethnography, 82
Wyatt, G.E., 46

Xavier, T.L., 181